MISSED
THE RAPTURE?

MISSED THE RAPTURE?

How to Overcome During the Great Tribulation

JOHN F. BALCH, MDiv AND
JAMES B. DE YOUNG, ThD

XULON PRESS

Xulon Press
2301 Lucien Way #415
Maitland, FL 32751
407.339.4217
www.xulonpress.com

Paperback ISBN-13: 978-1-66285-177-3
Ebook ISBN-13: 978-1-66285-178-0

A Note About Our Cover

Jesus spoke about the importance of understanding the "signs of the times" (Matt 16:3). At no time is this more important than prior to his Second Coming (Matt 24:3ff). We hope we've captured his urgency through the various symbols on our cover:

- The background of a wildfire bearing down on a town speaks of the natural catastrophes that signal his return;
- The biohazard warning sign represents the diseases and other physical afflictions that will plague an unbelieving world;
- The jagged "A" is an internationally used symbol for anarchy, alluding to the rampant lawlessness and deception that will characterize human culture at the end of the age;
- The symbol in green represents one-world government under the Antichrist. Note the stylized "666" above the "peoples" of the world. The surrounding wreath stands for the false peace that he will offer to all at the outset of his rise to power;
- The tsunami warning sign? Again, it could represent widespread natural disaster. But let's let it speak here of the tidal wave of additional miseries that will successively sweep the planet before the return of Christ.

Be on the alert!

Table of Contents

Preface

This book is written before the fact. Let us explain.

The instantaneous disappearance of hundreds of millions of people will be the most dramatic event of world history to that point. Bar none. It will also be the most controversial. And it will happen at the beginning of a period in history unlike any other. What will follow this disappearance will see an accelerated degeneration of society and culture, the rise of a totalitarian world-wide government, and the unleashing of divine judgement upon the planet.

The disappearance will remove from the earth every living person that is a true believer in Jesus Christ. All unbelievers and pretenders will be left behind. The popular term for this event is the Rapture. There are many things about this event that are startling:

- it will come without warning;

- it will include so many;

- it will happen all across the planet at the same moment;

- it will have effects on society and commerce that will be immediate and unmeasurable;

- it will raise questions for which the unbelieving world will have no answers.

But perhaps the most surprising thing about it will be this: it's been predicted in the pages of the Bible for almost 2000 years.

The first chapter of our book will discuss the what, who, and why of the Rapture. It will relate what the Bible says about the event. And what the Bible says about it will not be acceptable to most, for reasons that will become apparent. But it will make sense to many. And if it does to you, you'll have to deal with its personal implications—and the decision to be made that those implications make plain.

During his short ministry to Israel, Jesus performed many miracles. They were foretold centuries before, in the writings of the Old Testament prophets. Jesus's performance of these miracles proved two things, at least to anyone who was paying any spiritual attention. First, they identified Jesus as the promised Messiah. Second, their fulfilment proved the authority of the scriptures that had predicted his coming.

Because the Rapture is also predicted in the Bible, its fulfilment leads to the same conclusions. It will lead many to place their faith in Christ after it happens. But what then? These will be new believers in a period where Bible-believing churches have disappeared, along with their pastors and teachers. Open preaching of the gospel will likely become outlawed in fairly short order. Normal access to Christian material will soon be restricted or forbidden. Practically speaking, only Bibles and other materials that were left in private hands will be available—and that haphazardly.

Most important, very little of that material *will have been designed specifically for those "left behind."* And that especially applies to things written on the basic principles of discipleship and early growth in Christ. This book is intended to address that shortage. In providing this book, the authors aren't at all dismissing the capacity of the Holy Spirit to see that evangelism and discipleship continue during the last days, even in truly miraculous ways. We're merely offering it as a tool for his purposes; kind of sending it forward for use then.

Even so, the authors expect that many will read this book even before the Rapture. We hope that these earlier readers will want to leave copies behind, intended for unsaved family members, friends and neighbors. Many may wish to attach letters of encouragement to consider the Gospel. The authors also expect that some people left after the Rapture might gain access to empty church buildings and Christian schools. Church and school leaders should consider stocking copies of the book and other materials intended especially for these searchers.

The event of the Rapture will prove its prediction. It will also establish the reliability of all the other prophecies about the end of the age. And it will validate, in kind, the contents of this book.

We provide it with the following understandings:

- The practical and authoritative nature of the Bible is the basis for the book's content (2 Tim 3:16-17).

- It isn't intended to be a replacement for the Scriptures, but simply a tool to highlight what the Bible says about the matters being discussed here.

- It's expected that the reader will be able to find a quality, readable version of the Bible. If one's not nearby this book, it might take a bit of extra effort.

- Every believer's experience of the coming times will be unique. The authors are not prophets, but teachers. The major issues that our book covers come from our familiarity with what the Bible teaches, on top of what we see of both human nature and current trends in society.

- The book is comprehensive, but can't be exhaustive.

- It isn't intended to be read once and then put away or passed on. It's expected that various portions of the book will be re-read as world events and personal experiences dictate.

- The particular end-time perspective of the authors is based on a literal approach to interpretation. This is the standard means of interpreting the rest of the Bible and there's no inherent reason to change it when dealing with issues of prophecy. This doesn't deny the use of symbols or figurative language (particularly in the books of Daniel, the other prophets, and Revelation), but asserts that the text and context—and them only—will make it plain where such language is being used.

A Note to Early Readers with a Different Perspective

Biblical Christianity encompasses folks with differences of understanding on a number of important issues. But nowhere are these differences more obvious than when believers begin to talk about what will happen on the earth during and following the end of this age. This is especially true regarding the nature and timing of the Rapture, the nature and extent of the Tribulation, the place of Israel, and the nature of the Millennium. On these issues, most folks tend to adopt the views of their preferred Bible teachers or church affiliations. But at their root, these major differences are due to variations in the way prophecy is interpreted.

The writers of this book believe that the entire Bible should be interpreted literally, unless other factors demand that a word or phrase be used figuratively or symbolically. That's the normal way people communicate. Using this approach, we think that God's Word makes a very strong case for the literal reality of the Rapture, a following seven-year Tribulation, *an actual* Battle of Armageddon, and a thousand-year earthly reign of Christ—in that order.

But we acknowledge the possibility that some of our views might, in the end, turn out differently in a few particulars. Frankly, there's nothing that settles the interpretation of a prophecy better than its literal and final fulfilment! But as the first of these major events, the Rapture was yet to come at the time of our book's writing. We're currently like folks who are near-sighted but have not yet gotten a prescription for glasses. If our condition isn't too bad, we can find ways to manage stuff at arm's reach. But things farther off are somewhat fuzzy.

As an example, there are many true believers in Jesus that believe that the Rapture and resurrection of dead believers will happen *at the end* of the Tribulation, and even that this period is not a strict seven years. Others believe that the Rapture may occur in the *middle*. Some think that the Rapture or the Millennium (or both) are entirely symbolic. Many don't think that national Israel is still in God's plans at all, whether before or after Jesus returns as King over all the earth. There are even believers that think that the world will get better and better until it's fit for Jesus' return (they're currently having a tough time making their case!).

We don't wish to marginalize the differing views that others may have on these things. We welcome them as thoughtful readers, not so much to try to change their minds (we'll let God do that as he unfolds events). If nothing else, they can take away the truths and helps to godly perseverance that will be indispensable in terrible times without regard to when Jesus returns. For the run-up to the end will be a steady downward spiral of deception, lawlessness, and persecution that will surround them—even before the beginning of what Daniel, Jesus and Paul described as the Tribulation.

Regardless of the time of the Rapture, Jesus makes it plain that people should both turn to him in faith and be prepared for his return. However you see the End of the Age, there's plenty in this book to cover each of these necessities.

On Our Use of "Tribulation" and "Great Tribulation"

It's very common for today's believers to use the terms "Tribulation" and "Great Tribulation" interchangeably. That is, both are commonly applied to the entire seven-year period between the Rapture and the Second Coming of Christ "in power and great glory." Both expressions are basically synonymous with the common Old Testament phrase for this period, "the Day of the Lord," a description that is also picked up in the New Testament.

In our book, John usually refers to the entire period simply with "Tribulation." James generally refers to it by the "Great Tribulation" (or, simply "GT"). However, when the Bible adds the word "great" it usually does so in particular reference to the last 3 ½ years (Dan 12:1; Matt 24:21; Rev 7:14).

In either case, readers of our book will understand the use of each by the immediate context.

A Note on the Book's Unusual Features

Because of our personal backgrounds and interests, we've chosen to write this book in two parts. John, the Bible teacher, is responsible for Part One. It addresses the Rapture, the Gospel and your response to it, and the basics of growing as a disciple of Jesus Christ. James, the Bible scholar and seminary professor, has done Part Two, about the Antichrist and the events of the Tribulation. Our styles are rather different, as you'd expect. But we're very much on the same page with what each of us has to say.

There are four unusual features that will be apparent from the beginning:

1) Most chapters will begin with a short fictional episode. We hope that the story of Bill Archer and the other characters will increase your interest. And that they will provide a realistic backdrop for the explanation of the issues that follow.

2) A list of bullet points will precede the text of each chapter. The times and events that the book addresses will be unlike anything the world has ever experienced before. It may be so intense that some readers will want to know the bare bones or

"nitty-gritty" of the subject matter immediately. These bullet points will simplify things greatly.

3) The tone of the book is very personal. It's not so much addressed to "an audience" as it's addressed to *you*. That noticeably affects its style, especially in Part One. There'll be lots of contractions and fragmented sentences (which will surely frustrate our editors). Think of it as conversational in nature, but perhaps like a one-sided talk with the proverbial "Dutch uncle." Actually, James *is* Dutch, and John has real Dutch uncles as in-laws, so we've got that covered nicely. We've worked hard to keep the keep the book from becoming something too academic in style. You'll have to decide if we've succeeded. If we can't avoid using a technical or theological term, we'll make an attempt to explain it simply.

4) Our chapters are loaded with Bible references. This will not be so unusual for early readers who've been believers for some time and have done a lot of reading on biblical issues. But it will certainly be new for those who haven't had their nose in this kind of book before. We want you to have confidence that our points are based on the Scriptures, and to see that God's word is understandable.

First, we want you to understand that the book's content is based on what can be found *and readily understood* in the word of God. We want you to be confident in what we've written surrounding these quotes. But even more, we want you to be confident in what *God* has written! We write only because we believe he has something to say to you.

Second, if you're not accustomed to checking out things in the scriptures, it will give you lots of practice. A great first place to start will be your Bible's Table of Contents. Use it often to start. It won't be long before you're able to latch on to the general location of most books without having to resort to it. You should make an effort to look up the references in parentheses that are a part of the general text. It's important to see things in their context. And we think that it will give you good experience in both finding things in the Bible and in encouraging you to read elsewhere on your own. Remember, God has far, far more that he'd like you to know than just what's in the pages in *this* book.

If You Read Nothing Else...

But before we begin, here's a list of seven absolutely essential things you'll need to do to negotiate successfully the months and years ahead. Everything else in the book is pretty much just an expansion on these points. The list is pretty much in order of the items' relative importance:

1. Respond to the Gospel by placing your faith in Christ as your Savior and Lord. It all starts here. Don't mess around with this issue! Go right to Chapter Two if you're at all unsure what this is about.

2. Do not—*under any circumstances*—accept any mark, imprint, tattoo, or device on or in your hand or forehead. Half way into the Tribulation, it will be something that will be required for essential transactions. But it will be directly linked to the worship of a counterfeit Christ, and taking it will forfeit one's opportunity to be saved. We will cover this in more detail in Chapter Ten.

3. Get hold of a Bible and begin to read it. Start with John's gospel and then Ephesians. We'll have more suggestions on this in Chapter Seven.

4. Begin a pattern of prayer. We'll talk more about that later, also in Chapter Seven. Talk with God anytime, anywhere, in any

situation. It's an expression of your trust in him and a source of personal strength.

5. Be on the lookout for other new believers nearby. Others who will have come to know Christ should be a great source of encouragement.

6. Look for occasions to tell others about Jesus and what you've seen him doing in your life.

7. Begin to prepare for a lifestyle of rugged self-sufficiency.

Grace, mercy, and peace to you!!

John Balch
James De Young
Portland, Oregon
Damascus, Oregon
July, 2022

PART I

WHAT JUST HAPPENED? – AND WHAT TO DO ABOUT IT

Chapter 1

"What Just Happened?"

The What, Who, and Why of the Rapture

Bill Archer left the small office of his engineering company in a hurry. One of his employees had just come through the side door with an urgent but confusing alert. Something about a strange occurrence in the equipment yard behind the building. On his way to investigate, Bill noted that Carolyn, the new receptionist, was missing from her desk. As he passed it, he noticed that her clothes were strewn askew across the front of her chair, her upset coffee cup's contents flooding the keyboard in front of a screen showing a document still filling with an endless string of the letter "u". An odd realization began to grip him. Bill didn't make it to the side door. Instead, he turned and trotted past Frank Simms, his junior partner, asking him to handle whatever had happened in the equipment yard. "Gotta check on what may be an emergency at home, Frank. We'll talk later..."

He muttered an oath against his misfortune as he jumped in his car. Even though his house was only six minutes away, he'd hoped to be able to get something from the news station that his car radio was set to. But he'd yanked out that old Sony the previous evening and hadn't finished the installation of its much better Alpine replacement. Thomas, his 14-year-old, had been at wit's end over an advanced algebra problem—and the two that followed, of course. It had killed the install for the rest of the evening. Thus, the empty space in his dash at what seemed to be developing as the worst possible moment. He'd thought about using his smart phone to find some news from the internet but there'd been some sort of connectivity issue. Hitting the gas, he'd have to deal with all this tech stuff later.

Short as it was, the drive home was also odd. If only for the two, well, not quite "accidents" that he'd seen along the way. The first was a car that apparently had been backing out of a driveway. But it hadn't made it to the street. Instead, its rear bumper was jammed against the trunk of a maple tree in the extension between the sidewalk and the curb. It's still turning wheels were creating deepening ruts in the slick turf beneath their treads. The other was an SUV that was "parked" with its right front wheel on the grass above the curb. Was it the driver that was leaned against the passenger door sobbing? Then three people at the corner of Sixth and Elm in seemingly heated conversation, arms and fingers pointing down Elm and at the hardware store that was kitty-corner. A couple of doors farther on, a man was sitting in the middle of his front yard in boxers, weeping.

Rushing into the house, he called out, "Sue!" No answer. Again, as he crossed through the living room. Nothing. Except for the strange whir of a kitchen appliance, accompanied by some very rapid thumping. Turning the corner through the dining room, he'd almost expected the essence of what he saw, if not the detail. First was the hand mixer, running at medium speed, clattering on the floor beside the island. Cake batter was splattered everywhere, a broken egg on the counter beside a half-filled glass bowl of that cherry chip stuff their kids loved so much. And a shoe on the floor, empty, peeking around the corner of the island. Another hesitant seven feet and he saw the rest: the haphazard heap of Sue's favourite sweatshirt, joggers, and an apron. He slowly unplugged the mixer and turned toward the bedroom down the hall, at the same time hoping he'd not find what he now expected—and wishing he would.

Stephanie had been picked up from her second-grade class yesterday afternoon by Susan, brought home with a temperature and upset stomach. Flu, no doubt. Not much better at breakfast this morning. She stayed home with the good medicine of a doting mom. The bedroom door was open and it was just as Bill had pictured it on the way from the kitchen. The covers fairly tidy, but Stephanie's empty PJs—the ones with the unicorns—stretched out above them, an open picture book resting atop them in the now strangely silent home. "Oh, my God", Bill, said softly, his eyes beginning to mist.

His smart phone rang. Bill mumbled grudging approval: at least a small step in the right direction. It was Thomas. "Dad! Come and pick me up! School is bedlam – a bunch of kids just disappeared, some teachers, too! Everyone's freakin' out! They said we should go home, if we could get through to anybody!" "I know", Bill said. "I just got home and your mom and sister are both missing, too. I think I know what's happened. I'll be right there. It'll be a zoo—meet me down the street at Dean's Drug Store."

Before he hopped back into his car to fetch his son, he remembered the book that Susan kept on the third shelf of the book case next to the entertainment center in the den. She'd said— only twice—that someday he might find it not just useful, but necessary. He knew was about some critical spiritual matter or another. She was devout in her beliefs but had never pestered him about such things. And oddly, she'd never opened that paperback. Not quite buying into her "relationship with Jesus", he hadn't either. But in deference to their marriage, and the quiet sincerity of her faith, he'd never asked that it be moved. And it had sat there, dusted dutifully like everything else, for the last four years.

On a hunch, he crossed the room and picked it up. The cover read: "Missed the Rapture?" *But Thomas couldn't wait. He'd have time to read later.*

Chapter 1

"What Just Happened?"

The What, Who, and Why of the Rapture

The Bare Bones

- The recent instant disappearance of millions was the "Rapture". It was predicted by the Bible to occur before the judgements of God that bring about the return of Christ and the end of this age.

- The Rapture was the removal from the earth of living believers in Christ and the resurrection of Christians that had died previously.

- It represents God's mercy on living believers by not exposing them to martyrdom and his judgements upon the world system.

- It represents a fulfilled prophecy; certifying the authority of the Bible and what God has said in it about sin, salvation, and future events.

- It represents a final chance for you to find eternal life through faith in Christ.

This book was written before the Rapture and in anticipation of questions about what that disappearance could mean. Even though it was published before the event, *it was written primarily for you*, who find yourself here after the fact.

Your questions are being asked everywhere. Media and government won't make an honest effort to explain it as a spiritual event. And especially not as the Bible does. All the standard sources have a radically different agenda, after all. And yet, how can they avoid dealing with it? Instead, they'll offer alternate explanations—by the fistful. They'll be loaded with speculations and conspiracy theories. Don't be surprised if one of them includes a world-wide "alien abduction"!

By simply opening the cover of this book you indicate that you've been shaken by this event. And that you're sceptical of the tales being spun by the normal information sources. Or, you've taken it up because you heard about it in the past, probably through a Christian family member or friend. You opened this book because you're looking for an explanation with substance. But you want more than just an explanation. You want direction and hope in the midst of chaos and uncertainty.

So, what just happened? "Rapture" comes from a Latin word that means to "seize" or "snatch". Remember the veloci*raptors* in *Jurrasic Park*? But the Latin term is just the intermediate translation of the original Greek word that has the same meanings. It's the word that the Apostle Paul used in a letter to a small church in the Greek city of Thessalonica. Here's the passage:

> For the Lord himself will come down from heaven, with a loud command, with the voice of the archangel and with the trumpet call of God, and the dead in Christ will rise first. After that, we who are still alive and are left will be *caught up* together with them in the clouds to meet the Lord in the air. And so we will be with the Lord forever. (1 Thess 4:16–17)

And there it is: "caught up", describing something being snatched away in an instant. But in this case, it's people. What people? Well, Paul is very particular when he says "we". He's referring to himself and the folks he's writing to. Nobody else. Here's how he describes them: "...To the church of the Thessalonians in God the Father and the Lord Jesus Christ..." (1 Thess 1:1) and who "turned to God from idols to serve the living and true God, and to wait for his Son from heaven, whom he raised from the dead—Jesus, who rescues us from the coming wrath" (1 Thess 1:9b–10).

These were not people that simply had some generic or informational belief in God. They had an intimate trust in him, and in Jesus Christ, His Son. These were people that were not *in* that church, they *were* that church. As such, they were "in both God the Father and the Lord Jesus Christ." And there's one last, critical item: as believers in Christ, they were waiting for Him to return "from heaven", as the One who would "rescue" them from the wrath to come. By extension, it applies to all true believers in Jesus.

That's the essentials of the event; the what, the who, and the why. The rest of this chapter will flesh these out for the sake of clarity. And the rest of the book will answer the basics of the question that remains in the back of your mind: "What now?" We're pretty sure that on that subject, you're not just looking for information, you're looking for what you should *do* in response.

The Great Snatch

The disappearance was instantaneous. As Paul would put it later to another church, it happened in an "eye-blink". And it occurred in that same moment everywhere. Because this book was written prior to the Rapture, the authors can only speculate on how this disappearance may have appeared to you and others. But it certainly had to be astonishing and unnerving. Undeniable, yet also unexplainable. And if it didn't happen in front of you personally, it became apparent in other ways.

Folks returning home to find the garage door and a car trunk open, a spilled bag of groceries, a vacated pile of rumpled clothing, a neighbor across the street scratching her head. Office phones left off the hook, half-eaten meals and spilled beverages at restaurant tables. An unoccupied Post Office truck idling next to an open mailbox, scattered painter's equipment at the base of a ladder against the side of the house next door. Shoes, clothes, and personal items askew on sidewalks, in hardware store aisles, in office buildings and school hallways. The stories are endless. And some may have had disastrous consequences attached.

In any case, the ripple effects were felt everywhere, but especially where Christianity was common. The most terrible effects may well have involved infants and children that simply vanished, leaving devastated parents and families behind. The stress, grief, and bewilderment experienced was both immeasurable and catastrophic.

But very quickly glad voices began to appear. Popular personalities and commentators, maybe even some of your neighbors and friends, expressing their gratitude for the departure of these believers in Jesus. Because they were perceived as social and moral irritants, people whose promotion of civil and personal justice, self-control, modesty, and responsibility threw cold water on everyone else's parade. They were viewed as self-righteous, narrow-minded, and spiritually arrogant. Good riddance, for some. Maybe even for many.

The "Other Half" of the Rapture: A Massive Resurrection

But this instant departure of living believers was only half the story. It also included the remains of those who'd previously died as followers of Christ, remains that God had brought back to life in the instant before they were taken up. It didn't take long for reports to surface of bodies missing from funeral homes, and of cremation containers found to be empty. Maybe even of disinterred but empty caskets.

There are multiple things that united these two groups in this single event:

- both groups were made up of those who had previously placed their personal faith in Jesus as their Savior;

- both were responding to Jesus's descent from heaven, to his command (see John 5:28), to an announcement by an archangel, and to a heavenly trumpet call;

- both were taken up to meet the Lord in the air;

- both were given incorruptible human bodies of similar nature; and

- both arose to the same glorious future.

Paul spoke of this resurrection in a letter to the church at Corinth:

> Listen, I tell you a mystery: We will not all sleep, but we will all be changed—in a flash, in the twinkling of an eye, at the last trumpet. For the trumpet will sound, the dead will be raised imperishable, and we will be changed (1 Cor 15:51–52).

To Paul, "mystery" represents something previously unknown or cloudy but now to be revealed plainly. "Sleep" is a common biblical metaphor for death. He goes on to say that the dead will be raised imperishable, transformed into new, immortal bodies. But also note that he says that "we shall not *all* sleep". That implies that a portion of those called into the heavens will be living when that moment of change occurs. And they'll all get the same kind of new bodies: "we will *all* be changed". Paul makes it plain that both groups participate in the same event. And that's just what he told the Thessalonians.

Paul was not the only early church leader to make the resurrection an essential point in what he wrote and preached. So did Peter, John, and the writer of the Book of Hebrews. All these merely followed the lead of Jesus himself, who spoke of it repeatedly. And, of course, he himself would be the ultimate proof of its reality.

The resurrection of believers was foretold through similar events both before and after the resurrection of Jesus. These include the raising of a widow's son (1 Kgs 17:17ff), the raising of the Shunammite's son (2 Kgs 4:18ff), of a man hastily thrown in the hollow of Elisha's grave (2 Kgs 13:20–21), of the widow's son in Nain (Luke 7:11ff), of Jairus' daughter (Luke 8:40ff), of Lazarus (John 11:1ff), of many at the time of Jesus's death on the cross (Matt 27:52–53), of Tabitha (Acts 9:36ff), and of Eutychus (Acts 20:9ff). Every one of these resurrections was verifiable by witnesses.

There are lots of folks that find the idea of a bodily resurrection to be an absurdity. It supposedly contradicts logic. It's scientifically impossible. Don't be surprised, these dismissals go way back. In the First Century, some major players in Jewish religion rejected a bodily resurrection out of hand. Chief among them were the Sadducees (Acts 23:8). Many of the Greeks that Paul preached to considered it bizarre (Acts 17:18, 32; 1 Cor 15:12). The same scepticism remains to this day.

Many dismiss the physical resurrection by spiritualizing it. They say that it's only figurative or symbolic of some non-material event or change. There are those that spiritualized the Rapture, too—before it actually happened. The proof of the physical, bodily reality of both came with their occurrence. They can no longer be explained away by something else.

The gathering of God's *living* servants directly into heaven was also previewed in the Bible. The Old Testament speaks of what happened to both Enoch (Gen 5:21–24) and Elijah (2 Kgs 2:10–11). In the New Testament, Jesus appeared to his disciples for over 40 days after his resurrection (Acts 1:3). And after that, he also physically ascended into heaven (Acts 1:9–11). In the cases of both Elijah and Christ, the Bible says there were eyewitnesses.

So, it can't be said that history has no precedents for either a massive resurrection or the snatching up to heaven of God's living servants. What just happened has certified the reality of all these miraculous occurrences. This should be a tremendous encouragement to trust the reliability of the Bible. And that same trust should also be applied to what it says is still future for you.

The Rapture Had a Purpose

It's reasonable for a person to ask what purpose God had in promising the Rapture. He is gracious in not leaving us with the necessity to speculate. It's right there in our quote of Paul from 1 Thessalonians 1:10; ". . .who delivers us from the wrath to come." The apostle John says the same thing in the Book of Revelation. Here he records Christ's commendation to the first century church in Philadelphia (in what is now western Turkey): "Since you have kept my command to endure patiently, I will also keep you from the hour of trial that is going to come on the whole world to test the inhabitants of the earth" (Rev 3:10). To be kept out of a coming trial of the entire world is an evidence of Gods' mercy!

But what is this "wrath" that Paul speaks about, or that Jesus calls an "hour of trial"? It's God's righteous judgement upon a world that has finally "filled up the measure of its sin" (1 Thess 2:16).

Now many folks are inclined to think that the world is pretty benign or neutral from a spiritual perspective. Yes, there are instances or pockets of evil and rebellion against God and his standards. But surely, aren't they the exception rather than the rule? After all, look at all the progress mankind has made! How can it be that the world has descended to the point where God has "had enough"? Did you once have this opinion? Has it changed as you've seen the world around you descend into moral and philosophical chaos?

God doesn't see the world as benign at all. Here's his assessment of the world and its rulers (with the spiritual forces of evil lurking in the shadows):

> Why do the nations conspire
> and the peoples plot in vain?
> The kings of the earth rise up
> and the rulers band together
> against the Lord and against
> his anointed, saying,
> "Let us break their chains
> and throw off their shackles." (Ps 2:1–3)

And here's what the world looks like right now:

> But mark this: There will be terrible times in the last days. People will be lovers of themselves, lovers of money, boastful, proud, abusive, disobedient to their parents, ungrateful, unholy, without love, unforgiving, slanderous, without self-control, brutal, not lovers of the good, treacherous, rash, conceited, lovers of pleasure rather than lovers of God—having a form of godliness but denying its power. (2 Tim 3:1–5a)

And regarding mankind across the ages, Paul quotes from several other Psalms and Isaiah, saying:

> As it is written:
> There is no one righteous, not even one;
> there is no one who understands;
> there is no one who seeks God.
> All have turned away,
> they have together become worthless;

there is no one who does good,
not even one.
Their throats are open graves;
their tongues practice deceit.
The poison of vipers is on their lips.
Their mouths are full of cursing and bitterness.
Their feet are swift to shed blood;
ruin and misery mark their ways,
and the way of peace they do not know.
There is no fear of God before their eyes. (Rom 3:10–18)

God's just judgement is based on the perfections of his nature and on the authority that he carries as the Creator. He can no more indefinitely delay his judgement of sin and rebellion than you would indefinitely fail to deal with graffiti painted on your house or car! Someone might argue that the harshness of this judgement conflicts with his love. Alright, let's see how Peter keeps these two in proper balance when speaking of things to come:

By the same word the present heavens and earth are reserved for fire, being kept for the day of judgment and destruction of the ungodly. But do not forget this one thing, dear friends: With the Lord a day is like a thousand years, and a thousand years are like a day. The Lord is not slow in keeping his promise, as some understand slowness. Instead, he is patient with you, not wanting anyone to perish, but everyone to come to repentance. (2 Pet 3:7–9)

His judgement is found in the first sentence above. His love in the last, expressed in the salvation that he provided through the sacrifice of Christ, and his patience in waiting for folks to do something with it. My friend, this love is still personally on offer to you, in the Gospel.

It Represented a Fulfilled Prophecy

The Rapture was predicted almost two thousand years ago. It's been fulfilled in your day, and you've already confirmed its occurrence. In that sense, consider it a prophecy intended by God *especially for you!* It's appropriate, then, to ask what purposes God has in fulfilling prophecy. Basically, they boil down to four:

- to establish the certainty of his promises,

- to stimulate the trust or faith of those who recognize their fulfillment,

- to have that faith applied to the rest of what God has said in the Scriptures, and

- to serve as a rebuke for those who continue in willful unbelief.

The Rapture was the first of a series of fulfilments of major events predicted in the Bible that will come to pass over a period of seven years. This seven-year period is referred to as the Tribulation. It will end with Jesus physically returning to the earth to defeat the enemies of God, and to establish his thousand-year reign of righteousness and peace.

This period was first spoken of in detail in the Book of Daniel. It includes natural catastrophe, social unrest and war, widespread spiritual deception, and violence. But it speaks also of the rise to world dominance of a person known elsewhere in the Bible as the Antichrist.

Jesus spoke to his disciples of this period in the final days before his arrest, illegal trial, and crucifixion. That message is called the Olivet Discourse and it's found in the twenty-fourth and twenty-fifth chapters of Matthew's gospel. He describes the latter half of this period as the *Great* Tribulation (Matt 24:21, although both words are often used in this book for the entire period). The major characteristic of these last three and a half years will be the consecutive judgments of God to be visited upon the earth and its population. More will be said of this short era in the final five chapters of our book.

It's Another Opportunity for You – Don't Make It Your Last!

Here is the bottom line: you've been left behind. Left behind because, whatever you may have *thought* about Jesus Christ before, you haven't yet placed your faith in him. But it's not too late to do that! An eternity of joy in His presence is still available to you. And a life, here and now, that is more than equal to the harrowing days ahead. Now, that's some really *good* news! And that's fitting, because "good news" is the literal meaning of the word "gospel".

But to place your faith in Christ requires an understanding of what the Gospel really is. After that, everything boils down to a simple choice that you need to make. Let's talk about the essentials of the Gospel in the next chapter, and finish it up by discussing your choice.

Chapter 2

The Essentials of the Gospel – and Your Decision

What You Must Know and Do to Be Saved

Susan's brother Art was a graduate of Union Theological Seminary, with a subsequent doctorate from Harvard Divinity School. He had risen through a succession of church assignments and was now rector at a large Episcopal church in suburban Washington, D.C. It was a prominent one, attended by senators, congressional reps, agency heads, and foreign diplomats. Art had written two books which had sold well and been well received in both academic and social circles. His first was on the biblical roots of open-border immigration, the second on commonalities between Islam and Christianity. He was occasionally interviewed on religious events and topics by both CNN and ABC. Affable, articulate, generous, and photogenic to boot. What was not to admire about him?

But Bill occasionally wondered how it was that his wife and brother-in-law seemed to swim in such contrasting versions of Christianity. What was more curious than that was Susan's remark about six months ago over dessert, concluding one of their monthly dinner dates. She'd ordered Tiramisu, he was making unsuccessful efforts at slowing his destruction of a Chocolate Indulgence. Her comment certainly diverted his attention—while speaking of her brother, she'd simply and quietly said, "I pray for him." It was so startling that Bill had forgotten how the conversation had led up to that moment. And so startling that he'd chosen not to ask her what she meant by it. Neither then, nor since.

For a long time, Bill had delighted in listening to Art converse during holiday visits and the bi-annual family reunion on his wife's side of the family. His brother-in-law talked about religion and the love of God as easily as Bill had heard his own grandfather talk about flyfishing during childhood vacations in Maine. Bill had found Art's discussions not just well-reasoned and persuasive, but soothing to his spirit as well. He was especially relieved to learn that all his efforts in civic affairs and charitable organizations over the last fifteen years really counted with God. Art had no clue that these good works often played in Bill's mind against a lengthy string of terrible deeds that he'd done in his youth. Misadventures that continued both in and after four years of military service practically ordered by his folks—wishes supported by the "suggestion" of a local Circuit Court judge.

Bill had finally turned a corner eleven months after he'd been discharged from the Navy. A night on the town had ended with a terrible auto accident. It had killed his best high school friend and left Bill with major leg and internal injuries. And his scientifically inclined mind finally began to speak loud enough to be heard: "Bill, you're a complete jerk! You've pushed the envelope so hard for so long that you should have killed yourself a half dozen times by now. As it is, Sam is now the second friend you've seen under a sheet. Give it a rest already!"

Through that tragedy he'd gotten a grip on himself. Off to college and then engineering school on the GI Bill. It was at college that he'd met Susan. She'd quickly latched on to his relative maturity, especially as compared with that of the other guys at school. Hey, at the same point in their education he was five years older, after all. But Susan didn't know just how recent that apparent "maturity" was—or how precisely he'd come by it. She was quiet and had not pressed him about either it or the adventures that might have attended his youth. Bill didn't know if it was good sense or abject shame that kept his lips well sealed on any number of items from his past. Thankfully, his folks had kept mum as well, not wanting to ruin what looked like a good thing developing with this young lady.

"That was then, this is now", he thought, observing that never had an old, hackneyed phase sounded so bitter. He'd continued to churn over the devastations that had now befallen him and Thomas, who'd been spending more time than ever with his buddies. Bill wasn't sure if that was good or bad. At least it was a break of sorts; hopefully one that wouldn't end up being too costly in other respects. On top of the loss of his wife and daughter, practical matters had immediately become almost unmanageable. He'd gotten no help from his lawyer, who was unexpectedly swamped and curt. Phone calls and emails to his insurance company went unanswered. His own company was in shambles, and he couldn't provide adequate responses to HR questions from the families of the three employees that had disappeared.

Rumors abounded. The news was as chaotic as the entire society had suddenly become.

His mind drifted back to the book. Again. It had been doing that for the last four days, rather naggingly, he observed. He'd read only the first chapter but found it so—so outlandish that he'd read it twice, closing it up each time without going farther. Yeah, he'd heard Susan mention the Rapture on scattered occasions in the past, but passed it off as an oddity that she'd picked up at the church she attended. Not being disrespectful to her, of course, but the folks there certainly fit his picture of what some friends and media people called "Bible-thumpers".

But he couldn't seem to shake off what he'd read about it in the book; particularly in that opening Bible verse that the authors had quoted to describe it. It was pretty outrageous that someone writing in the First Century could have described so closely what had just happened across the globe, and quite cruelly in this very house. Bill had never before seriously considered the implications of what his wife had said would be a "fulfilled prophecy". Was the Bible something different than what Art had once called "living literature", a mere collection the moral pronouncements—and fantasies—of its many authors?

For some unexplained reason, Bill again reflected on his response to that auto accident, the one that had killed his friend, but also turned his own life around. Here was another life moment staring him in the face, a moment when he really needed to get a grip on himself. And he found himself praying.

He presumed that there was a God out there. But this time he sensed as never before that it was a God who was personally interested in Bill's welfare and would hear the cry of his heart: "Oh, God, this is all more than I can deal with. And it isn't just me. It's demolishing Thomas, too. I've understood before that you're a God of love. Sue and Art have both said that often enough. But what's happened to us—to everyone—makes me wonder. It's like the world has been cursed. It's like I have been cursed! But also, that if I don't call out to you, I will be cursed."

For a prayer, it certainly didn't seem like much. Totally one-sided. Not even an "Amen" at the end, let alone saying it in Jesus's name (why did people do that, anyway?). All it had going for it was its brutal honesty. Bill figured God could handle that. Maybe, just maybe, there was something important to gain by it. Certainly, there was nothing—at least nothing more—to lose. He decided to consider this "voicemail" to God as, well, experimental.

It was 11:30. Thomas had shuffled off to bed twenty minutes ago, sullen and dead tired. Suspecting that it would probably be another long night, Bill toyed with reading in Sue's well-worn Bible. Then again, he didn't feel ready for that just yet. And besides, he had utterly no idea where it would be best to begin. At the beginning, with Genesis? Genesis? That was old stuff. What could it possibly have to say about the current mess? Instead, he picked up the book on the Rapture and opened it to Chapter Two.

Chapter 2

The Essentials of the Gospel – and Your Decision

What You Must Know and Do to Be Saved

The Bare Bones

- The Gospel is God's offer of salvation to all. Satan seeks to make it unattractive or irrelevant by any possible means.

- The Gospel begins to make sense when a person admits to being a sinner and that being so places him or her under the sentence of death: eternal separation from God.

- The Gospel is the only means by which sinners may be reconciled to God and given eternal life.

- Jesus Christ is qualified to be our Savior by his sinless nature. But his nature includes his being God in the flesh. This is the substance of his inherent authority as Lord.

- The Bible states that Jesus's resurrection from the dead certified the effectiveness of his sacrifice on the cross. Personal belief in the resurrection is fundamental to saving faith in Christ.

• The salvation that is offered through the Gospel is appropriated solely by faith. Faith in Christ is a willful choice to rely upon the sacrifice of Christ as the payment for one's personal debt of sin.

Let's be straight up about this: Satan is a sore loser. The resurrection of Christ attested the devil's future defeat at the end of history. This guarantee of his judgement and pending eternity in Hell only fuels his wrath against God. And in the interim, he'll do all he can to take as many people with him as possible. He does so by keeping them out of the arms of the Savior. His primary strategy in doing this is to cloud the essentials of the Gospel. And he uses at least ten devices to do it:

• by making the Gospel appear irrelevant through atheism or agnosticism,

• by making it appear irrelevant by worldly attractions and distractions,

• by offering the deceptive substitutes of other religions or "faiths",

• by confusing the essentials of the Gospel with the surface behaviors and activities that people associate with Christianity,

• by convincing people that their sin is too small to keep them out of heaven,

• by convincing people that their sin is too great to be covered by God's mercy and redemption,

• by convincing people that good works or a favorable comparison with other sinners (God "grading them on the curve") will save them,

- by changing the definition of sin altogether, or convincing people it has no eternal consequences,

- by tainting the Gospel as the plan of an unjust, capricious, or "blood-thirsty" God, or

- by distracting people with thorny issues, with disagreements with what God says about something in the Bible, or by his failure to act when they think he should have.

If you were left on the earth in the wake of the Rapture, you've probably been victimized by one or more of these deceptions. This chapter is written to clear the air on what the genuine Good News is all about—and to leave false notions about it in the dust.

The Background of the Gospel

There are three wonderful terms that characterize what the Gospel is all about: grace, mercy, and peace. Here's some thumbnail descriptions for each. They don't reflect the breadth and depth of each term, but they'll do for starters:

Grace is God's giving us what we don't deserve;

Mercy is God *not* giving us what we *do* deserve;

Peace is God reconciling us to himself in the person of Christ.

Grace is about salvation, adoption into God's family, heaven, and everything else that comes with faith in Jesus. Given our inherent condition, none of these are deserved. Nor can they be earned. Mercy is about pardon from judgement. Given our condition and God's holiness, judgement is what we *do* deserve. Peace is about establishing the kind of relationship that God has intended men and women to have with him from the beginning.

Of course, each of these three terms also have huge application for folks *after* they become believers. But here at the start, they're an easy to memorize backdrop for what the Bible teaches as the kernels of the Good News. And "good news" is precisely what the word "gospel" means.

The Essentials of the Gospel

Paul identifies the fundamentals of the Gospel in the opening verses of 1 Corinthians 15:

> Now, brothers and sisters, I want to remind you of the gospel I preached to you, which you received and on which you have taken your stand. By this gospel you are saved, if you hold firmly to the word I preached to you. Otherwise, you have believed in vain. For what I received I passed on to you as of first importance: that Christ died for our sins according to the Scriptures, that he was buried, that he was raised on the third day according to the Scriptures... , (1 Cor 15:1–4)

These are the matters "of first importance":

- *Christ* (it's the Greek word for "Anointed One", the Messiah, as promised in the Old Testament; many of those passages reflect his divine nature);

- *died for our sins* according to the Scriptures (that is, the sins of each particular person that needs a savior);

- *and was raised to life on the third day*—again, according to the Scriptures.

Note that each one of these things is based on what God had previously established as biblical truth.

When he wrote to the early Christians at Rome, Paul covered these things this way: "If you declare with your mouth, 'Jesus is Lord,' and believe in your heart that God raised him from the dead, you will be saved" (Rom 10:9).

This is shorter, but essentially covers the same things. Here he also speaks of Jesus as divine (the essence of his being "Lord") and that he was raised from the dead. Implied in his death is that it had a purpose: to be a substitute for us, as the payment of the penalty due for our sins. Paul says that a person has two resulting obligations: they must be believed and they must be declared. Belief is your personal reliance on their actuality. Declaration is a verbal admission that you've availed yourself of them, that you want them to be effective for you personally.

"Believe" and "declare" in this verse from Romans 10 parallel "receive" and "stand upon" in the opening verse of 1st Corinthians 15. They reflect your conscious choice to agree with God about what he says of your lost and guilty condition. They also reflect your wish to personally lay hold of his remedy for it, the sacrifice of his son on the cross. Finally, they reflect your willingness to affirm these truths as occasion arises.

Christ... died for our sins... and was raised on the third day. This is the essence of the Gospel. Anything different from these three fundamentals either confuses or negates them (remember those ten "devices" itemized at the beginning of this chapter?). The Gospel is the message that Satan seeks to suppress by any and every means. That's because it's the only means by which we can be brought out of darkness into Jesus's marvellous light. It's the only means by which we get to heaven. And it's the only means by which God lifts us out of the hands of the evil one, who has taken us captive to do his will (1 John 5:19).

The False Notion of Many Ways to Heaven

We're sure you've often heard that there are "many ways to heaven." Folks say that because they don't want to deal with these truths. Or they may say that Jesus's being the *only* way of salvation is arbitrary, arrogant, narrow-minded, or ungracious—and that the Gospel must therefore be false. In settling your opinion, wouldn't you conclude that Jesus Christ himself should be the expert on the matter?

Well then, here's what he said: "I am the way, the truth, and the life. No one comes to the Father except through me" (John 14:6). Jesus being the way to be saved and to go to heaven doesn't ultimately rest on the teachings of Christianity *as a religion*. And it certainly doesn't rest on the opinion of any particular person, whether believer or not. In the end, it rests on the claims of Christ alone.

Pay special attention to Jesus's use of the word "the" with each essential in this statement. Jesus is not "a" way (that is, one of many), he's not "a" truth (among others of equal standing), nor is he simply some mystical kind of "a" life, some sort of existence that we're left to speculate about. No, he's the fundamental essence of these three things. And it's because he's the *embodiment* of them that salvation is available through him—and through him only.

Peter also puts to rest any notion of there being many ways to God and to heaven. He said, "There is no other name under heaven by which we must be saved" (Acts 4:12). He does more than just say that Jesus is the *only* way, he says that he's the absolutely *necessary* way. He didn't say "can be saved," he said "must." That makes believing in Christ for salvation a moral obligation—with all the implied eternal consequences. Heaven if we do, hell if we don't. And that, my friend, should really focus your attention.

The Primary Admission: That I Am a Sinner

For many, the greatest hurdle in trusting in Christ is accepting the real need for it. It's admitting that they're sinners, not just in their deeds, but by their very nature. If they've convinced themselves that sin isn't a significant issue, Jesus becomes no more relevant than any other person from the dusty pages of history. If a person can dismiss the issue of sin, then they can dismiss with a single wave both their own true condition and the One who was sent by God to save them from it.

Look, nobody likes talking about sin. But especially as a personal matter. Being a "sinner" smacks of failure, imperfection, unacceptability to God, even social disgrace. It has to be avoided because our pride demands that we not fall short, but especially by comparison with others. And so, we delude ourselves by thinking we are better than most: "Why, look at what I've made of myself!" Or, we buy into the deception that our good deeds will work as some self-printed admission ticket to heaven. But if that's true, then Christ died for nothing (Gal 2:21)!

But Just What Is "Sin"?

So, let's get down the nitty-gritty: Just what is sin? It's breadth and depth are seen in how many words are used in the Bible to describe it. The Old Testament uses at least ten separate Hebrew terms for sin, and the Greek New Testament has at least fifteen. Each of them has a particular nuance, of course. But all of them ultimately boil down to two basic components:

- our lack of conformity to God's character, and

- our willful independence before him.

Independence and not coming up to God's standards are more than just our inclinations. Sin (in the singular) is at the very root of our being: it's our inherent condition (see Ps 51:5; Eph 2:1–3). It's this condition that produces all of our behaviors and attitudes that fall short of God's standard (that's *sins*, in the plural).

On Sin, Death, and Judgement

Both the condition of sin and the deeds it generates place us under God's righteous judgement. Perhaps a bit too simply, sin is the basis of his legal charge against us, sins are the evidence. Paul puts the penalty very plainly: "The wages of sin is death" (Rom 6:23; see also Jas 1:15).

Consider what Paul wrote about the condition of his readers before they believed in Christ: "As for you, you were dead in your transgressions and sins" (Eph 2:1). Almost without exception, when most people speak of death, they're thinking only biologically. But if we limit death simply to its physical aspect (Rom 5:12; 1 Cor 15:22a), we make a serious error. Because the Bible reveals two *non-physical* effects that also apply, even while we're alive.

The first is a profound separation from God himself (see Gen 3:8–11; Isa 59:2). This is death in the spiritual realm. It's an absence of the intimacy that we were intended to have with him from the beginning. It's an estrangement that makes it impossible for a person to properly please him (Rom 8:7–8; Heb 11:6). Those who don't pass from death to life by belief in Jesus (John 3:18; 5:24) remain under the judgement of God, not just in this life (John 3:36), but in the next (Rev 20:15).

The second effect is the death of one's own spirit. Being dead in trespasses and sins is described as being in a condition of spiritual darkness (Eph 5:8). It's an inability to properly recognize, access, and employ the truth (Rom 1:21). It's no wonder Jesus said that a person "must be born again" through their trust in him (John 3:3, 7, 16).

Can One's Sins Be Beyond Remedy?

We've just spoken about folks who dismiss sin as a personal issue. Well, there are others with just the opposite problem. They have no difficulty at all in understanding that they're sinners. Recognition isn't the problem, magnitude is. They're conscious of sin so much—or of sins so many or terrible—that they think they're beyond redemption. They think that there has to be at least *some* limit to God's mercy in Christ, and what they've done has certainly exceeded it! From the opposite perspective, it's just another case of "Why, look at what I've made of myself!"

God deals with this faulty thinking with an unexpected and dramatic example. Of all people, it comes from the Apostle Paul himself! Check this out:

> I thank Christ Jesus our Lord, who has given me strength, that he considered me trustworthy, appointing me to his service. Even though I was once a blasphemer and a persecutor and a violent man, I was shown mercy because I acted in ignorance and unbelief. The grace of our Lord was poured out on me abundantly, along with the faith and love that are in Christ Jesus.
>
> Here is a trustworthy saying that deserves full acceptance: Christ Jesus came into the world to save sinners—of whom I am the worst. But for that very reason I was shown mercy so that in me, the worst of sinners, Christ Jesus might display his immense patience as an example for those who would believe in him and receive eternal life. (1 Tim 1:12–16)

This is his description of his former days as a Pharisee, a person who made it his business to expose the sins of others and see that it brought them to appropriate misery. What an admission! But that's not all. In the book of Acts, we find Paul openly admitting his involvement in putting people to *death* for having believed in Jesus (Acts 7:58; 9:1–2; 22:19–20; 26:9–11)!

Can't get any worse than that. And yet, he was shown mercy, even *as the "worst of sinners"*. This was so that others would not be able to persuade themselves that Jesus couldn't—or wouldn't—save them.

However hefty the list of God's charges against Paul, they all grew out of his ignorance and unbelief. And that, friend, can be remedied in a moment through God's grace and mercy. But only if you're humbled enough to want Christ's death on the cross to count for you.

A Fundamental Implication: The Lordship of Christ

This is a good place to mention a critical truth about the person of Christ. It was mentioned above from 1 Corinthians 15 and Romans 10 and deals with Jesus's divinity. Put a bit more simply, Jesus Christ is God in the flesh. Paul says that "in Christ all the fullness of the Deity lives in bodily form" (Col 2:9). This divine nature was his even from before what we conceive of as time (John 1:1). It wasn't a condition that was bestowed upon him at his birth in Bethlehem. It wasn't something that he later gained by some act, such as being baptized by John the Baptist. It wasn't something that was only temporary and passed from him when he died on the cross. It's a timeless aspect of his very nature (see Col 1:17; Heb 13:8).

Jesus Christ's divinity is essential to his being. It was also essential to his sacrifice on the cross, which required the perfection of sinlessness (Heb 9:14; 1 Pet 1:19). His divinity was at the source of his resurrection (John 10:17–18). And it's what he currently demonstrates to believers as their intercessor and High Priest (Heb 5:5–6; 7:24–28). It's his divinity that makes him Lord. *The* Lord, far beyond anything a mere human could lay claim to.

Anyone who trusts in him for their salvation is brought into an intimate relationship with everything about him. Yes, he becomes a person's Savior when they appropriate his death for their sins by faith, but he is Lord regardless. That's why, in the end, *every* knee shall bow in that acknowledgement (Phil 2:10–11).

Here's the gist of the matter: he holds all authority in heaven and earth (Matt 28:18). He therefore has a right to expect a responsiveness to that authority. But especially from those who place their faith in him (Luke 6:46; John 13:13–17). Every believer in Christ is obliged to respond to him in obedience.

This may sound to some as something a bit more than they want to buy into from the start. But that's a flawed perspective, a leftover from our previous history of willful independence toward God. Instead, we should think that our responsiveness to his lordship is just a part of a very special and intimate relationship with him. We will naturally want to please him (Eph 5:8–10).

Because Jesus's lordship isn't limiting or oppressive, he can give this unique perspective on obedience: "My yoke is easy and my burden is light" (Matt 11:30). The apostle John tells us that "his commands are not burdensome" (1 John 5:3). Think of this as real freedom. That's what's gifted to every person that places their faith in Christ (John 8:32–36; Gal 5:1). It's a freedom not just from slavery to sin, but into the liberty to be of service to God (Rom 6:7, 18, 22; Gal 5:13; 1 Pet 2:16).

For the believer, Jesus is both Savior and Lord. Together, they produce both gratitude and obedience.

A Necessary Personal Decision: How to Receive Christ as Savior and Lord

All of this is about the fundamentals of the Gospel, the good news about forgiveness of sin and how to obtain it. It all brings you to a decision that you must make. You need to do some personal business with Christ.

You may have other questions, but they can wait. We'll probably address many of them in the rest of this book anyway. Don't let them be excuses to delay this decision or kick it down the road for some other day. There is a whole new life that awaits you on the other side of that wall of separation, but it's without any meaning for you until you go through the door. Jesus is the door. The Gospel is the knob.

You can apply the Good News to yourself by prayer. Don't be intimidated. He's listening and expects you to use your own language and style. Don't be "religious," just be honest. You can do it aloud or silently: he'll hear it either way. Here's the gist of what to say:

- Tell Jesus that you know you're a sinner and recognize that it places you under eternal judgement.

- Tell him that you've chosen to believe that he died on the cross in *your* place so that you can be forgiven and removed from that judgement.

- Tell him that you believe that he rose from the grave.

- Tell him that you acknowledge him as Lord, the final authority over how your life should be lived from this point onward.

He'll know you're thankful without you mentioning it—but feel free to mention it anyway. Say an "amen" if you like: it just means "and that's the way it is." It's kind of like your nod to Jesus that you've said your peace—while requesting his.

Chapter 3

An Introduction to Eternal Life

Being a New Person in a Crumbling World

*Problem planning and management issues: forget the engi-
neering business, Bill now had these in spades everywhere
else. Never before had he faced so many knotty questions,
each with monumental implications and consequences. Four
nights ago, he'd read the second chapter of the book that
Susan had left him. Actually, he'd read it twice. It was all
about his need for making a personal commitment to faith in
Jesus as Savior and Lord. Intellectually, what he'd read had
cleared up a number of issues on which he'd had false notions.
If he were to accept what the Bible had to say about them
as true, there was no question about the decision that he
needed to make. That was the rub: it wasn't the content that
immobilized him, but the* decision. *Bill had finally come to
this: "Well, if what is said here is true, I have everything to
gain and nothing lose—certainly nothing more than I've
lost already."*

*He'd decided to say aloud his prayer to be saved. He'd sup-
posed that Jesus would have "heard" it if he'd done it silently,
but he sensed that he needed to hear himself speaking the
words. He wanted to distinguish them from all the other*

35

words that had been surging back and forth in his mind. And he knew from personal experience that speaking aloud helped to manage his train of thought. As much as anything he'd ever said in the past, he didn't want these words to lose their focus.

By the time that Bill had placed his faith in Christ, he had been worn out. After his prayer, he'd closed Susan's book, set it aside, then sat back to consider the decision that he'd just made. It wasn't long before he found himself reaching for the lever on the side of the chair and throwing it into its full-recline position. Moments later, turning off the lamp beside him had been a no-brainer.

He'd been awakened in the morning by Thomas sticking his head in the library door and announcing that he was off to school. And he'd been awakened also to a cacophony of thoughts. Not just about what had happened to Susan and Stephanie, and the mess that the Rapture had left in its wake. That continued to nag his consciousness as something that had lots of "loose ends," and particularly regarding God's involvement in it. But what was added to it now was the recollection of what he'd read just hours before, and the decision that he'd made in response. His prayer had been a response to a curious inner assurance, one that it was the right thing to do, even the chief necessity. And he realized after his prayer that the decision was not just for the moment: it appeared to extend, rather loudly, into an as yet uncongealed future.

Chapter 3

An Introduction to Eternal Life

Being a New Person in a Crumbling World

<u>The Bare Bones</u>

- God's promises establish that your salvation is both certain and lasting.

- When you become a believer in Christ, you are "born again", becoming a new person, whose spirit is no longer dead but alive to God.

- God's own spirit, the Holy Spirit, takes up permanent residence in you. The Holy Spirit's presence is a "down payment" guaranteeing your redemption and heavenly future.

- The Holy Spirit is intent on changing you into a person that demonstrates a likeness to Christ himself. Jesus's nature will begin to be evident in your character and your actions to the extent that you stay humble and devour his word.

- You become an agent of God, one in whom he displays his mercy and power while the world descends into increasing chaos.

- The central figure in this chaos will be the Antichrist.

The Certainty of Eternal Life in Christ

If you've just made that decision and said that prayer, I'd suggest two things that you'll find very helpful in the days to come:

1) Grab a little slip of paper and write down the date and the following: "On this date I received Jesus Christ as my Savior and Lord". Slip it in your wallet. This isn't because you're liable to forget either the date or the circumstances. But there's going to be a time that someone on this planet—or a dark spirit in Satan's realm—will call into question the decision you've just made. You'll find it helpful in that moment to fish it out and wave it in the air in front of them as evidence. Pretty soon, you'll simply tell them what it says—and probably adding on what you've recently been learning about Jesus.

2) Find an appropriate someone and tell them the same thing that you just wrote down and slipped into your wallet. Don't feel obliged to get into a heavy conversation about it. It's the declaration, not the discussion, that's important. Consider it your first spiritual "adventure"!

These steps will provide a practical confirmation of the step you've just taken. But, frankly, they're just circumstantial reminders. There's something far more substantial than these two tips. It's what God says in the Bible about what you've done. Here's what Jesus said (and still does, by the way): "All that the Father gives me will come to me, and the one who comes to me I will certainly not cast out" (John 6:37, NASB).

And here's another promise from him:

My sheep listen to my voice; I know them, and they follow me. I give them eternal life, and they shall never perish; no one will snatch them out of my hand. My Father, who has given them to me, is greater than all; no one can snatch them out of my Father's hand. (John 10:27–29)

And the apostle John in his first letter: "I write these things to you who believe in the name of the Son of God so that you may know that you have eternal life" (1 John 5:13). Did you catch that word "know"? John didn't say "guess," or "presume," or "wonder," or even "hope." He said "know": it's something to be certain of.

And finally, here's something hefty from Paul:

What, then, shall we say in response to these things? If God is for us, who can be against us? He who did not spare his own Son, but gave him up for us all—how will he not also, along with him, graciously give us all things? Who will bring any charge against those whom God has chosen? It is God who justifies. Who then is the one who condemns? No one. Christ Jesus who died—more than that, who was raised to life—is at the right hand of God and is also interceding for us. Who shall separate us from the love of Christ? Shall trouble or hardship or persecution or famine or nakedness or danger or sword? As it is written:

"For your sake we face death all day long;
we are considered as sheep to be slaughtered."

No, in all these things we are more than conquerors through him who loved us. For I am convinced that neither death nor life, neither angels nor demons, neither the present nor the future, nor any powers, neither height nor depth, nor anything else in all creation, will be able to separate us from the love of God that is in Christ Jesus our Lord. (Romans 8:31–39)

Well, friend, that pretty much covers every eventuality. Did you notice that there's no quibbling or hedging in these statements? No one who has placed their faith in Christ Jesus as Savior and Lord should ever have any reason to doubt the security of their salvation. It's a fact that stems from being justified before God; permanently off the hook because Jesus stepped up and paid the penalty for you. It's a standing or state of being in Christ that exists apart from both your feelings and your circumstances. That's because it's founded on the promises that God has made in his word, promises in which it is impossible for him to lie (see Heb 6:17–19).

On Being a New Person...

The Bible says that you become a new person at the moment you place your trust in Christ. This doesn't imply that you've become fully renovated in an instant. But it does mean that your essential nature has undergone—by God's doing—a fundamental change. Jesus says you have been "born again" (see John 3:3–8).

Here's how Paul put it: "Therefore, if anyone is in Christ, he is a new creation. The old has passed away; behold, the new has come" (2 Cor 5:17). That speaks of an entirely new kind of life based upon the regeneration of your spirit. And here's Paul in another place:

As for you, you were dead in your transgressions and sins, in which you used to live when you followed the ways of this world and of the ruler of the kingdom of the air, the spirit who is now at work in those who are disobedient. All of us also lived among them at one time, gratifying the cravings of our flesh and following its desires and thoughts. Like the rest, we were by nature deserving of wrath. But because of his great love for us, God, who is rich in mercy, made us alive with Christ even when we were dead in transgressions - it is by grace you have been saved. (Eph 2:1–5)

And Jesus himself: "When Jesus spoke again to the people, he said, 'I am the light of the world. Whoever follows me will never walk in darkness, but will have the light of life.'" (John 8:12)

Your new person, brought about by your faith in Christ, is one in whom his Spirit has taken up residence. It's a transformation in your essential *nature or being*. And it's the starting point for a gradual transformation in your *character and actions*. You will begin to outwardly express more and more what Jesus himself is like (see Eph 4:15; Rom 8:29; Luke 6:40). That change will be pretty much proportional to how much you seek his direction, rely upon him, and spend time reading his word. We'll talk more about this a few paragraphs farther on.

...In Whom God's Spirit Dwells

Once again, let's listen to Paul:

> "And you also were included in Christ when you heard the message of truth, the gospel of your salvation. When you believed, you were marked in him with a seal, the promised Holy Spirit, who is a deposit guaranteeing our inheritance..." (Eph 1:13–14a).

And,

> You, however, are not in the realm of the flesh but are in the realm of the Spirit, if indeed the Spirit of God

lives in you. And if anyone does not have the Spirit of Christ, they do not belong to Christ. But if Christ is in you, then even though your body is subject to death because of sin, the Spirit gives life because of righteousness. And if the Spirit of him who raised Jesus from the dead is living in you, he who raised Christ from the dead will also give life to your mortal bodies because of his Spirit who lives in you. (Rom 8:9–11)

And there you have it. Now, Paul throws a lot of heavy stuff in here. But here's the essence: when you recognize that something is of interest to God, it is from the prompting of the Holy Spirit within you. When you are sensitive to sin and deception, it's from the Spirit. When you find yourself yearning to learn more and more of Christ and what's in God's word, it's a work of the Spirit. These are all a consequence of the Holy Spirit's being in you (Rom 8:14).

But beyond merely being led by God's Spirit, there are other major benefits that he provides:

- spiritual understanding and perception (John 16:13; 1 Cor 2:12–13),

- special capacities to serve God through serving others (Rom 12:6–8; 1 Cor 12:4–11),

- the expression of spiritual attitudes and traits (Gal 5:18, 22–23).

And more. Lots more.

When you accepted Christ as your Savior and Lord, you were given access to all the essentials necessary to be pleasing and useful to God. Here's how Peter describes your new status: "His divine power has given us everything we need for a godly life through our knowledge of him who called us by his own glory and goodness" (2 Pet 1:3). The only thing that you need to supply is growth in your knowledge of Jesus Christ and how he wishes to make you into his likeness. That comes through the study of his word (see 1 Pet 2:2). We'll take up this particular subject in the next chapter in more detail.

As for a heavenly future, here's something from Paul: "Now the one who has fashioned us for this very purpose is God, who has given us the Spirit as a deposit, guaranteeing what is to come" (2 Cor 5:5). Did you note that Paul uses the word "deposit"? What he's saying is that, when you believed, God sent his Spirit to reside in you as a *down payment* to guarantee your possession of that inheritance. People have the terrible habit of welching on their promises. God never does—and takes up residence in you to prove it!

Here's the same from Peter's perspective:

> Praise be to the God and Father of our Lord Jesus Christ! In his great mercy he has given us new birth into a living hope through the resurrection of Jesus Christ from the dead, and into an inheritance that can never perish, spoil or fade. This inheritance is kept in heaven for you, who through faith are shielded by God's power until the coming of the salvation that is ready to be revealed in the last time. (1 Pet 1:3–5)

This all speaks about the promise made to you of an eternal future in heaven. It's an "inheritance" that's reserved for you (see John 14:1–3).

Salvation – From the Inside Out

God has done all the "heavy lifting," but that doesn't mean that you can now kick back and coast leisurely into heaven at some point down the road. Your daily circumstances will prove that soon enough. For a perspective on what we're talking about here, consider this: "...being confident of this, that he who began a good work in you will carry it on to completion until the day of Christ Jesus" (Phil 1:6).

Paul says that God, from within, will move forward with his plans for you until the day that Jesus returns. That's *his* part. But as his new son or daughter in Christ (see John 1:12), he intends for you to be a partner in the process. Here's Paul a few verses later:

> Therefore, my dear friends, as you have always obeyed—not only in my presence, but now much more in my absence—continue to work out your salvation with fear and trembling, for it is God who works in you to will and to act in order to fulfil his good purpose. (Phil 2:12–13)

Right there in the middle of those two verses is this: "work out your salvation." Don't misunderstand what's being said here. Paul doesn't say "work *for*," but "work *out*." The distinction is massive. Salvation isn't something you can work *for* because it's a gift, something that cost you nothing (see Eph 2:8–9). But now that you've got it, it needs to be exercised, demonstrated, made evident in your daily life. That's what's *your* part.

Look, you placed your faith in Jesus for salvation. It was offered to you as a gift, something that you couldn't possibly earn or secure by your own effort. But having accepted it, you'll now have a constant string of opportunities to demonstrate the results of what's happened to you. That is, you'll use that very same faith to make choices that will express his presence within you. This is the process that not only makes you useful to God, but accompanies your development of a Christlike character. It's one aspect of what the Bible calls "sanctification," being set apart as holy. These opportunities become what the New Testament describes as a "walk." It's a life that isn't *earning* salvation, but one that's proving its existence by what it produces in you.

Here's how this process is expressed in a few other places: "So then, just as you received Christ Jesus as Lord, continue to live your lives in him, rooted and built up in him, strengthened in the faith as you were taught, and overflowing with thankfulness" (Col 2:6–7). And, "we are God's handiwork, created in Christ Jesus to do good works, which God prepared in advance for us to do" (Eph 2:10). And:

> We continually ask God to fill you with the knowledge of his will through all the wisdom and understanding that the Spirit gives, so that you may live a life worthy of the Lord and please him in every way: bearing fruit in every good work, growing in the knowledge of God, being strengthened with all power according to his glorious might so that you may have great endurance and patience, and giving joyful thanks to the Father, who has qualified you to share in the inheritance of his holy people in the kingdom of light. (Col 1:9–12)

And:

> We know that we have come to know him if we keep his commands. Whoever says, "I know him," but does not do what he commands is a liar, and the truth is not in that person. But if anyone obeys his word, love for God is truly made complete in them. This is how we know we are in him: Whoever claims to live in him must live as Jesus did. (1 John 2:3–6)

Now, all of these are essentially saying the same thing: God intends that you act like the believer that you've just become—and he intends that you keep at it. Keeping at it is what the Bible calls endurance or perseverance. We'll address that in more detail in Chapter Six.

An Informed Perspective on the Near Future

Life is tough. It always has been. That's nothing new to you. But the Rapture was the unique introduction to a relatively short period of time when everything is going to *really* come unglued. The Book of Daniel indicates that this period covers only seven years. It will involve an unprecedented collection of miseries that give it its name: the Tribulation. And those difficulties will be experienced, at one level or another, by everyone, whether they continue in their unbelief or are newly-minted Christians.

The trials that will mark these days will be both environmental (natural disasters, pestilence, famine) and social (outbreaks of war, civil unrest, anarchy, and violence). You can see these descriptions previewed in Matthew 24, Luke 21, and the first four verses of 2 Timothy 3. Much of this will be directed toward Christians and the nation and people of Israel. Satan is behind the scenes, pulling all the levers.

A person of unique charisma and influence will arise on the world stage to offer an initial measure of peace and stability. He is the Antichrist. He'll perform miracles and wonders to establish his credibility. And to the relief of most, he'll appear to deliver on his promises. But only for a while. Like all of the other deceptions that will mark this period, it will turn out to be a sham. The stability he provides will come by political, economic, or military persuasion and force. Most won't make any noise about the human and constitutional rights they've kissed goodbye. They'll surrender them willingly for the short-term benefit of what they will call "peace and safety" (1 Thess 5:3). But he won't be able to stem an increasing frequency of natural catastrophes. In short order, he will consolidate his sweeping power to become a global tyrant. But all of this is just a prelude to his final demand.

Half way into this period he will require that he be worshiped by the entire world. And then the world will experience a terrible series of divine judgements, their magnitude being unimaginable except that they've also been predicted in the Scriptures. They will be so great that the last three and a half years have their own title: the *Great* Tribulation. All of these issues will be covered in more detail in Chapters Twelve through Sixteen.

What's critical for you to understand is that you will have the resources available to deal with all of it from the outset. Actually, they were all supplied when your accepted Christ as your Savior. It's just that you're not yet fully aware of them and how to put them to use. These resources will enable you not only to endure, but to prosper spiritually in the process. From another angle, God intends for you to be all in—and has equipped you accordingly. Chapters Five and Six will cover the primary principles that will contribute to your being successful in negotiating your coming circumstances.

Chapter 4

Reorienting Your Life to God's Word

The Importance of the Scriptures to Your New Life

This was not the first occasion he'd recognized that his mind had become a shambles. Bill chaffed at the disorder. For a few moments, he considered the possibility of calling Frank Simms and begging off coming in to work because of a "headache." Frank had become the go-to person for such things because Carolyn hadn't been replaced yet as the receptionist—or even found, for that matter. Her circumstances, and what they left him with, had become just something else on the pile, a pile that was growing at an alarming rate. No, he needed to go in to the office. There was pressing work to be done there. Perhaps the tyranny of the urgent would require some orderliness to his thinking, at least until he began to wrap up his work day. He'd come home to check up after Thomas and then throw together some dinner—or order out, again.

Bill planned to pick up the book again that evening. It was becoming a pattern once the mundane issues of the day had ebbed away. "Mundane?" Ha! Another term to add to the collection of words that were gathering new definitions. He seemed to recall that the book's next chapter was about the importance of "truth" or some such subject. Perhaps it would provide some direction. Before he crashed again in his recliner.

Hours later, he'd classified his day as being fairly uneventful, at least in comparison to the week before. Everything was becoming a sea of relativity, after all. No new crisis had arisen, only the further mysteries—or complications—of the recent ones. He'd called Thomas just after school had ended. At least the cellular networks seemed to be back to normal. Bill had offered to bring home pizza, thinking it was both convenient and a sure thing to boot. Thomas never turned down anything from Angelino's. Bill had gotten the first six words out of his mouth before he heard, "Sorry, dad, Jim asked me over for din. His folks are ordering out from Angelino's. And I also got an invite to stay overnight." "Okay, but at least offer to provide the sodas. You got bucks for that?" "Thanks, Dad. And I can cover the sodas, too. Be in touch."

Bill was grateful on three accounts. First, it gave him a night off from seeing those shadows of both anger and sadness that would appear on his son's face without warning. Shadows that gnawed at Bill's heart as much as did Sue's and Stephanie's absences. Second, and on the slightly brighter side, there couldn't have been a better home for Thomas to hang out at overnight. He and Jim had been close buddies since grade school and the Caberman family was refreshingly friendly and stable.

The third reason was that he could digest the next chapter in Susan's book without domestic distractions. This one was about the importance of the Bible; he'd peeked when he got home. Bill was sensing an interest to begin reading the Bible, *but he had a jumble of conflicting thoughts. Not just about where to start, but which copy to use. Would using Susan's just trip his emotional circuits and be another distraction? Maybe the one that was "his," the one that he'd opened only twice. Would he find it too difficult to understand? The verses that were quoted in the book on the Rapture were pretty straight forward, but surely they'd been selected and isolated by the authors. This would be an entirely new venture. Susan knew her Bible like the back of her hand. By comparison, he had no clue what reading through it would be like.*

Chapter 4

Reorienting Your Life to God's Word

The Importance of the Scriptures to Your New Life

<u>The Bare Bones</u>

- Your new life must be founded on the truth contained in the Bible. It's the basis for the reorientation of the way you look at everything.

- The Bible is as dependable as the unchangeability of its Author. It's comprehensible and capable to form you into the person God intends you to be—regardless of the adversities you may face.

- God's perspective is expressed in a biblical worldview. Because that worldview is drawn from the Scriptures, it takes on their characteristics of truth and wisdom. A biblical worldview is integrated, consistent, and fully compatible with God's will.

- A secular worldview is the default perspective of all outside of Christ. It is drawn from human wisdom and speculation. For that reason, a secular worldview is arbitrary, ever-changing, incoherent, and is incompatible with a biblical worldview.

It is therefore fundamentally contrary to the truth and the will of God.

- Secular world views are a chief means of Satan's progressive deception of mankind. They are also his means to provoke conflict and disorder in personal, national, and international affairs.

The Indispensable Word of God

Have you noticed that we've really been piling up all these Bible quotations? Well, we could easily have added more. Their number reflects just how important these things are to God. He covers the essential issues many times, and from all sorts of angles. And all for your benefit.

Your new life is to be founded on and reoriented by the truth that's found in the pages of the Bible. Peter describes this with an appropriate picture: "Like newborn babies, long for the pure milk of the word, so that by it you may grow in respect to salvation" (1 Pet 2:2).

Everything that is contained in the Scriptures is underwritten by God's unchanging character. That's why his word will be your primary source of stability in a period that's already woefully unstable—and will become even more so. Folks around you will really begin to come unwound. But you'll have the resources to stand secure. As we've said previously, when you received Christ as Savior and Lord, you were gifted with everything necessary for life and godliness. All you need to supply is your continued trust in him and your diligence in becoming familiar with what's written in God's word.

You're now faced with the necessity of choosing between two radically different ways of thinking. Let's call them competing worldviews. We'll pick this up in more detail shortly. But for openers, think of a worldview as a perspective that governs how you think about what happens both around and to you. It's about what you hold to be real, true, and moral. The biblical worldview is how the Bible explains them. The secular worldview is the vast assortment of ideas and opinions that have their roots in the world system and the forces behind it. One represents the truth of God himself; the other is the attempt of humanity to create answers from its own reference points, a pretty shaky approach when it's applied to moral and eternal matters.

Although you have the freedom to constantly choose between these two perspectives, we think that you'll quickly adopt what the Scriptures say, rather than how the world explains the things that really matter. And that you'll find yourself gravitating quickly to the Bible for two reasons. First, its dependability has just been verified by the undeniable evidence of the Rapture. The event proved the assertion. You've pretty much acknowledged this by getting this far in our book. Just extend that confirmation to the rest of the Bible.

The second reason comes not so much from logic as from an inner testimony. If you've responded to the Gospel by faith, the Holy Spirit will be giving you an inner sense that what you've read is the truth of God. Just before his death on their behalf, Jesus spoke to the disciples of this work of the Spirit:

> But when he, the Spirit of truth, comes, he will guide you into all the truth. He will not speak on his own; he will speak only what he hears, and he will tell you what is yet to come. He will glorify me because it is from me that he will receive what he will make known to you. All that belongs to the Father is mine. That is why I said the Spirit will receive from me what he will make known to you. (John 16:13–15)

If you recognize a confirmation of the truth of the Scriptures that you have read to this point, you simply need to apply that same sense of their authority to what you'll read from the Bible from here on.

The Dependability of the Word of God

Paul speaks about the dependability of the content of the entire Bible; and also of its purpose: "All Scripture is inspired by God and profitable for teaching, for reproof, for correction, for training in righteousness; so that the man of God may be adequate, equipped for every good work" (2 Tim 3:16 (NASB)). The word of God has the inherent capacity to reorient a person's thinking away from what previously had darkened their understanding and lured them from a grasp of the Gospel. And it's your source for being able to perceive everything in and around you from God's perspective.

The Bible is complete and comprehensible in regard to the issues about which it speaks. These include what it says about God's nature, his work as the creator and sustainer of all things, angels and the realities of the spiritual realm, the nature of man, salvation, the development of Christian character, the flow of history, and its consummation at the end of this age. And that's just for starters.

Being complete and comprehensible applies regardless of the enormous difficulties that lie ahead. For the Bible, and especially the New Testament, has always contained everything necessary for believers to negotiate heavy testing and persecution. The only thing different about what's ahead for you is the extent, frequency, and severity of those issues. The principles of Scripture are the same, and will apply as equally in the future as they have in the past.

In Chapter Seven we will provide some helpful tips on how to get started in reading the Bible profitably. If you want to get a jump on that, begin reading in the Gospel of John. Then a reading of Ephesians would be in order, or perhaps First Peter, especially considering the times in which you find yourself. If you want to read a narration of how First Century Christians managed their trials, you can find it in the book of Acts. Wherever you read, you'll be surprised to find out how much has *not* changed in 2000 years!

Reorienting Your Thinking

Handling matters in a fallen world has always been the great, new adventure for those that come to faith in Christ. It's natural to expect that becoming a new person should require a new way of looking at that world and your place in it. That new perspective is a matter of how you change your *thinking* about that world. Here's what Paul has to say on this subject:

> Therefore, I urge you, brothers and sisters, in view of God's mercy, to offer your bodies as a living sacrifice, holy and pleasing to God—this is your true and proper worship. Do not conform to the pattern of this world, but be transformed by the renewing of your mind. Then you will be able to test and approve what God's will is— his good, pleasing and perfect will. (Romans 12:1–2)

As you're probably beginning to notice, Paul can pack a lot of hefty stuff into a few words. That's the case here. But let's focus for the moment on what's right in the middle of this quotation. He says that it's a believer's responsibility to no longer "conform" to the pattern of life that characterized their past existence, but to be transformed by the renewing of the way they think about things.

Paul describes this transformation with a distinctive word. The word that he uses here is the verb form of "metamorphosis." Remember that from high school biology, the process of a caterpillar being changed into a butterfly? Talk about a great metaphor for becoming a new person!

The New Testament has some important things to say about God's part in this transformation process (like Eph 2:10, Phil 2:13, 1 Cor 5:17, and Rom 6:3–11 for starters). But let's speak here of the contribution that *you* will make to the "renewing of your mind". Something from Psalm 119 captures the key to what it's all about: "I have more insight than all my teachers, for I meditate on your statutes" (Ps 119:99).

It's your exposure to the word of God that will change the way you think about things. And the way you think about things governs the way you react to them (see Prov 23:7a; Luke 6:45).

One's Worldview: Everyone's Frame of Reference

Let's expand here on the concept of worldview that we introduced above. Most of our thought processes are governed by our worldview. A worldview is our collection of ideas not just on the what and why of the way things are, but on how we think they ought to be. Perhaps too simply, it's a combination our perceptions of reality and our values. Into this pot we throw our past experiences, our present emotions, and the opinions of those we admire and respect—just for seasoning, of course.

It's not just philosophers, professors, and politicians that have world-views, everyone does. If people are inclined to think they don't have one, it's because they don't think much about what forms the bedrock of their own values and opinions. And the less they think about it, the greater the inconsistencies and contradictions that their worldview contains. The proof that everybody has a worldview is that they have general patterns of thinking, preferences, standards, and behavior. It's their worldview that directs those patterns.

As we've already mentioned, worldviews come in two distinct varieties: biblical or secular. You can get your perspective from what God has revealed in the Scriptures or from somewhere else. At their core, these two types are built upon radically different premises. The differences are so great that the two worldviews can't logically co-exist with one another.

Paul puts this contrast in a rather descriptive and practical light:

> See to it that no one takes you captive through philosophy and empty deception, according to the tradition of men, according to the elementary principles of the world, rather than according to Christ. (Col 3:8 (NASB))

Now, in the context here, Paul is not addressing worldviews directly. He's talking about an assault on his teaching by Jewish traditionalists and people with other religious agendas (see vv. 4 and 11–23). And yet a conflict between competing thought systems is at the core of what he says.

In dealing with his opposition, he plainly identifies two major factors that contribute to a secular worldview: popular philosophy and deception. And he says that these two are directly tied to two others: human traditions and to the basic concepts that drive the world-system. It should not be forgotten that all of this is under the current control of the devil (2 Cor 4:4; Eph 2:2; 6:12; 1 John 5:9).

But Paul also wants to emphasise the capacity of all this stuff to captivate a person's thinking. To make the point he uses a term to describe the booty or spoils of war being hauled off by a conquering army. Except that here Paul has *people* in mind: "see to it that no one takes *you* captive! That's because a person is largely a product of his or her thought processes (Prov 23:7; Matt 12:34).

Oh, and one other thing. Paul is not addressing this verse to the lost (though they're the easiest victims), he's addressing believers. And that means they're not immune to the infectious thinking that dominates a world in rebellion to God. It's everywhere. And it gobbles up the unsuspecting.

Colossians 2:8 is the secular worldview versus the biblical worldview all rolled up into one verse. Now let's now explain the essence of each.

The Biblical Worldview

A biblical worldview concerns what is true and good. We'll be the first to admit that non-biblical worldviews are concerned with these things, too. But the critical difference lies in the source that produces or informs their particular system's values. The biblical worldview is always centered in the revelation of the nature and character of God (which are unchanging), and in the expressions of his being that are seen or revealed in the creation.

God's revelation is two-fold. What we see in the creation is called the *general* revelation. It speaks to our conscience about the orderliness, power, and majesty of God. From that derives our essential accountability to him. Good places to read about this are Psalm 19:1-6 and Romans 1:8-23.

Then there's what's called the *special* revelation. That's what we learn from God in his word, the Bible (see Ps 19:7–11 and 2 Tim 3:16–17). It speaks more specifically about the nature of the creation and mankind, about God's actions in history, his principles for living, and most importantly about the person of Christ and the redemption from sin that is available only through him. And quite a few other matters, of course.

All of these factors contribute to an integrated understanding of God, ourselves, the world at large, and our place in it. And also of the world to come. Because it comes from God as its single source, and because it comes with his intention to establish us upon the truth, a well-developed biblical worldview is always integrated and consistent. These factors give the biblical worldview an inherent stability and coherency. It also guarantees its compatibility with God's will.

The Secular Worldview

A few folks will get technical with the title of this section. "Hey," they'll say, "there's lots of secular worldviews!" And indeed, there are. Actually, it's not uncommon for people to have more than one secular worldview, depending on just what they're considering at the moment. But for our purposes, we can treat them as one because they all have one glaring characteristic in common. They are all—and always—founded on human reasoning and speculation. The Bible declares that this speculation stands in opposition to God and acts as a replacement for his revealed truth (see Romans 1:21–23; Eph 4:17–19).

By having no root in the revealed truth of God, all secular world-views are subject to relativism and ever-shifting human opinion. This gives them a corresponding level of instability and disorder, one that affects every level of human thought and perception. And because behavior is the product of thought and perception, this disorder and inconsistency ends up characterizing how individuals conduct their affairs.

This same effect is also seen in the conflicts between groups and nations. That's because the bigger the group, the greater the smorgas-bord of secular worldviews it entertains and has to satisfy. The world system is an ever-changing buffet line of philosophy and thought, of values and ethics. Add to this mix all the self-interests that individuals, collectives, and nations pursue. Is it any wonder that the world is in chaos?

Here's something else to consider: individuals, cultures and nations tend to equate progress in technology to progress in non-material issues. Issues like values, ethics, and social theories. This, of course, is a monumental deception. For the world's conflicts, inequities, and moral decay prove that progress in science and technology has pro-duced no similar progress in non-material areas. The spiritual state of the world is really no better than it's ever been. Some would even say it's worse. If only because the most technologically advanced and sophisticated cultures also seem to be those where "me" most reigns supreme. The world simply continues a downward slide in finer fab-rics and with more complicated gizmos.

But there's a final, most telling aspect to secular worldviews. Listen to what Paul has to say:

> As for you, you were dead in your transgressions and sins, in which you used to live when you followed the ways of this world and of the ruler of the kingdom of the air, the spirit who is now at work in those who are disobedient. (Eph 2:2)

Paul ties the thinking and behavior of those outside of Christ to the thinking of "this world." But that is directly tied to "the ruler of the kingdom of the air." And that's Satan, the evil one. Ultimately, secular worldviews are the product of darkness, the fruit of the schemes of the devil. He's challenged God from the beginning, reigning in the world as the prince of deceit and destruction (see John 8:44). John wrote that "the whole world lies in the power of the evil one" (1 John 5:19). Everything he offers mankind is a substitute for the real thing. In the end he will parade before the world his greatest servant, the Antichrist, as the ultimate substitute for Jesus Christ himself. In the end he will manage all secular worldviews to serve in worship of himself.

Your worldview will govern how you handle the issues and adversities of the Tribulation. Make sure you're cultivating the right one.

Lawlessness and Deception: The Nature of the End of the Age

The Bible teaches that the Tribulation that concludes this age will have two primary features: lawlessness and deception (Matt 24:3–28; 2 Thess 2:7–12). Both of these are aspects of disorder, a prime characteristic of Satan's schemes and activities. Lawlessness is disorder in relation to behavior. Deception is disorder in relation to truth. We have already established in Chapter Two that all people are fallen and sinners both in nature and deed, that they're "dead in trespasses and sins" (Eph 2:1). But there is an intellectual component that's a part of that condition.

Paul says that, prior to new life in Christ, we are "darkened in our understanding" (Rom 1:21; Eph 4:18). It's really a fundamental disturbance in an unbeliever's rational capacities. Little wonder, then, that those outside of Christ are susceptible to deception. Deception comes from outside ourselves through our unrelenting exposure to error, and to the guile by which it's camouflaged. Deception also comes from within by our capacity to dismiss conscience and rationalize bad choices. Frankly, before a person places their faith in Jesus, even the things that are said in the Bible are apt to be dismissed as foolishness (1 Cor 2:14).

Partners in Crime: Disorder and the Secular Worldview

As we've said before, our behaviors are driven by our thinking. But unless we're renewed through faith in Christ, our capacity to think clearly remains darkened. This is far more than just an inability to think logically and critically. That's a condition that's become particularly prevalent in America in recent decades. And it draws upon the *natural bent* of those outside of Christ to reject the truth (Rom 1:18). In time, it becomes apparent that this rejection is willful. It begins with the truth about God, but expands to apply also to what he says about moral and ethical values. And even about the principles that are fundamental to the proper operation of society (John 3:19–20). This is what the Bible describes as "darkness".

A secular worldview works together with man's fallen nature to produce immorality, vanity, social disorder, violence, anarchy, and war. That makes it a fertile field for the destructive schemes of the devil, and particularly in a period when divine restraint has been lifted from his activities (2 Thess 2:6–7). This will reach its peak in the period in which you're now living! The evil one's increasing manipulation of deceit and secularism is the primary instrument behind the unparalleled chaos that already surrounds you, a chaos that will increase in the months ahead.

This world of disorder is the pool in which everyone alive in the Tribulation must swim at one depth or another. God intends that you not just tread water, but actually pile up a good number of profitable laps before he calls you out of the pool. That requires that you recognize what you've already been given by him to accomplish this purpose.

Let's consider what you've been given under the two categories of *perspectives* and *resources*. We'll talk about the first of these in the next two chapters. We'll hold our discussion of resources for later, where we will address them as disciplines for profitable living.

Chapter 5

Profitable Principles for Tribulation Living – I

On Promise, Hope, Presence, Peace, and Power

Bill's engineering principles governed how he looked at things. Everything boiled down to task management. He saw that as resting on two essentials: managing the process and employing the right tools. According to a popular expression, Bill was very "left brain." Everyone noticed. It was a characteristic that Susan would jokingly rib him about, but only on an irregular basis. She had the insight and discretion to never mention it when he might be apt to take it as a personal dig or as nagging. He thought about how fortunate he was. There was another guy in his office, a draftsman, who had the same approach when dealing with issues. And it was not uncommon for him to grumble at work about how his wife would regularly needle him about his "heartless approach to problem-solving." Bill occasionally mused about where Susan's artful timing came from.

He'd read about the renewing of the mind as a necessity for someone who'd become a new Christian. And what he'd read was only logical. To be honest about it, Bill had always noted that Susan had quietly operated on a different level. It was one that he found both fascinating and admirable, yet somehow not quite accessible to him. It suddenly dawned on him: she'd filtered everything through a biblical worldview. It was something that had always escaped him—until now.

He was sensing that he was getting closer to something that he could really lay hold of in his turmoil. What he'd read about the different kinds of worldviews had also made sense. He'd lived his life to this point very much under the secular approach. And the more he began to apply real-world and personal illustrations to that realization, the more sense it all made. But the issues that faced him now were still somehow beyond the concepts that had been explained in the third chapter of the book. Chapter Four was entirely reasonable, but didn't register as particularly practical for the daily issues he seemed to be facing.

Bill suddenly realized what he was looking for in his whirling circumstances. He thought it might be reliability. There was plenty of that in physics, mathematics, and chemistry, the building blocks not only of the engineering profession but also of the materials that it employed. But the heaviest things he was now facing were not matters of roof truss stress loading or options for bridge piers sunk beneath riverbeds. No, it wasn't reliability—at least regarding the Bible. That had been addressed to his satisfaction in the fourth chapter. What he was really looking for was how he could apply what he learned from the Bible. Learning didn't mean much if you couldn't do anything concrete with it. That involved practical life issues as much as the moral values that lay behind them.

No, it wasn't reliability, it was perspective.

Chapter 5

Profitable Principles for Tribulation Living – I

On Promise, Hope, Presence, Peace, and Power

<u>The Bare Bones</u>

- Life during the Tribulation will be tough. But it will be much easier for those who can employ practical principles that put its difficulties in perspective.

- A believer's purpose is the accomplishment of God's will. It's a privilege to partner with Christ in demonstrating both his power and his grace in the face of adversity.

- Promise is gifted to believers by God himself. Promise is direction. Promise is stability. Promise is hope. It's the principle upon which our access to divine resources rests. It's the principle that guarantees our future. It's a direct expression of God's faithfulness.

- Hope for the believer rests upon the surety of God's promises. For the lost, hope is merely a dream because it can't be guaranteed by anything in this world.

- God's presence insures constant access to his sufficiency in everything. The presence of Christ is the perfect defense against the fear of what awaits at the hands of man.

- God's peace is accessible only through Jesus himself. Jesus's peace surpasses circumstance because it's rooted in his own nature. It's realized in the believer when it's accepted as real and then acted upon.

- God's power is his means of accomplishing his will. It's always for good. It's made available to believers for the same purpose. It's furnished because we aren't able to accomplish his will in our own strength. That makes believers vessels for the demonstration of his power—and advertisements for his glory. Just like peace, divine power is reckoned into use.

We mentioned in Chapter Three that life is tough and always has been. It's kind of a recurring sub-theme in this book. But it's one of the major themes of the Bible, even from its opening pages. "Tough" is the consequence of sin in the world (see Gen 3:16–19). Tough is an evidence of the disorder that followed Satan's seduction of Adam and Eve in the Garden. Tough plays no favorites; it falls upon everyone. Rich and poor, young and old, great and small. But even though it produces all sorts of miseries and destructions, tough can also produce surprising positives. Things like invention, endurance, sympathy, care, and philanthropy.

But tough also becomes the tool of God, especially when he uses it to refine the faith and character of believers. It's the great purifier of his children. And the great occasion for his power to be put on display in them. But, in the whole of history, nothing will be able to compare with the tough that will occur during the seven years of the Tribulation.

Just before his arrest, trial, and crucifixion, Jesus was asked by his disciples about the sign of his second coming and of the end of the age. The most detailed account of his answer is found in chapters 24 and 25 of Matthew's gospel. Jesus paints a chilling picture there of the character and events of this period. Not far into his answer he says this:

> For then there will be great tribulation, such as has not been from the beginning of the world until now, no, and never will be. And if those days had not been cut short, no human being would be saved. But for the sake of the elect those days will be cut short. (Matt 24:21–22)

Chapters Twelve through Sixteen will describe the events, personalities, and issues of this period in detail. But the next two chapters will provide some principles that will help you maintain both your wits and your progress as you face them. Before we discuss those principles, let's paint a backdrop.

The Appreciation of Purpose

God intends that you not just get through this adversity, but that your endurance produce something valuable. Peter wrote two letters that are found toward the end of the New Testament. He wrote them to believers who were enduring great testing. And behind all their difficulties was the work of the devil himself. He's always been involved in producing misery, but especially for God's people (read the first two chapters of Job for a hairy example). Here's one of the things that Peter had to say to these folks regarding Satan's troublemaking: "Resist him, firm in your faith, knowing that the same kinds of suffering are being experienced by your brotherhood throughout the world" (1 Pet 5:9).

The word "experienced" is a pretty bland translation here. It leaves you with a sort of "been there, done that" sense. That's because it misses the gist of the Greek word that Peter used. He chose a term that describes something *being brought to an intended end*. It's a word for a purpose that is being "accomplished." The world always looks on suffering as something destructive. But God sees suffering as a short-term means to a greater accomplishment.

This means that Jesus has divine purposes in mind when we success-fully handle adversity. And that's a whole lot more than just "toughing" something out. In your love for Christ, his purposes become yours. You've heard folks fret because they sense they have no purpose, no great reason for being. Have you noticed that it never sits well when you hear this from someone? And it's even worse when you come up with the thought regarding yourself! So, let's re-orient and give you a purpose, a reason for being.

When you come to Christ you make yourself available to him. It's not inappropriate to say that *he* becomes your reason for being. But from another perspective, he has reached out and chosen *you*. He wants you to participate with him as he prepares for his rule over the earth. That's a great honor and makes you uniquely valuable. It's something worth hitching your wagon to.

From this perspective, your accomplishment becomes a great wit-ness. It's a testimony both to his power and mercy, not to mention your faith. Your perseverance in the face of tribulation pleases Christ and brings him glory. And it's an encouraging proof to you that you can overcome pretty much anything that arrives at your doorstep.

What follows are seven principles to help you survive these times in a spiritually successful manner. Each of the following principles is an important perspective that you can apply to the issues that the coming days will bring. They'll be touchpoints to direct how you can profit from those issues. What we present in the rest of this chapter and the next isn't exhaustive. There are other principles that govern living for Christ that are found in God's word. We're just offering these as some major starters. God will lead you to others in due time.

Here's the first thing to know: each of the seven principles below is based on divine promises. Because these promises are as firm as the God who gives them, the principles will apply regardless of your cir-cumstances. They're unqualified and always dependable. You can take them to God's bank and cash them in time and time again. That's intended to give you confidence and resolve. And what you're about to face is sure to give that confidence and resolve a real workout.

The Paramount Principle of Promise

God intends that his children shine as lights in a dark world (Matt 5:14–16; Phil 2:15). But because it's a world in rebellion against him, it calls for Christians to develop substantial personal character and resilience. Here is something absolutely fundamental: God doesn't expect you to rise to the occasion in your own strength. Instead, he gives you two necessary tools for the task: his power and his promises. We'll speak of his power below. But it's appropriate to speak of the importance of promise as the first principle. That's because it's the basis for each of the ones to follow.

Promise is direction. Promise is stability. Promise is hope. The whole matter of promise is essential to a satisfying and effective experience of life in Christ.

In one sense, promise in the Bible is just like it is elsewhere: a person makes a statement with the intention of performing it for the person to whom it was made. It's made to give a confidence that what's been promised will indeed happen. But there's a rub with promises made by people: they're all too often unkept.

They decay into disappointment because they go unfulfilled. And they aren't kept for two basic reasons. The first is that the person making the promise is *human*. And that introduces a whole boatload of undependabilities. The second is that the person making the promise *has no ultimate control* over many of the circumstances that affect its fulfilment.

God transcends these two failings by underwriting his promises with his unchanging nature. First, through his *faithfulness*. This represents his perfect dependability. It's a part of his nature that he can't suspend (Heb 10:23). Second, God is *sovereign* over every circumstance. That means he can exercise his limitless power to secure the outcome of any event just as he has intended it (Isa 46:9–11; 55:11; Jer 1:12). These are just two things out of his nature that guarantee what he's promised. You'll discover that there are other divine characteristics that also lie behind what he's said.

The promises of God aren't idealisms or nice-sounding phrases without any real substance. They are powerful and intensely practical. Here's how Peter speaks of them: "...he has granted to us his precious and very great promises, so that through them you may become partakers of the divine nature, having escaped from the corruption that is in the world because of sinful desire" (2 Pet 1:4).

These promises are conditioned only by the extent of our trust in them; the depth of our willingness to rest our actions on them. Note that he says three other things about them. First, they are "granted" by God. That means that they've been given to you permanently: they're always at hand, always redeemable! Then there's the adjectives he adds. "Precious" speaks of their tremendous value; "very great" speaks here of their magnificence or capacity—literally, they are the "most mega" possible.

But finally, Peter discloses their purpose. And it's a very personal one for you: God's promises are your means of experiencing things that reflect his own nature. This is a result of his being at work within you (see Phil 2:13). This speaks not just of your *potential*, but also of your *purpose*: to be an example of life in the midst of death, of light in the midst of darkness (see Eph 5:8).

In both of his letters Peter spoke about God's promises to believers that faced hefty trials and persecutions. Their response to adversity is the major theme of each. In the first one, he describes them as "aliens and strangers" (1 Pet 2:11). That seems a bit odd, as they were living among friends and neighbors in a familiar society and culture. But what had happened was that they'd experienced a radical change in both their person and their purpose. Don't be surprised if you begin to feel the same way, now that you've become a Christian. It will probably be very quickly!

An Aside: Promise is Hope

A few paragraphs above we said, "Promise is hope." That doesn't mean that promise and hope are identical; instead, think of promise as being the root from which hope blossoms. Hope focuses on what God has guaranteed that he will do. Hope is certainty. It's the assurance of what lies ahead (see also Heb 11:1). And that's why hope for a believer is so much different than it is for a person who doesn't believe.

People without Christ are "foreigners to the covenants of the promise, without hope and without God in the world" (Eph 2:12). That's bad anytime, but even more when that world is picking up speed on a downward spiral. For them, the best that hope can offer is limited to something that *might* happen. For them, hope is essentially a dream, a product of human imagination. That's a far cry from what God has intended, promised, and has the power to accomplish (see Isa 46:9-10).

The importance of hope can't be over-emphasized at any time. But especially in light of the trials of the Tribulation. Hope really flowers in the New Testament because of the promises given there to believers. Look up the following and see for yourself:

- Hope produces endurance (Rom 8:25; 1 Thess 1:3)

- Hope produces joy (Rom 12:12)

- Hope produces boldness (2 Cor 3:12)

- Hope anticipates a full renovation of our character (Gal 5:5)

- Hope will be fully realized in heaven (Col 1:5; Titus 1:2; 3:7)

- Hope is a natural outgrowth of the Gospel (Col 1:23)

- Hope anticipates future "glory" (a pregnant term if ever there was one) and it is inseparable from the presence of Christ *in* every believer (Col 1:27)

- Hope looks forward to our own resurrection (1 Thess 4:12)

- Hope is a defense in spiritual conflict with the forces of evil (1 Thess 5:8)

- Hope is a possession of honor and privilege (Heb 3:6)

- Hope is a sure anchor for the soul (Heb 6:18–19)

- Hope is our eager expectation for the return to the earth of Jesus himself (1 Pet 1:13).

- Hope in seeing Jesus face-to-face stimulates our desire to grow into his likeness (1 John 3:2–3)

We've taken a short side trip on this issue because hope is what God's promises are intended to produce in you. Later in this chapter we'll talk about the principle of perspective. Hope is the basis of perspective. It's a primary factor in how the Bible puts adversity into an acceptable context. But first let's consider God's presence, peace, and power.

The Principle of Presence

God is never absent. He can't be, because it's part of his nature to be everywhere, all the time. The two-dollar word for this is "omnipresence." Another divine trait that goes along with it is "omniscience," the two-dollar, twenty-five cent word for his knowing everything. A great place to read about both of these is Psalm 139. King David speaks there in very practical terms about what they mean. If you feel you're in need of a break at this point, look it up and read it. Slowly. Then maybe just sit for a while to let it sink in. We can wait.

Now, Psalm 139 is a fabulous starter on the subject of God always being with us. But when we think about God's presence, Jesus adds a unique perspective. And it's one especially fitting for believers experiencing the troubles that will come with the conclusion of history as we've known it.

> Go therefore and make disciples of all the nations, baptizing them in the name of the Father and the Son and the Holy Spirit, teaching them to observe all that I commanded you; and lo, I am with you always, even to the end of the age. (Matt 28:19–20 (NASB))

This passage is known as Jesus's "Great Commission." It's his "marching orders" for his disciples. But look particularly at how he finishes them. First, he says, "lo." It means "behold," or better yet, "Look at this!" What he's about to say should get special attention: "I am with you always." This, friend, represents the promise of his *personal* presence with every Christian. Finally, he wants to be sure that his hearers understand the extent of that promise: "even to the end of the age." Well, lo and behold, here you are. Right in the middle of the conclusion of what he said 2000 years ago! The "end of the age" is a phrase that Jesus used in Matthew 13:40–50 and it goes back more than 500 years earlier to the last chapter of the Book of Daniel. It's about the very period that you're now a part of.

Here's something written to believers under duress in the Book of Hebrews: "...be content with what you have, because God has said, 'Never will I leave you; never will I forsake you.' So we say with confidence, 'The Lord is my helper; I will not be afraid. What can mere mortals do to me?'" (Heb 13:5b–6).

So, let's also take apart this nugget. Being "content with what you have" means far more than simply being satisfied with your "stuff." In the end, it covers all your circumstances, too. Contentment is being satisfied that God has given you everything you need to deal with your present situation, whatever it is. You can be content with whatever it includes because God, who is all-sufficient, is with you. And he'll never leave or forsake you. The author of Hebrews went back to quote God's promise to Joshua (Josh 1:5). As the successor to Moses, he'd just been charged with leading Israel to conquer the godless nations that were squatting on the Promised Land. No easy task. Nor will yours be.

Now, the worst of our circumstances are often caused by other people. So, what does the writer choose for his second quote from the Old Testament? Psalm 118:6: "I won't be afraid because the Lord himself is my helper." It's pretty plain that this requires his presence. This confidence produces a particular observation: "What can mere mortals do to me?"

Well, frankly, quite a lot—but only if you look at it from an earthly perspective. Yes, it's possible, and particularly during the latter part of the Tribulation, that you could even be put to death. But *you get that life back again*, and in far better shape than the one you'd be giving up. Because you get it back in heaven! Being put to death would certainly be a big deal if your life here was the only one you had. But it's not. You now have one that will last forever! We'll refocus on all of this when we take up the matter of persecution at the end of this chapter.

The Principle of Peace

"Peace I leave with you; my peace I give you. I do not give to you as the world gives. Do not let your hearts be troubled and do not be afraid." (John 14:27)

How does a person keep his wits when everyone around seems to be losing theirs? Well, largely it's an issue of peace. And especially, the nature of that peace. It's where that peace comes from that's the key.

As a believer, you have three choices. When stress gets great enough that it begins to topple your sense of equilibrium and security, you can try to generate it in your imagination, you can seek peace from your surroundings, or you can get it from Jesus. You're probably already discovering that you can't get it from any combination of the three, if only because these three are never on the same page.

Let's dismiss imagined peace right out of the box: it isn't real. There is no possible way some "power of positive thinking" will be a match for the last days. When the heat is on, you can't pretend it away. Nor can you use some mental "sleight of hand" and say that the nasties are just a figment of your imagination. The troubles are all too real, imagined peace is not.

Okay, how about peace from your surroundings, the secular or worldly perspective? Well, the world generally defines peace as the absence of war. But, more broadly, as the absence of conflict in whatever form. Peace then becomes the removal of discomfort, uncertainty, or anything else that would disturb us. That's why, in the world's understanding, peace is entirely *circumstantial*. And because it's circumstantial, it's undependable and ultimately insufficient to the need. That's why the world's peace is a false hope. It's dependent upon one's surroundings, which are always subject to change in the next moment. In the world, lasting and fundamental peace can only be offered as a fuzzy dream. It's something that can never really be realized as long as sin reigns in the Creation. For where there is sin, there is sure to be disorder and conflict. Not the stuff of peace. Not at all.

Jesus's peace is dramatically different. It proceeds from the nature of his own being. That's why he pointedly describes it above as *his* peace. And because it's derived from his nature, it carries with it all the stability, assurance, and security that he himself represents by being God in the flesh. The writer of Hebrews says "Jesus Christ is the same yesterday and today and forever" (Heb 13:8). As a result, his peace reaches out beyond the ravages of time and nations, of oppression and catastrophe. And it reaches over and beyond the intentions of the Prince of Demons.

But we're not done yet. Jesus goes on: "Let not your heart be troubled, nor let it be fearful." This is *your* part. The *only* part for which you're responsible. "Troubled" speaks of a heart that's agitated to the point of instability by the circumstances it faces. "Fearful" is being hesitant or faint-hearted, someone who flinches in the face of adversity. When Jesus says, "let not," he's saying you can actually set aside those *feelings* as irrelevant in the face of his peace. Peace is the remedy. We need to understand just *how* it is the remedy. Better said, how you lay hold of it.

Go back and read the Savior's words again. Did you notice that Jesus didn't tell his disciples that they had to *ask* for this peace? It is right there in front of them. They simply needed to grab it, to live in it, or as previous generations would say, to "reckon" it. Well, what do we mean by that term?

To "reckon" means to count something as true, to consider it as existing in fact. And then, most importantly, to act on that basis. Webster defines it as "to depend, to rely (on)." It helps to be able to picture this concept in action. You reckon that a healthy-looking chair can support you. And so, you plant yourself in it without concern. Or, because you keep your car battery charged and topped off, you reckon that the engine will turn over the next time you turn your ignition key. And when you do, you're not concerned about the car starting, only about the next-door kid who likes to play in your driveway. In the end, to reckon something is to put your faith in it. And putting your faith in something means that you can *do* something because of it.

Jesus's peace is there, always. You merely need to acknowledge it, believe it, and allow it to soak through what you're about to do in the next moment. You'll discover that the more mature you become in Christ, the more familiar this peace will be, the more it will characterize your response to trouble. And the more often it will bloom, unbidden, in the field of your most troubling circumstances.

Jesus's words are more than just an antidote to anxiety. They're a vaccine against it. They will enable you to continue to "fight the good fight, finish the course, keep the faith" (2 Tim 4:7), to continue to "bear up under sorrows" (1 Pet 2:19). None of the issues that the Tribulation will offer are a match for either Jesus or the peace that he has promised and laid before you to seize. That's because he is the one who has overcome the world:

> "I have told you these things, so that in me you may have peace. In this world you will have trouble. But take heart! I have overcome the world." (John 16:33)

Let's add to all this what Paul says:

> Do not be anxious about anything, but in every situation, by prayer and petition, with thanksgiving, present your requests to God. And the peace of God, which transcends all understanding, will guard your hearts and your minds in Christ Jesus. (Phil 4:6–7)

The Principle of Power

Power. What a concept! But let's remove it from the realm of hydro-electric dams, rocket engines, and explosives. Let's talk about it in relation to people. Everybody finds power desirable in one way or another. After all, isn't it one of the chief ingredients of getting things done? But some find it essential, not so much for what it can do, but for what they think comes along with it. In other words, power not over things or circumstances, but power over people. It can become intoxicating. Think of personalities in sports or entertainment that use their celebrity as a cultural opinion platform. Think of wheeler-dealers in business, government, and politics who use their reputation and position to climb higher both in their field and out of it. Feel free to add your own examples. But, once again, how the world sees power is not how God sees it.

The issue of his power is far more complex, but for the sake of our discussion let's get to the basics. For God, power is the exercise of his authority to accomplish his will. You might ask, "How is that any different than how power in the world works?" Well, for one thing, his exercise of power is always for good. It either benefits his creatures or demonstrates his justice, his holiness, or some other aspect of his divinity. Sometimes combinations of these things all at once. From another angle, his power is never contaminated by sin, in either its motive or its execution. His exercise of power is never arbitrary or for its own sake. It's always compatible with his purpose, justice, mercy, grace, wisdom, and any other divine attribute we could name.

Paul had a depth of personal experience of that power that's hard for us to grasp. He was afflicted with some sort of physical disability that really took a bite out of his physical capacities to serve Christ and his people. We're not sure precisely what it was, although there's evidence that he at least had really bad eyes (Gal 4:15; 6:11). But whatever it might have been, it was bad and nagging enough that he pictured it as a thorn constantly stuck in his flesh. Bad enough that he asked God three times to remove it (2 Cor 12:1–8). Listen to what God said in response:

> But he said to me, "My grace is sufficient for you, for my power is made perfect in weakness." Therefore, I will boast all the more gladly about my weaknesses, so that Christ's power may rest on me. That is why, for Christ's sake, I delight in weaknesses, in insults, in hardships, in persecutions, in difficulties. For when I am weak, then I am strong. (2 Cor 12:9–10)

It sounds like Paul learned this principle the hard way. Think, then, about how wonderful it is that God is offering you this lesson right out of the box! "When I am weak, then I am strong." This is really an outlandish concept, until you begin to realize what it represents: your personal strength is insufficient for the task at hand, so God supplies his own. As Paul said earlier in this letter: "But we have this treasure in jars of clay to show that this all-surpassing power is from God and not from us" (2 Cor 4:7).

God demonstrates himself in those occasions when people see you accomplishing things others cannot. It brings him glory. It's one of the greatest lessons every new believer needs to learn. And learn well. Be encouraged, you will get lots of laboratory exercises!

Expect to see his power directed to you so that you are:

- able to stand and proceed when you'd otherwise be apt to collapse for lack of strength.

- able to serve him, not in your own strength but in his.

We could probably say that these are really just two different expressions of the same work of God in you. But here's something to keep in mind: God's power is his enablement to do what you ought, but not necessarily what you wish. It's sufficient for the accomplishment of God's will, not your own.

How do you access this power? Well, just like peace, it's already there for the need at hand. You don't really need to ask for it. Again, you simply *reckon* it – consider that it's both present and sufficient. Then you act on it.

Chapter 6

Profitable Principles for Tribulation Living - II

On Perspective, Perseverance, and Persecution

The Bare Bones

- Perspective balances your present difficulties against your promised glory.

- Perspective finds its ultimate example in the perseverance of Jesus.

- Perseverance is continuing to do the right thing by seeing what it produces in the end.

- Perseverance is essential in the experience of salvation, hope, ministry, and reward. It's the evidence of your faith and the backdrop of your testimony.

- Perseverance is both a sacrificial exercise and a choice.

- Persecution comes to believers because Jesus isn't present to be its focus.

- Persecution ranges from social isolation and harassment, through betrayal and job loss, to imprisonment and even death.

- Persecution becomes an occasion for blessing. Personally, through receipt of divine grace and power; for others, as the you share with them the Good News.

The Principle of Perspective

The eleventh chapter of the book of Hebrews is all about faith. The writer begins with a few verses on its nature (verses 1 and 6 are worth special attention) and then illustrates this with a pile of examples from the chief characters of the Old Testament. But though faith is the central theme of the chapter, there's another thread woven alongside it. It's about perspective.

> By faith Abraham, when called to go to a place he would later receive as his inheritance, obeyed and went, even though he did not know where he was going. By faith he made his home in the promised land like a stranger in a foreign country; he lived in tents, as did Isaac and Jacob, who were heirs with him of the same promise. For he was looking forward to the city with foundations, whose architect and builder is God. (Heb 11:8–10)

Abraham faithfully obeyed his call because "he was *looking forward* to the city... whose architect and builder is God". Abraham perceived that where he ended up geographically was not his final destination. That's proven by two things. First, when he got to the foreign land to which God lead him, he made a home "like a stranger". That reflected his attitude toward his surroundings. Second, he lived in tents—as did both his son and grandson and their families. That was the physical

81

expression of the attitude. This perspective was so strong that it was taken up by his succeeding generations! That's how committed they all were to what they believed God held out for them long into the future.

The writer goes on:

> All these people were still living by faith when they died. They did not receive the things promised; they only saw them and welcomed them from a distance, admitting that they were foreigners and strangers on earth. People who say such things show that they are looking for a country of their own. If they had been thinking of the country they had left, they would have had opportunity to return. Instead, they were longing for a better country – a heavenly one. Therefore, God is not ashamed to be called their God, for he has prepared a city for them. (Heb 11:12–16)

And there you have it: "*... they were longing for a better country—a heavenly one.*" There is the biblical perspective in black and white. It governed not only the ultimate hopes of Abraham and his family, but how they viewed their present circumstances by comparison.

Let's pick up that thread again from the life of Moses. In his case, it wasn't so much about where he was, but about whom he chose to be among:

> He chose to be mistreated along with the people of God rather than to enjoy the fleeting pleasures of sin. He regarded disgrace for the sake of Christ as of greater value than the treasures of Egypt, because he was looking ahead to his reward. By faith he left Egypt, not fearing the king's anger; he persevered because he saw him who is invisible" (Heb 11:25–27)

Moses grew up, from infancy, in the palace of Pharaoh himself. Why, he even became Pharaoh's adopted grandson (Exod 3:9–10) . Power, privilege, wealth, influence, education, pleasure; you name it, it was at his fingertips. But he chucked it all in favor of the disgrace of mistreatment as an Israelite. Note carefully that the writer considered this disgrace as being on behalf of the Messiah, who wouldn't appear for another 14 centuries! Why do something so radical? "He persevered because he saw him who is invisible". He wasn't just looking toward heaven, but to the God who guaranteed it *and would ordain his circumstances so that he got there!* We can't overstate the importance of this principle. It has the capacity to make even the most terrible trials endurable. And even profitable, from an eternal standpoint.

Let's see how this worked out practically with the apostle Paul. First the principal again:

> Therefore, we do not lose heart. Though outwardly we are wasting away, yet inwardly we are being renewed day by day. For our light and momentary troubles are achieving for us an eternal glory that far outweighs them all. So, we fix our eyes not on what is seen, but on what is unseen, since what is seen is temporary, but what is unseen is eternal. (2 Cor 4:16–18)

Now we're getting down to the real nitty-gritty. We need to understand what he has in mind when he speaks of "light and momentary troubles". Well, here's what he has in mind:

> I have worked much harder, been in prison more frequently, been flogged more severely, and been exposed to death again and again. Five times I received from the Jews the forty lashes minus one. Three times I was beaten with rods, once I was pelted with stones, three times I was shipwrecked, I spent a night and a day in

the open sea, I have been constantly on the move. I have been in danger from rivers, in danger from bandits, in danger from my fellow Jews, in danger from Gentiles; in danger in the city, in danger in the country, in danger at sea; and in danger from false believers. I have labored and toiled and have often gone without sleep; I have known hunger and thirst and have often gone without food; I have been cold and naked. Besides everything else, I face daily the pressure of my concern for all the churches. (2 Cor 11:23b–28)

Based on when he wrote this letter, all this happened to Paul in a period of just six or seven years. It doesn't include what he endured in the nine or ten years that followed what he wrote here. Those ended with his death as a prisoner of the Roman Emperor Nero, likely by beheading.

It seems outlandish that Paul should take the stuff in this list and classify it as "light and momentary troubles". Are you kidding? How can Paul dismiss so lightly such terrible experiences? Only by looking ahead. It's simply a matter of perspective. He could do it because of his certainty of the reward that awaited at the finish line. And not just his certainty of the reward, but of its surpassing nature.

You, friend, have joined the fraternity of these saints, and of countless others that go back across thousands of years. These were people that were called by God to believe in him. What shall we say of them all? Just this: "...anyone who comes to him must believe that he exists and that he rewards those who earnestly seek him" (Heb 11:6b). We'd like you to focus on that last line, and to expand your normal notions of what "reward" means.

Folks that don't have a close relationship with the Lord of Glory have to limit the word to worldly definitions. But God doesn't reward believers according to those limited standards. That's why all the folks we've just talked about *looked ahead* to a reward far more than anything the world could ever provide or even imagine. Take another break and read the last two chapters of Revelation, fittingly, the last two chapters in your Bible. The wonders that you'll find in those verses are just the basics (see also 1 Cor 2:9).

To close discussion of perspective, here's the first three verses of Hebrews 12:

> Therefore, since we are surrounded by such a great cloud of witnesses, let us throw off everything that hinders and the sin that so easily entangles. And let us run with perseverance the race marked out for us, fixing our eyes on Jesus, the pioneer and perfecter of faith. For the joy set before him he endured the cross, scorning its shame, and sat down at the right hand of the throne of God. Consider him who endured such opposition from sinners, so that you will not grow weary and lose heart. (Heb 12:1–3)

Jesus Christ is the ultimate example of perspective. And therefore, of perseverance.

The Principle of Perseverance

Perspective and perseverance are like fraternal twins. Not identical, but with lots in common. Not identical, but always in partnership toward the same end. With what you've learned above about perspective, it won't be hard to see how it walks hand-in-hand with perseverance.

To persevere means to continue to stand, to maintain, or perform under difficult circumstances. But especially when those conditions make the effort a whopper. It applies where most folks would just give out and give in. Perseverance goes by a fistful of other words: endurance, resolve, persistence, determination. But like other important things that we've talked about, what's really important is where they come from. There are really only two options.

Perseverance can be an expression of your own "grit" or it can come from the strength that God supplies through your faith. You get to choose between the two. But be aware that if you try to persevere from your own resources, you'll probably wilt pretty quickly when the battle's a spiritual one. And all the critical battles you'll face in the Tribulation will be spiritual ones at their core.

Let's get practical again. Perseverance is just a matter of repeated steps taken toward a particular goal. The illustrations are endless. Think about running to get in shape. Early on, you'll hear internal voices asking if you really want to continue. The ones hollering the loudest will be your lungs and your legs. Let's say they lose the argument and you keep at it. Initially, you've got nothing to show for your labor but shortness of breath now and sore muscles tomorrow. But after a while you notice you can run both harder and longer, and probably faster!

We're all familiar with this process in all sorts of activities. Why, you might think that it's a fundamental mechanism of life. It probably is. But don't forget the end product: it produces a condition where you can accomplish things that months before would have totally wiped you out. Is it still uncomfortable when you're really pushing it? Sure. But not enough to make you quit. And that's precisely the point.

The same process applies to living for God in the midst of a twisted age. Even before the Tribulation, doing the right thing wasn't easy. The easy way out has always cost very little—in the short run. But we can pay pretty dearly in the end. The easy way out is always short-sighted. When it comes to perseverance, it's precisely the end that you have to look at. Though endurance may be only a succession of present moments, it's really about the long game.

Think about Jesus's example as seen above in Hebrews 12. He endured "for the joy that was set before him". He fixed his eyes on what lay *beyond* the finish line to get him past his death for us on the cross. In the same way, your faith in what God has promised in the future generates the motivation to proceed by faith in the meantime. The rewards of heaven, and hearing Jesus say "Well done, good and faithful servant" (Matt 25:23) will encourage your legs to keep moving into the next lap.

Perseverance is so important that the New Testament treats it as one of the prime proofs of genuine faith in Christ. That's because it can't be expressed *without* faith. Don't get the cart before the horse here: perseverance is the *consequence* of faith, not what produces it. From another angle, your faith saves you, your endurance merely testifies to that salvation (Ac14:22; Col 1:22–23; Heb 3:14; 1 Pet 1:6–7).

The New Testament connects perseverance with these four major issues of the Christian life:

- Salvation (Matt 10:22; Rom 2:7; Col 1:22–23; Heb 3:6, 14; Rev 14:12)

- Spiritual life and ministry (2 Cor 6:4; 12:12; Col 1:11; Heb 12:7; 1 Pet 2:20)

- Present hope (Rom 5:3, 4; 8:25; 15:4; 1 Thess 1:3)

- Future reward (1 Cor 15:58; Gal 6:9, 1 Thess 2:19; 2 Tim 4:7–8; Heb 10:36)

Take the time to read the references above. Take them one at a time and don't hurry though them. You'll be impressed with just how critical a good perspective on endurance really is.

Let's finish this section with two final observations. First, *perseverance is a sacrificial exercise.* You'll discover that the last days will challenge you to give up a lot of things that you've previously considered as well deserved: ease, convenience, security, preservation of your resources, expectations of situations, expectations of people. That's just to name a few. Don't worry about trying to figure out when perseverance is called for. Circumstances and God's Spirit will make its necessity obvious.

Second, *perseverance is a choice*. That means it can't be considered in a detached manner. It's the obligation that comes with the grace bestowed upon us in Christ. It's the essential test of our faith and obedience. When things get tough, nobody *feels* like keeping on, they *choose* to. It's an issue of the will. Expect God to strengthen yours (Phil 2:13).

The Probability of Persecution

While we were writing this book, America was in the growing grip of a "cancel culture". A person's relevance was becoming more and more dependent on their agreement with the social and political views of the country's loudest influencers. If you didn't agree with their positions—or were simply silent—you were marginalized, ridiculed, or oppressed. People had social media accounts suspended, reputations smeared, even jobs lost. That's because the movement was also being taken up by organizations and corporations. But that was chicken feed by comparison: during the Tribulation, the power to coerce acceptable thought and behavior will reach its pinnacle. As will the consequences for those who don't cave in to it.

You'll continue to be strong-armed by others for what you believe. But more than ever before, you'll be attacked for Who you believe in. This is because the main personality that will come to dominate this period will be the Antichrist. And because he's directly empowered by Satan. At one level or another, he'll be driving the agenda of everything and, except for believers, everybody. The Antichrist's entire program will revolve around two purposes: the world's worship of himself, and its rejection of Jesus Christ. But because the world is unable to take out its anger against Christ directly, it will search out his representatives.

Paul spoke of this kind of opposition in an interesting way:

"Now I rejoice in my sufferings for your sake, and in my
flesh I am filling up what is lacking in Christ's afflictions
for the sake of his body, that is, the church," (Col 1:24)

What? Something was *lacking* in Jesus's afflictions? Well, let's
explain. The resurrection was the certification that Jesus's sufferings
and death satisfied God's just demands against each believer's sin. Your
faith in that sacrifice is what has saved you. What was *not* satisfied by
the death of Christ was the hostility of the world against him, and of
the dark spiritual forces that generate that antagonism. This hostility
goes back a long, long way (see Psalm 2). Ever since the Lord arose into
heaven following his resurrection (Acts 1:9–11), he's no longer been
available as a direct object of that hostility. Only those that love him.

Jesus described it in this way:

> If the world hates you, know that it has hated me before
> it hated you. If you were of the world, the world would
> love you as its own; but because you are not of the world,
> but I chose you out of the world, therefore the world
> hates you. Remember the word that I said to you: 'A ser-
> vant is not greater than his master.' If they persecuted
> me, they will also persecute you. If they kept my word,
> they will also keep yours. But all these things they will
> do to you on account of my name, because they do not
> know him who sent me. (John 15:18–21)

As we've said, the chief world-conflict of the Tribulation will be
a spiritual one. You and all the others that Christ will bring to himself after the Rapture will become the chief *earthly* enemy of both the
Antichrist and the evil one. There is no honest way to sugar coat the
matter. Sooner or later, you will be unable to avoid the impact of this
conflict. And your personal experience of it could be very costly.

You're probably already asking, "Just how far could this opposition go?" And your question is personal, not hypothetical. Well, recall what happened in the end to the apostle Paul. But let's see what more Jesus himself has to say. After all, he's the primary teacher on the subject:

> Blessed are you when people insult you, persecute you and falsely say all kinds of evil against you because of me. Rejoice and be glad, because great is your reward in heaven, for in the same way they persecuted the prophets who were before you. (Matt 5:11–12)

> All this I have told you so that you will not fall away. They will put you out of the synagogue; in fact, the time is coming when anyone who kills you will think they are offering a service to God. They will do such things because they have not known the Father or me. I have told you this, so that when their time comes you will remember that I warned you about them. (John 16:1–4a)

> Whenever you are arrested and brought to trial, do not worry beforehand about what to say. Just say whatever is given you at the time, for it is not you speaking, but the Holy Spirit. Brother will betray brother to death, and a father his child. Children will rebel against their parents and have them put to death. Everyone will hate you because of me, but the one who stands firm to the end will be saved. (Mark 13:11–13)

> Then you will be handed over to be persecuted and put to death, and you will be hated by all nations because of me. (Matt 24:9)

To this we can add what the apostles wrote:

You, however, know all about my teaching, my way of life, my purpose, faith, patience, love, endurance, persecutions, sufferings—what kinds of things happened to me in Antioch, Iconium and Lystra, the persecutions I endured. Yet the Lord rescued me from all of them. In fact, everyone who wants to live a godly life in Christ Jesus will be persecuted. (2 Tim 3:10–12)

Dear friends, do not be surprised at the fiery ordeal that has come on you to test you, as though something strange were happening to you. But rejoice inasmuch as you participate in the sufferings of Christ, so that you may be overjoyed when his glory is revealed. If you are insulted because of the name of Christ, you are blessed, for the Spirit of glory and of God rests on you. (1 Pet 4:12–14)

All this was familiar treatment for the early believers. And, frankly, it has been for great numbers of Christians over the centuries in most of the world. And if that weren't enough, folks who look into these things report that there were more martyrs for Christ during the last century before the Rapture than in the 1900 previous years. Is the same treatment in store for Christians during the Tribulation? Well, you decide:

I saw thrones on which were seated those who had been given authority to judge. And I saw the souls of those who had been beheaded because of their testimony about Jesus and because of the word of God. They had not worshiped the beast or its image and had not received its mark on their foreheads or their hands. They came to life and reigned with Christ a thousand years. (Rev 20:4)

Note that these saints "had not worshipped the beast or his image". That's a reference to the Antichrist, during the last three and a half years of the Tribulation (we'll say more about this "mark" in Chapters Nine and Thirteen).

That's some heavy stuff! We haven't piled up these verses just to be melodramatic. Instead, you're being well-served by having a picture of the breath of this opposition. But don't be afraid or immobilized by the prospect. The Scriptures speak often of the divine grace and power that falls upon believers in these circumstances. But just as important is what the Bible says about the reward they're granted in the future.

Much of this will be new for American believers. But little is new from the perspective of God's people in other countries, and particularly over the last twenty centuries. Historically, the United States has accommodated freedom of religion as virtually no other country on the face of the planet. It's a matter of constitutional law from the nation's founding. But the times have become so corrupt that the provisions of the Constitution are being systematically dismissed. Regrettably, Christians in our land will now be playing catch-up with many of the saints from former generations and elsewhere.

This captures the gist of the subject. We can summarize persecution in the last days as an increasing progression of the following:

- social isolation;

- economic isolation;

- betrayal by families, neighbors, schools, organizations, agencies, and law enforcement;

- investigation and pursuit by religious and government authorities;

- threats, coercion, physical abuse;

- imprisonment; and

- execution and martyrdom

Having said all this, it's important to close with what God says about our responses to persecution. Not about how we feel about it, but how he expects us to act when it happens:

> I am sending you out like sheep among wolves. Therefore, be as shrewd as snakes and as innocent as doves. Be on your guard; you will be handed over to the local councils and be flogged in the synagogues. On my account you will be brought before governors and kings as witnesses to them and to the Gentiles. But when they arrest you, do not worry about what to say or how to say it. At that time you will be given what to say. (Matt 10:16–19)

> But we have this treasure in jars of clay to show that this all-surpassing power is from God and not from us. We are hard pressed on every side, but not crushed; perplexed, but not in despair; persecuted, but not abandoned; struck down, but not destroyed. We always carry around in our body the death of Jesus, so that the life of Jesus may also be revealed in our body. For we who are alive are always being given over to death for Jesus's sake, so that his life may also be revealed in our mortal body. (2 Cor 4:7–11)

> But even if you should suffer for what is right, you are blessed. Do not fear their threats; do not be frightened. But in your hearts revere Christ as Lord. Always be prepared to give an answer to everyone who asks you to

give the reason for the hope that you have. But do this with gentleness and respect,... (1 Pet 3:14–15)

Rather than give a short commentary on each of these passages, we'll just mention something from the first two lines of the one from Matthew: "shrewd as serpents, meek as doves". Functionally, it directs you to be perceptive, maybe even cagey, with the people you meet. And don't feel obliged go looking for trouble. It will find you easily enough by itself.

Some final thumbnail thoughts are in order:

- persecution may be prevalent, but it's not permanent;

- persecution isn't ultimately personal; it's directed at a Jesus folks perceive as a threat because they don't know him;

- God takes the persecution of his saints seriously, as seen in how strongly he will vindicate those who've received it in his name (read 2 Thess 1:3–10);

- persecution becomes a blessing: those who endure it are the recipients of God's comforts and enablements. They may even lead others to Christ through it.

Here's a fitting quote in conclusion: "And the God of all grace, who called you to his eternal glory in Christ, after you have suffered a little while, will himself restore you and make you strong, firm and steadfast. To him be the power for ever and ever. Amen." (1 Pet 5:10–11)

God's promises and these principles put into your hands the major tools to manage all your coming challenges. Without the concern that you'll be in over your head. They will also will enable you to begin a new life that's an ever-growing pattern of good choices. They will strengthen you and help you bring honor to Jesus.

Chapter 7

Basic Christian Disciplines – I

The Essence of Discipleship, Bible Study, and Prayer

Bill was standing at his garage workbench. He'd finally put back in place the tools he'd used in replacing his car radio. That job had been finished three weeks ago—at two in the morning—and his gear had been in a heap on the bench ever since. Bill mused about the disorderly pile: "Yeah, kinda like you, buddy."

His thoughts turned to Thomas. He'd been spending an increasing amount of time over at the home of his best friend, Jim. The Cabermans were gracious and generous hosts, and their home was clean and orderly. Bill had no concerns for Thomas' welfare at their place, which was only two miles away. Not inconvenient at all. He was beginning to have a glimmer of new concern for his son, though. Thomas seemed to be more self-absorbed and prone to mood swings. "Well, hoopdy-do,", Bill thought, "it's not like you haven't been the same for the last four weeks. This place is like a morgue. Give him a break—he's lost his mom and little sister. And a fistful of other friends at school. School! I can't imagine what it must be like for the teachers to have to deal with this stuff. It's no wonder

Parkside's been in the news, with all those student body problems."

If there was an upside, Thomas' time at his friend's house gave Bill more time to read. He'd decided that his time for it was becoming more precious. And he'd made a corresponding, conscious decision to restrict the time he watched cable news and the growing number of TV "special reports" on the Great Disappearance. It was all loaded with hype and speculation. And increasingly, heaped with reminders of the occasion for local, state, and federal governments to apply all sorts of new regulations and restrictions on individuals and businesses. He'd found himself becoming unexpectedly suspicious of it all. It seemed in some ways like another stanza to the song they'd first written together back in 2020, when the China Bug had hit the world like a bomb. A new verse being sung even louder this time around. Bill had enough on his mind; he didn't need either the news or the cheeses in government to stir the pot.

He recognized that he'd been staring absent-mindedly at the tools on the pegboard above his workbench. TOOLS! And a realization began to form in his mind.

Bill had taken a break from "Susan's Book", as he'd found himself calling it. It did provide a kind of physical connection with her, after all. Instead, he'd begun reading in the Gospel of John. He'd decided not to rush it. It was new stuff. Not just in content, but in style. For someone who probably wasn't highly educated in his day, John seemed to have a rather unique, even philosophical, bent to his writing. But, more particularly, it was the things that Jesus himself had said that were really heavy. In all sorts of ways. It seemed that they had a ring to them that lifted them, well, right out of time. It didn't seem like Jesus was speaking 2000 years ago; he was speaking to him—right there in his den! No, Bill was taking it slowly in John, often pausing to think far longer than it took to read a particular story.

Bill sensed that reading in this gospel had been great for his spirit. He imagined that his response was like a kid's first reaction to ice cream. Chocolate, of course. But here, looking at his tools, he realized that there was another part of him that needed some attention. After all, ideas weren't really useful until they could be put into practice. And, for him, putting an idea into practice involved the employment of tools. Yes! Tools! Of whatever sort. Tools got things done. Tools turned energy into products; things that produced benefits, orderliness, and efficiency in people's worlds. Bill was of little use without his tools, either at work or at home.

He'd recalled leafing ahead in Susan's book. The next two chapters had covered the subject of Christian disciplines, apparently areas of study and activity that had special functions. Tools also have distinct functions, he thought. They work together to build something of value. Could the disciplines in the book be considered as "tools"? If so, they could lend a good measure of order and purpose to the project—as he was now starting to think of it—of his new life in Christ. But he wouldn't know until he read more about them.

Bill turned off the light above the workbench, closed the garage door, and hot-footed it into the kitchen. He drew a quick cup out of the coffee maker and walked to the den.

[Note: Bill has bitten off a rather large chunk here. There's a lot of critical tools that God has provided those who love him to manage their circumstances. It's probably best that we deal with them without further interruption. We'll get back to Bill, Thomas, and their further "adventures" with Chapter Ten.]

Chapter 7

Basic Christian Disciplines – I

The Essence of Discipleship, Bible Study, and Prayer

The Bare Bones

- A disciple is a learner. A disciple of Christ is one who commits not only to leaning of and from him, but also to becoming like him in character and action.

- A disciple is a witness. He or she not only increasingly demonstrates who Jesus is, but willingly speaks of him as occasion arises.

- A discipline is an activity that gets a person's concerted time and attention. Christian disciplines are regular activities that make believers useful to God for both his purposes and his glory. They are the pursuits of discipleship.

- Time in the Bible is the first of two primary personal disciplines that will govern the quality, vitality, and consistency of your growth as a believer in Christ.

- Time in prayer is the second essential discipline that will attend your growth as a believer.

What Is a Disciple?

What does it mean to a disciple? We can look at that from two related perspectives: one as an imitator, the other as a witness. The first of these comes from the word itself. A disciple is a "learner", the meaning of the term used in the New Testament. It presupposes that the disciple values both the teacher and the content presented. And it's a given that the disciple will become an imitator of his teacher (see Paul's use of the principle in 1 Cor 11:1). Jesus expressed it in this way: "A disciple is not above his teacher, but everyone when he is fully trained will be like his teacher" (Luke 6:40, ESV). All of this is heightened, of course, when the teacher is Christ himself.

Jesus's intention is that every believer becomes conformed to his likeness (Rom 8:29; Eph 4:15). That's fundamentally the *kind of person* he intends you to become. He prioritized the importance of discipleship when he made it the main thrust when he commissioned his followers (Matt 28:19–20).

The second perspective of being a disciple is being a witness. Just before his ascension into heaven, he left the disciples with this final obligation: "But you will receive power when the Holy Spirit comes on you; and you will be my witnesses in Jerusalem, and in all Judea and Samaria, and to the ends of the earth" (Acts 1:8).

Being a witness includes what a believer looks like to others. That's the association with being an imitator. But it heavily leans toward what he or she *says* about Jesus Christ and his teaching. Even at the end of the age there will be some "nice" people that don't believe in Jesus. To many, real Christian character may not look a lot different than those of these folks, at least not at first glance. In these cases, the distinctions may only become plain when the subject of the Savior is brought up.

There are two other relevant things that Jesus said here. One covers the *extent* of this witness. It's to the "end of the earth". That covers not just a lot of geography and the breadth of human culture, but a lot of time. You get to join the saints from everywhere over the last 2000 years

by participating in the process at its very conclusion. But the fundamental point is that this testimony is a work of the Holy Spirit. Every
believer should have an appreciation that when they speak up for Christ,
it's God's Spirit at work behind the scenes.

Don't talk yourself out of your capacity to say something impactful
about Jesus with some excuse you're "not a good speaker", or aren't elo-
quent or loaded with debating skills. Or even because you don't think
you have much knowledge of the Bible. Moses offered up a similar
opt-out (among others) when God called him (Exod 4:10). Strange
that the Holy Spirit saw him a bit differently (Acts 7:22). But better yet,
consider the case of a man healed by Jesus who was born blind. Take
a break here and read the story in the ninth chapter of John's gospel.
We'll wait...

Now his healing was indeed miraculous. But it's what happened
following that's the point here. Look at the simplicity— and power—of
his witness. This man merely told his doubters what Jesus had done for
him. Having had his eyes opened (in more ways than one!), he opened
his mouth. And you can be sure that it was God's Spirit that spoke
through him, if only because it ended up in the Bible! But also note
that he said what he did without any particular concern for its results.
That he left in God's hands.

The testimony of the early Christians was so potent that many were
put to death for it. How they lived could get them in trouble. But for
many, it was what they *said* that sealed their earthly end. Their testimony was so powerful that our word "martyr" is the direct equivalent of
the Greek word for "witness". Yet, in the broader sense, every believer in
Jesus is a "martyr", even if he or she isn't put to death for their testimony.
That's why living and speaking for Christ is costly. (see 1 Cor 4:10–11).

What Is a Discipline?

Being a disciple presumes a Christian's attention to some basic activities. Here, we'll call these activities "disciplines", obviously a derivative

term. They're activities that are to get your special time and attention. They're things for which you're responsible; they don't happen by themselves. Think of it this way: no one ever—ever—got in shape by being a couch potato. This is especially true in the spiritual realm.

These next four chapters address a handful of the essential disciplines that have been the building blocks of believers ever since the First Century. To continue the analogy, if going to the gym represents the progress of our lives as disciples, Christian disciplines represent the individual machines in the gym that ensure we're strong from top to bottom. Think of them as "skill-makers". Maybe better, think of them as "strength-makers". These activities haven't just proven their worth over the centuries, they've demonstrated their necessity. And all the more so in times of great stress and testing.

The Importance of Spending Time In Your Bible

Right out of the gate is what you will learn in the Bible. As we discussed earlier in Chapter Three, the importance of the Bible in your life can't be overstated. Jeremiah paints a unique picture of the satisfaction that grows out of this: "When your words came, I ate them; they were my joy and my heart's delight, for I bear your name, LORD God Almighty" (Jer 15:16).

The Scriptures are right up there with the Holy Spirit's work as a primary key to your growth as a believer. It's essential in your understanding of God's will. And it's indispensable in your being able to distinguish between truth and error, especially now that deception is everywhere.

On Its Nature. The first thing that you need to adopt is an understanding of the inspiration of the Scriptures. Their inspiration is the basis of their authority. The extent to which a person thinks the Bible is simply the writer's invention or opinion becomes the extent to which the Bible has no authority or impact in their lives. Here are two of the texts that deal with this matter:

> All Scripture is God-breathed and is useful for teaching, rebuking, correcting and training in righteousness, so that the servant of God may be thoroughly equipped for every good work. (2 Tim 3:16–17)

And,

> We also have the prophetic message as something completely reliable, and you will do well to pay attention to it, as to a light shining in a dark place, until the day dawns and the morning star rises in your hearts. Above all, you must understand that no prophecy of Scripture came about by the prophet's own interpretation of things. For prophecy never had its origin in the human will, but prophets, though human, spoke from God as they were carried along by the Holy Spirit. (2 Pet 1:19–21)

Note from the first passage that "all Scripture is God-breathed". Paul doesn't tip-toe around the *extent* of what he's about to say. He's very purposeful in choosing "all": what he's going to say next extends to everything contained in the Bible.

And what does he say next? He says that it's "God-breathed"; a unique term to express that God's Spirit directly inspired or invested in the minds of the Bible's writers precisely what he intended to be passed down. Peter said the same thing at the end of his quote above. That's not to say that the writers didn't bring their own vocabularies and writing style to the table as the pen and ink for God to use. They certainly did, and God honored their diversity in doing so. But his use of human writers in this process was no more difficult for him than his use of Mary as the means of bringing to us a Savior in all his divine and sinless perfections (see Luke 1:35). We should note that in both cases it was specifically the work of the Holy Spirit.

One other thing that Paul includes is the all-encompassing *effect* of the Bible: it's profitable for "teaching, rebuking, correcting, and training in righteousness". You shouldn't have much problem in understanding the different functions covered by these four words. What's really critical is noting that they're all geared to one divine intention: making you into a man or woman that is fully capable of accomplishing God's purposes.

What Paul says in a single sentence, Peter expands to three. The writers of Scripture, though human, "spoke from God as they were carried along by the Holy Spirit". That's why these two apostles use terms like "useful" and "completely reliable", It's why Scripture is capable to "thoroughly equip", and why we "do well to pay attention to it". It's directly infused with God's authority. Of course, these men were speaking primarily of the Old Testament texts, what was already at hand in the First Century. But, by extension, the process applies to the New Testament writers as well (see how Peter directly ties the character of Paul's letters to the Old Testament in 2 Pet 3:15–16).

On the Old Testament and the New. Having identified its fundamental Author, let's now address the book itself. It's obviously in two major parts: what we call the Old and the New Testaments. The Old recounts God's actions in the ancient past, but especially with the nation of Israel. It reveals both God's nature and his deeds on behalf of his people. It's loaded with divine wisdom and history. And it discloses things to come, not only for Israel, but for the whole of humanity. Most importantly, it's where the person and coming of Jesus Christ (the Messiah) is first revealed. You can read Jesus's view of this in John 5:39 and Luke 24:27. Finally, it's all about faith—from every conceivable perspective.

Don't get caught up by any sort of idea that the Old Testament is somehow inferior to the New. Something on the order that it's primarily a revelation of God's anger, or judgement, or the strictness of his laws—in contrast with the New Testament being a revelation of his love and grace. This is a phony notion that comes from folks who don't know the Bible well, and are woefully unfamiliar with the true nature of God. The Old Testament is loaded with examples of God's love and mercy (just as the New is filled with warnings of his judgement on the unrepentant). In the Old Testament the godly are people of faith. Just like in the New. Yes, there's a lot about God's law, particularly about the Law given to Israel through Moses. But remember this about the Law: it was never intended to be a means of earning eternal reward, but a tool to reveal each person's need for a Redeemer (see Gal 3:21–24).

The New Testament doesn't replace the Old, it builds on it. But especially as it reveals the person and work of the Messiah as the central Person of history. A great way to become familiar with his nature, his personality, his purpose, and his power is by reading the four gospels. Each has a distinctive flavor. The history of the first few decades of the Church is in the Book of Acts. Then there's the epistles (letters) from Paul and other apostles to local churches, to larger groups of believers, and to a handful of individuals.

The epistles are the backbone of New Testament teaching on a believer's relationship to the Savior. They do this by two major means: first, by discussing the nature of that relationship, and then by exploring its practical obligations.

Finally, the New Testament closes with the Book of Revelation (the Apocalypse). It has Jesus's instructions to representative churches, a survey of the events of the Tribulation (including God's judgments upon the unbelieving), a summary of the following 1000-year earthly reign of Christ (the Millennium), and then what awaits the saints in eternity. Wow, what a load for your very soul!

On Choosing a Bible. Early on, whatever kind of Bible you can find will be better than nothing. Unless it's offered to you or published by a group that has its own distinctive translation or additions (the major cults have their own proprietary translations or extra "scriptures"; that's always a big red flag for false teaching). Be looking for a Bible that is a readable but *direct translation*. If you can find one right away, latch onto it. Good examples are the New American Standard Bible (NASB), New King James Version (NKJV), New International Version (NIV), and English Standard Version (ESV). Reading the preface will generally say how the translators approached their task.

You might come across a "Study Bible" that includes not only the biblical text, but the editor's explanations of passages or short articles on specific subjects. These are certainly helpful, but they may represent a particular theological "slant" on certain points.

Other versions will openly admit to being very free in rendering the Bible's original languages in more contemporary terms and expressions. They may even be described as "paraphrases" or "dynamic translations". These versions are willing to sacrifice a measure of accuracy in favor of readability. As a consequence, they sometimes miss how the Holy Spirit has lead a writer to use particular terms or grammar to communicate a critical point. The end result is that the important point gets lost in the shuffle. Paraphrases may be sufficient for a comfortable read by the fireplace on a cold day, but not so much for careful study and understanding. Once again, far better than nothing, but not really preferable.

On Understanding What It Says. Listen up! God didn't write the Scriptures for philosophers, or academics, or even for theologians and ministers. He wrote the Bible, and then superintended its preservation, for everyday folks like you! That means that it's understandable by its very nature. We won't deny that there are occasional things in its pages that will leave you scratching your head. Why, even Peter admitted that (see 2 Pet 3:16). Here's the key: *read it in context.* That means paying attention to what leads up to what's being said (and sometimes to what follows). It means developing a savvy for major background issues, and to what the words would mean to its first readers.

That's how you read everything else you come across, isn't it? You be the judge: if God wanted to break into your life by writing something to you, why would he pull a switcheroo and require you to adopt an entirely different way of reading? Why would he communicate in ways previously unknown, highly subjective, mystical, or open to misunderstanding? Truth is not fuzzy, speculative, or hard to come by. It's not "secret knowledge". It's accessible, present, plain, and potent. No riddles, no hidden meanings. God isn't one to require contortions of your intellect, he speaks to you face-to-face.

Does the Bible contain figures of speech, metaphors, and other devices for analogy? Sure. But so does everyone even today—even you. Oregon Ducks don't have feathers, do they? No, they're members and fans of the university's athletic teams. Psalm 57:1 is one of the places where King David speaks of refuge "in the shadow of (God's) wings". But wait, who says God has actual wings? Nobody. Instead, we recognize that it's a picture of his protection. Generally speaking, you know how to sort out these expressions: take something literally unless it's contrary to nature or that you readily know stands for something else. And keep this in mind: proportionally, very little of the Bible really falls into this category anyway.

The Bible directly affects your understanding of God, of his acts in history, of salvation, and of his will. The more you read, the more you'll gain familiarity with these issues. And don't forget that you also have an ever-present, internal teacher, the Holy Spirit (see John 14:26; 16:13; 1 John 2:27).

On Where to Begin. Giving you recommendations on where to begin reading is kind of a matter of our personal perspectives as this book's authors. But more importantly, our suggestions will also take into account the nature of the times you're facing. To start with, let's suggest that there are four major things from which you'll get immediate benefit:

1. First and foremost is *a deeper acquaintance with Jesus Christ as a person.* That means a gospel account. What you read there about him is still true—because he never changes (Heb 13:8). That's why we've already pointed out the Gospel of John as a starter. It's uniquely geared to the development of both your personal and practical relationship with him. That relationship should grow into something that's vibrant and dynamic. Far and away, it will be the best relationship you will ever have. And it couldn't be with anyone better; in him are found all the treasures of wisdom and knowledge (Col 2:3).

2. Next, some early reading on *how it is that you came to faith in Christ.* Obviously, you already have that from our perspective. But we're just gatherers and editors of what God's said on this. Now you need to read it from his own perspective, in its original broader contexts, and with its practical implications. Ephesians and Romans are called for here. Probably the former as it also has things to say about resources for spiritual conflict. Romans is broader in scope and, among other things, contains Paul's teaching on what will happen in your day with the people of Israel.

3. Then, familiarity with *how to respond to persecution.* The two letters of Peter are especially relevant to this subject. And his second letter gives a unique overview of the end of days from the perspective of God's nature and his plan for history.

4. And *something for the stuff that's generated in your spirit* by your circumstances. There's nothing like the psalms for this. They're the thoughts and prayers of Old Testament saints (remember, faith is the same in every age—Heb 11:1–2,6). The psalms are lessons both in praise and in the ponderings of hearts challenged by knotty questions. Like those arising from the assaults

of enemies and skeptics. Another thing to get exposed to is the practical wisdom (biblical wisdom is practical *by definition*) found in the Book of Proverbs. It's a tremendous primer on human nature from God's perspective, with all its lines in easily memorizeable form.

5. Finally, read it front to back. This will give you a perspective of the flow of history for God's people, of the issues they face, their victories and failures, and of a God who never deserts them.

A Few Tips on How to Get the Most Out of It.

• Set aside time and circumstance. Prioritize and cultivate consistency.

• Start with an attitude of dependence and expectation. You should do this consciously and purposefully. Many reorient themselves prior to a period of reading or study by starting with a short time of prayer to be profited by what's to be read.

• Become a careful listener. You'll find God "speaking" through the words set before you.

• There are two approaches to reading. One is more of an overview to become familiar with the content. The other is slower and more precise, with time taken to write notes, ask questions, look for practical advice and personal applications. And, of course, to pause in thanks and wonder for the truths you come across. Use both of these methods but remember that they have different purposes.

• Mark up your Bible. Use a highlighter. Make notes in the margins. Keep a separate journal of thoughts or notes. If your Bible has cross references noted in the margins, look them up (they're also a good exercise in locating other books in the Bible).

- Use a few common questions to guide your study. Things like, "What does this say about Jesus?" "What does it say about Me?" "What example is here for me to follow—or to avoid?" "What is here that I can thank God for?" "How does this relate to the other stuff nearby?"

- Finish what you start, don't skip around and lose all sense of context. Some verses may stick out, but most of them don't stand totally on their own. God isn't like todays media: he doesn't communicate through the Bible by "sound bites" and memes. If you need a break, read a psalm or two, or portion of the Proverbs; then get back to your journey through a book of the Bible.

- Don't expect God to accommodate any sort of magical or mystical approach. Like asking him to show you what you need to hear in the moment, closing your eyes, opening your Bible to a random page, and reading what your finger happens to point to. Be responsible.

- Some content is going to seem far more relevant than other portions, depending on what's going on in your present circumstances. That's to be expected. And it's common for believers to have read a certain passage multiple times before noticing a critical point or new application. The more often you dig, the more you find. Remember that the Holy Spirit is your companion when you read and study (John 14:16; 16:13; 1 John 2:27). He will sensitize you to things he considers to be relevant in the moment.

- Meditate on what you've read. Memorize verses that really grab you (it *really* helps to do this out loud!).

- Be on the prowl for a Bible handbook. It will be a great source for general questions on the content of the books of the Old and New Testament, its writers, historical and cultural backgrounds, meanings of what seem like technical terms, and lots of other items you'll have questions about as you read.

- When you're done, give thanks for what you've read.

- But you don't need to be done at all: you can keep chewing on and digesting what you've read at any time in between sessions (see Ps 1:2–3).

Delight yourself in God's word (see Jer 15:16). It's life to your soul (2 Tim 3:17; 1 Pet 2:2–3). You'll discover that there's virtually no end to either its depth or its treasures.

Prayer

Prayer is just as foundational as spending time in your Bible. They're like two legs, working together to get you where you're going. They're similar in that they are both means of communication. And also, because each will quickly reflect your own personality. And why not? God has taken you up as you are. You will be changing in many ways, but God has already been communicating with you based on your own characteristics.

You don't need to be formal or artificial in either listening to God or in speaking to him. By that we mean that you may speak to God with the same freedom and style that you would use in speaking to anyone you honor and trust. Say what you will without hesitancy. How this goes in the short term will fit the ways you presently process information. He may change that in months to come as your personality takes on new aspects and knowledge. Welcome to another facet of your new adventure.

But though these two "legs" are similar, they are also different, if only because communication goes in two directions. Think of your Bible reading as heavily weighted in the direction of God talking to you. On the other hand, prayer tends to be more weighted in the direction of your speaking to God. In both, the Holy Spirit will be in the background, quietly providing understanding and insight.

Now, in the matter of prayer, there's a unique feature at play: God already knows everything you're about to say (see Ps 139:1–4; Heb 4:13 for starters)! But if he already knows everything, why does anyone need to say anything to him at all? Well, for at least three reasons. The first is our natural inner *compulsion*. We're made to talk. From that standpoint, it doesn't matter that the person on the receiving end already knows what we're about to say. And since we know that he's intensely interested in everything about us (Ps 34:15–18; 66:19-20; 77:1; 102:20; etc.), we're sure that he wants to hear it direct from the horse's mouth. That's the second thing. Speaking to someone is a natural function of having a personal *relationship* with them.

But third, prayer is also a means of us *informing ourselves*. What? Yup, informing ourselves. Look, our minds are normally a jumble of observations, reasonings, emotional reactions, and questions. These all reflect our responses to the issues going on both around and in us. But this jumble isn't always *coherent*. One of the often-overlooked benefits of speaking to someone is its requirement that we sort out this stew in a coherent way. In having to articulate something for another person, we clarify issues for ourselves and make them more focused and purposeful. A real help to this greater precision is to pray aloud. It lends a sense of conviction not just to our praises and thanksgivings, but especially to our requests. If these three functions are so important in our conversations with other folks, how much more so are they with God himself!

Will it ever happen that you have a huge urge to pray but things are so hairy or overwhelming that you don't feel capable of making yourself understood? Yes. And especially in the unique days ahead. Guess what? You're covered! Listen to this from Paul: "...the Spirit helps us in our weakness. We do not know what we ought to pray for, but the Spirit himself intercedes for us through wordless groans" (Rom 8:26). That sounds a little strange—until you realize that you already know something about groans. They're what you utter when the heavies come but the words to describe them don't. Be encouraged that when that's the best you can do for the moment, the Holy Spirit steps in to "translate" perfectly for you! And besides, God already knows anyway.

The Priority of Prayer. We're directed to "pray without ceasing" (1 Thess 5:17). Of course, this doesn't mean a prayer that is endless. One has to eat and sleep and attend to other responsibilities, after all. To pray without ceasing means to be ready for it always, to be unrestricted to a set schedule or circumstances, to be free to converse with God as occasion arises. On the other hand, to set aside particular times or sessions to pray lends to the whole idea of discipline. To pray is to acknowledge gratitude and dependence, two things that are constantly in season. Prayer is a means of expressing his presence with you always, everywhere.

The Promise of Prayer. The promise of prayer is that you will be heard:

> For the eyes of the Lord are on the righteous,
> and his ears are open to their prayer.
> But the face of the Lord is against those who do evil.
> (1 Pet 3:12, quoting Ps 34:15-16a)

The qualification for this promise is centered on the word "righteous". In the Bible that's the status before God of those that have faith

(Hab 2:4b), but particularly the one who has faith in Jesus (Rom 1:17; Gal 3:9-14). Here's something else we're to have confidence in:

> For we do not have a high priest who is unable to empa-
> thize with our weaknesses, but we have one who has
> been tempted in every way, just as we are—yet he did
> not sin. Let us then approach God's throne of grace
> with confidence, so that we may receive mercy and find
> grace to help us in our time of need. (Heb 4:15–16)

Your access in prayer to God's very throne has already been secured by Jesus himself (Eph 2:18). Think of yourself as having been pre-qualified to pray with real intimacy and effectiveness! You've been given instant access into the very presence of God for that purpose. Consider the depth of privilege reflected in your being able to speak directly with the Creator of the universe, to approach not only the throne of his mercy but of his power. And to do so with confidence.

The Pattern of Prayer. There are many prayers in the Bible. Psalms are full of them; in fact, most of the psalms classify as prayers. Really, anything addressed to God qualifies as prayer. And remember that prayers are not defined merely by asking for something. As occasion dictates, prayer will also include praise, thanksgiving and confession of one's sins.

When you run across a prayer in the Bible, take some extra time to note any of these four things (praise, thanksgiving, confession, requests), then ask yourself why they were appropriate to the person that offered them. Consider these observations as one of God's means of updating your prayer life. Other subjects will certainly be your latest circumstances or the thanks and needs of others that pop into your head by the prompting of God's Spirit.

Of course, the primary example of prayer is the one Jesus used as a teaching aid to his followers. We know it commonly as the Lord's Prayer. Some think that it would be better known as the Disciple's

Prayer. Find it in Matthew 6:9–13 and read it. Even as a new believer, it may well roll off your tongue with very little prompting. But then read the next two verses (14 and 15). Did you note that Jesus closes the lesson by talking about forgiveness? Critical to prayer is eliminating the "spiritual baggage" of unfinished business. This baggage is sin going unaddressed (see Ps 66:18, Jas 4:3; 1 Pet 3:7).

This points up an important issue. The prayers of the Bible are filled with confession. It was commonly on the lips of even godly men and women. Why? Because they recognized that they were still imperfect. Confession is about agreeing with God regarding our spiritual short-comings—and being willing to "own" them before him. Sometimes we're aware of sins when we pray. Sometimes we're not, they just followed us into his presence tucked away in our back pocket. Confession enables us to keep "short accounts" so we can approach God openly, and without the devil pointing a finger at us while we're trying to do some serious spiritual business. One of the devil's common strategies is to torpedo your prayer life. Confession will send him packing.

The Power of Prayer. Here is a potent reminder of the power of prayer:

> The prayer of a righteous person has great power as it is working. Elijah was a man with a nature like ours, and he prayed fervently that it might not rain, and for three years and six months it did not rain on the earth. Then he prayed again, and heaven gave rain, and the earth bore its fruit. (Jas 5:16b–18 (ESV))

Note especially who the Holy Spirit directed James to write about here. And, what he prompted James to say about him. The subject was power in prayer. The example was the prophet Elijah, who was used by God to bring a massive judgment of drought upon an idolatrous and unrepentant Israel (see 1 Kgs 17:1ff). Well, that's not surprising as an illustration as Elijah was no minor-leaguer in either his faith or his service. But note that The Holy Spirit doesn't focus on that at all. Instead, he has James point out that Elijah had a human nature that was essentially no different than yours! A giant of faith? Of course. But as to the inherent weaknesses and limitations of his human nature, Elijah had the same ones that you do!

And that's the whole point of the matter. It isn't about capacities or experience, it's all about your status: being *righteous*. Elijah was righteous because of his faith (just like Abraham, Gen 15:6; Rom 4:1–5; etc.). And *you* are righteous in Christ because Jesus draped you in this condition the moment you were saved (Rom 4:5; 9:30; 1 Cor 1:30; 2 Cor 5:21). Don't be deceived in thinking that prayer power is primarily a function of using the right words. It's not a function of eloquence, persuasiveness, or special calling but of a right heart. And, as James points out, of being fervent. But that's just urgency and honesty working together.

It's interesting to read what the Lord Jesus had to say on this matter of power in prayer. Matthew reports an occasion when the disciples had failed miserably in casting a demon out of a young boy. But give them at least some credit: they came to Jesus to find out why. He said that it was because of their puny faith, probably connected with their lack of persistence in prayer or reliance on past accomplishment. Here's his rebuke—and his lesson:

> Then the disciples came to Jesus in private and asked, 'Why couldn't we drive it out?' He replied, "Because you have so little faith. Truly I tell you, if you have faith as small as a mustard seed, you can say to this mountain, 'Move from here to there,' and it will move. Nothing will be impossible for you. (Matt 17:19–20)

Now, it's fairly plain here that Jesus is using figurative language. "Like a mustard seed" refers to a really tiny one that still has the capacity, if constantly exposed to water and nutrients, to grow into a tree sufficient for birds to nest in (Matt 13:31–32). In context, "mountains" are also likely figurative for whatever seems beyond our capacity to handle. What mountains will you have the opportunity to move by faith? If they're his concern and you're his agent on the scene, you can do it simply by trusting in his power—and praying fervently.

The Posture of Prayer. Hands folded, knee bent, head bowed, eyes closed, quiet surroundings. You know the pictures. But there are many references throughout the Bible of folks talking to God that break these traditional poses. Actually, these traditional poses may be the exception. Don't wait until all the items on your list of supposed requirements for prayer have been checked off. The essential posture of prayer can't be seen, anyway. It's humility. And humility has a couple of siblings: honesty and earnestness, which we've already pointed out. They make a quiet but powerful threesome. Every effective prayer proceeds from them.

The Peace of Prayer. We could say much more about prayer, but here's a last one for these pages. It's about something that prayer accomplishes for you, and particularly, for your composure in trial.

> Do not be anxious about anything, but in every situation, by prayer and petition, with thanksgiving, present your requests to God. And the peace of God, which transcends all understanding, will guard your hearts and your minds in Christ Jesus. (Phil 4:6–7)

Paul knew what he was talking about: he wrote about all this while being in prison—again (Phil 1:7, 13)!

Chapter 8

Basic Christian Disciplines – II

Worship, Fellowship, and Holiness

The Bare Bones

- Worship is any personal activity that expresses the wonder and awe of God. Most often it's a verbal response to who he is and what he does. It is appropriate at any time and on any occasion, alone or in the company of others.

- Fellowship is sharing the commonalities of life in Christ. It's rooted in your relationship with him and flows out from there to others. Although some aspects may be experienced at a distance, fellowship's fullest expression is in the company of other saints. It is enjoyed when times are good. But it's most precious in times of distress. Perhaps its chief fruit is encouragement.

- Holiness is the process of developing a character that reflects Christ himself. It's a process that is a work of the Holy Spirit within willing hearts. The believer's contribution to it is a conscious, willful choice to turn away from the behaviors and attitudes of his or her old nature, and to draw upon the power of the Holy Spirit to act in ways that are consistent with God's will.

Worship

The subject of worship is so broad that entire books have been written on it. Lots of them. The essence of the Bible's Hebrew and Greek words for worship is that of bowing in reverence and service. It's background in the English language captures the gist of this nicely: worth-ship. Our spirits reach out to God in praise and gratitude because he is worthy of our esteem.

Worship is expressed to God throughout the Bible, first pages to last. There are tremendous expressions of it everywhere. Such as when Israel had been handed a great victory, or in the Old Testament's festivals and holy days, or when individuals were delivered from personal calamity. The chief celebration for God's people has always been worship. Because of his faith, Job could even worship in the midst of his great losses (Job 1:20–21). In the Psalms we see it from a personal perspective, in Revelation and in some of the prophets (particularly Isaiah and Ezekiel) we see it expressed by angels.

The Basis of Worship. Wherever it's found, worship is offered to God for two primary reasons: who he is and what he does. Who he is comprehends all the aspects of his nature. Adequate description of them—and therefore, of him—is almost beyond us. You'd do well to keep a list of the words that the Bible uses to describe these characteristics or "attributes". Begin to list them on one of those blank pages at the front or back of your Bible. If you come across a Bible handbook, theology book, or other guide that explains them, become familiar with what they mean. We can't express just how important each of his attributes is to you personally. That's because, in the person of Christ, God unreservedly offers you the totality of his nature for your comfort, encouragement and strength (Col 2:9–10).

And then there are God's deeds. These are his attributes being expressed in time, in creation, and in the affairs of mankind. His acts in the creation and in history are the testimony of his greatness and goodness to men and women, to the angels, and to the ages. His deeds demonstrate why everything is ultimately dependent upon him and why mankind ought to serve him without reservation.

If the primary things that drive worship are who God is and what he does, then worship is first a matter of thinking. It's an intellectual acknowledgement of what's true, either about God himself or about his actions. But it goes absolutely nowhere unless that acknowledgment is coupled with faith. Our responses, even our emotional ones, proceed out of that. But once worship has been founded on truth, the door is wide open in how it's seen.

The Breadth of Worship. It can be expressed through the full extent of your intellect, emotions, actions, and gifts. You can sing it, shout it, preach it, and dance it. You can draw it, paint it, write it, and serve God and others with it. It will accommodate both your ecstasy, your tears, and, with some self-control of your spirit, even your righteous indignation at evil. It's do-able morning, noon, and night. Everywhere, on any occasion. By yourself or along with others.

It's the speech of a spirit that's totally abandoned in its gratitude. It's thanks for being privileged to experience something of the fulness of God. It's honest but hard questions to him of why things are the way they are—and maybe even mention of your frustration that he hasn't told you more. In worship you might easily run out of words. But that's not a major problem: the Holy Spirit will gladly pass along what you can't express. You may run out of delight. Not an issue. Just take a breath, bask in wonder, and look for the next occasion to give it another round. The Father, Son, and Spirit are watching and listening. And so are others.

Beyond faith, worship seems to have only one additional requirement: honesty. In that sense, it's much like prayer. You'll probably sense when you've manufactured some artificial worship rather than turned it loose. Worship is something that God's Spirit will develop and hone, through your faith, your humility, and your growing knowledge of his word.

The Obligation of Worship. It's curious how the general culture has adopted some important biblical terms and concepts and redressed them for secular use. You'll hear folks that make no claim to being believers yet use words like "Amen!" and "Hallelujah!". We won't get into the current prevalence of "Oh, my God!", most always heard from people whose primary god is themselves. Almost always these words and phrases are just expressions of surprise, excitement, or hearty agreement with something. Let's look at this one: "Praise the Lord!"

It's the English translation of the Hebrew "hallelujah!". It's almost always used by non-believers as an exclamation. Curiously, even Christians use it this way, throwing it out as a mere reaction to something really awesome. But it's not inherently a reaction to something exciting. It's actually a *command*. Huh?

Read the psalms. "Praise the Lord!" is found everywhere. But if you were to ask David or any other of the psalm writers what they meant by it, they'd say that they were directing God's people *to express their own* wonder of God. As we've said, it's a command; that's its actual grammatical form. We identify the verb form as an *imperative!* And that's exactly what makes it an obligation for God's people. It's not just a phrase to throw out when you're glad something happened. Instead, the hearer is being directed to stand themselves in conscious wonder of God, for who he is and what he does—*and to verbally offer their own testimony of it.* In the end, praise and worship is the moral obligation of all who know him by faith in Christ Jesus.

Fellowship

Again, like a lot of important biblical concepts, the world's understanding of fellowship gives it no justice. In the world the emphasis is primarily one of getting together and having a good time. But the root word in the Bible is about the possession and sharing of things in common. Most importantly, non-material things. That's the substance out of which all the commonly understood expressions of fellowship grow. After some reflection, even those outside of Christ can grasp this. Yes, fellowship is a social matter. But it goes far deeper, and produces far more than just good times with good friends.

The Essence of Fellowship. True, biblical fellowship ultimately goes back to the intimate experience of Christ that he showers upon each of his followers. This is where it really parts company with the world's understanding of it. Listen to what John has to say about this: "We proclaim to you what we have seen and heard, so that you also may have fellowship with us. And our fellowship is with the Father and with his Son, Jesus Christ" (1 John 1:3).

Fellowship begins first with an intimate relationship with God the Father through Jesus Christ. Fellowship with other brothers and sisters in Christ proceeds out of that, and distinctively, out of that alone. This is the singular basis of our unity with other believers. In speaking of our unity in him, Paul says: "There is one body and one Spirit, just as you were called to one hope when you were called; one Lord, one faith, one baptism; one God and Father of all, who is over all and through all and in all" (Eph 4:4–6). When believers gather together, their mutual experience of all these things courses quietly in the background of all they say or do.

You know what it's like to have an affinity for certain other people. But that's all heightened by what you know that you have in common with them. Get two veterans together and within minutes one will drop a clue that will be picked up by the other. They'll be off and rolling. You might not get a word in edgewise for at least ten minutes while they question each other and share personal experiences. It doesn't matter if they were in supposedly "competing" branches. It doesn't matter that they didn't do the same job or were stationed in the same place, or even served in the same era! What does matter is that they had common experiences in a unique culture. But how much deeper is this sense of fraternity, when the common denominator is the mutual experience between believers of the riches found in the Lord of Glory!

Fellowship requires getting together. The techie gear of the last hundred years or so gives our age a big leg up on all the previous ones because actual, physical proximity is no longer necessary for folks to converse. Being together was limited to face-to-face for thousands of years, as writing letters didn't quite cut it. But even though you've got a smart phone and Zoom capability, even voice and eye interaction over distance *still* falls short of the real deal. Microsoft and Samsung can't get your arms around someone else who's six states away. Or enable their tears to wet *your* shirt. Sure, praying or sharing over the phone will do on occasion, but in the long run it somehow falls a bit short.

Actual presence is the essential. That's why God has chosen not to be distant (read Psalm 139 again). That's why the Spirit of Christ has taken up residence within you (Rom 8:9–11, 16–17, 26; Eph 1:13). It's natural then, that there's a quiet inner urgency for this kind of spiritual fellowship to be shared between believers. It's how he made you, and especially how he made you in Christ. It has its own unique capacity to provide mutual encouragement and strength. It's so potent that it even covers hard times (Job 2:11–13; Acts 20:36–38).

The Function of Fellowship. For your hairy, end-time circumstances, here's something to ponder:

> ...let us consider how we may spur one another on toward love and good deeds, not giving up meeting together, as some are in the habit of doing, but encouraging one another—and all the more as you see the Day approaching. (Heb 10:24–25)

Now we'll readily admit that the word "fellowship" does not appear above. But "meeting together" certainly fits the bill, especially when its purpose is mutual encouragement. Well, just what kind of encouragement? The kind necessary for the "Day approaching". The NIV's translators capitalized it to make it clear that it's ultimately a reference to *the* day when Jesus returns, which will be at the absolute height of the world's worst ordeals.

But long before that moment there will be plenty to tempt believers to cut back on their testimony. The hedge against such timidity is mutual encouragement, the kind that comes directly from another Tribulation saint. For a bottom line on the importance of mutual encouragement, read Hebrews 10:36–39.

Having hopefully made our case here, we're obliged to issue a word of caution. Your times will become increasingly dangerous, but especially if you're living and speaking for Christ. There will be people who could betray you to others (Luke 21:16–17, etc.). Even to the authorities who, in due time, will be under the control of the Antichrist. And as the age is one of deception, your enemies may even pose as believers themselves (see 2 Cor 11:14–15; Gal 2:4).

Spiritual counterfeits have always been the most dangerous. You'll need divine insight, not only to be able to discern who they really are, but how to deal with them. Choose carefully those with whom you fellowship. But in all of this, don't despair or cave in to fear. You are kept by God and the devil can't touch you for his own purposes (1 John 5:18).

Holiness

> As obedient children, do not conform to the evil desires you had when you lived in ignorance. But just as he who called you is holy, so be holy in all you do; for it is written: 'be holy, because I am holy. (1 Pet 1:14–16)

Holiness. Here's another Bible term that's been skewed (or skewered) by the world system. "Holier than thou" is usually a phrase and an attitude that comes to the mind of a person with no Bible or Christian background. And what kind of picture does that raise for most folks, maybe even believers? Not an attractive one. So, it's best that we back-track here and start from scratch. What does "holiness" really mean? To answer that, we first have to consider what it means when God says that *he* is "holy".

The Intrinsic Holiness of God. It must have something to do with his essential being, his nature. In both the Old and New Testaments, "holy" are words that speak of *separation*. So, let's put these things together. God is transcendent, superior, unequalled to anything or anyone else. Essentially, ethically, and morally, he is supreme. That means he is free from all impurity, whether in nature, intention, or action. He is totally *other*, separated by his perfections from anything we have ever known. It's one of the chief reasons he's to be worshipped.

But the word is also applied to the things and people that he's set aside (separated) for his own purposes. Like the objects in the old Tabernacle and Temple services. Like the nation of Israel. Like believers of all eras. And that now includes you.

The Positional Holiness of Believers. Now we can talk about holiness as God intends you to experience it. First, holy is your *positional* con-dition because you belong to God through your faith in Jesus Christ. And because the Holy Spirit resides in you. Fifty-eight times the New Testament refers to believers as "holy ones", generally translated as "saints". That's why we've used the term a few times already in this book.

You didn't make yourself a saint. And certainly, except for Jesus, nobody else could do so. Yes, there's some church traditions that have conferred "sainthood" on notable folks in their ranks, but there's never been any basis for that in the Bible. Only God can do that. And he did so with you at the moment you laid hold of eternal life in Christ, the moment he applied Jesus's own righteousness to you.

God has set you apart for his service, you've been "sanctified" by him. That's just a different rendering of the word for "made holy". Now you'll be in the know when you run across it in your reading.

The Practical Holiness of Believers. But there's more to be considered here than just your status or standing in Christ. And that's your obligation to see that such a standing is observable in the way you live. Note that God says, "*Be* holy". That's a command that he addresses to all the saints. And now, to you. And, as a command, it's addressed both to your mind and to your will. That's why holiness should be considered as another discipline. What Paul says on the matter will help to bring this all into better focus:

> But now you must also rid yourselves of all such things as these: anger, rage, malice, slander, and filthy language from your lips. Do not lie to each other, since you have taken off your old self with its practices and have put on the new self, which is being renewed in knowledge in the image of its Creator.
>
> Therefore, as God's chosen people, holy and dearly loved, clothe yourselves with compassion, kindness, humility, gentleness and patience. Bear with each other and forgive one another if any of you has a grievance against someone. Forgive as the Lord forgave you. And over all these virtues put on love, which binds them all together in perfect unity. (Col 3:8–10, 12–15)

The key verbs here paint a familiar picture. "Rid yourself", "taken off", "put on", "clothe yourselves". Think of removing some oily coveralls and dropping them in the dirty clothes basket. And putting on your nice threads because the person you're going to see deserves a lot better than your grubbies. The operation in both cases is exactly the same: you first choose not to wear one thing in favor of getting into something else. Then you do it. Catch this: the verbs that Paul used here were the actual terms used in his day for undressing and dressing. What an illustration!

Ah, but just what is it that you've put off—and put on? Paul says it's the old self and the new self. Or, we could say the old person and the new person. Okay, but how do you change "persons"? Well, self or person here represents old ways and new ways. Yes, it goes quite a bit deeper into our old and new natures, but we're not exactly doing a heavy theology course here. Fittingly, Paul comes to the rescue by defining in more recognizable terms what he's talking about.

He connects the old self with anger, rage, malice, slander, a foul mouth, and lying. And he says "such things as these", implying that this list isn't even close to being exhaustive. If you want to add a few more items to it, get your Bible and read verse five for another half dozen. We think you get the picture. But instead of being done up in these duds, we're directed to dress up in the deeds of the new self: compassion, kindness, humility, gentleness, patience, enduring and forgiving one another, and love. And that list's not exhaustive either.

The Process of Practical Holiness. This process of changing is conscious and decisive. And it's also progressive (in the sense of being continual). Again, that's why holiness is a discipline. Most of the key verbs in the quote above are present tense. Both negatively and positively, they are what you'll always be attending to. The key is in understanding that you don't rely on your own strength in the matter. Rather, you trust in the Spirit's power to work what you know is right at the proper moment.

Moments like this one: the blue Dodge Charger cuts you off just to get through the upcoming traffic light before you do. Guess what? Salt in the wound: he makes it, you get the red. Your initial reaction is to hit the horn and hope he gets pulled over somewhere down the road for speeding (oops, that's malice on top of anger). But you catch yourself, and recognize that you've also done a selfish thing or two behind the wheel. There's no dents or scratches to your rig, and there's a fair chance you're going to pull up right behind him at the next light anyway! Yeah, the guy certainly has some issues – ones that you also have some occasional personal familiarity with. Issues that are so familiar that *you* can pray for him pretty specifically, even though you have no clue who he is. But that's no big deal, because God already knows everything about him. And so, while you're waiting for the light to turn green, you ask a blessing on him (Rom 12:14, 18–21). You have *chosen* to dump the wrong response and latch on to the right one, the one that's consistent with God's will for you.

And there you go. It's just an illustration. You can change the details a half dozen or so times a day. The more you catch yourself and make the switch, the less frequent the necessity to catch yourself seem to be. It's the evidence that you're becoming more like Christ. It's the evidence that your spiritual status as holy is being expressed more and more in your outward behavior. This is what sanctification or personal holiness looks like in practical clothes.

You're the one responsible for getting the inward out to where it's visible. Not simply "for show" (though others will certainly start to notice), but to please God through your obedience to his will (see Col 3:22). You do this by making right choices and allowing the power of his Spirit to do the work. You're responsible, but he supplies the energy. It's not a contradiction. And it's a fabulous arrangement that God has established on your behalf.

The Issue of Temptation. We are presenting what believers are to shoot for. But we need to inject a little reality here: our progress toward holiness is not expected to be a rocket-journey of quick achievement. Using another analogy, it's not a sprint but a distance event requiring some endurance in the process. This means that it comprehends some stumbles along the way. How to get up from them we'll cover under the subject of confession in the section to follow. But before we do, we'd like to lay out a couple of promises regarding temptation.

The temptation to do what we want rather than what we ought is a normal part of life. No one is immune to it. Not even Jesus was. His temptations were as genuine as are yours (Heb 4:15), the distinction being that he never yielded to any.

A temptation is a beckoning or enticement to sin. As we're sure you're aware, some are rather sneaky, some are outrageously in your face. Some take advantage of poor thinking, some take advantage of mere weariness—of all sorts. But here's the double good news: first, no temptation ever comes from God himself, and second, when they do occur, God provides a way of escape. Try on these two promises:

> When tempted, no one should say, "God is tempting me." For God cannot be tempted by evil, nor does he tempt anyone (Jas 1:13)

And,

> No temptation has overtaken you except what is common to mankind. And God is faithful; he will not let you be tempted beyond what you can bear. But when you are tempted, he will also provide a way out so that you can endure it. (1 Cor 10:13)

Take what James says and chisel it onto your heart right now. The one who most wants you to question these words is Satan himself. You need to be ready to quote it back to him. The words of Paul are also pretty straight forward. Except that "a way out" is actually "*the* way out" in the original. Which leads to the rather important question: "Just what is this 'way out' that he says God will provide?" Well, Paul's underlying grammar indicates that it's *the capacity to endure* the moral ordeal at hand. It's out of God's faithfulness to you that no temptation will be irresistible, that you will be able to endure it.

That's the principle here. But we can offer a couple of tools from elsewhere in the New Testament to help you put the principle to work. First, *know God's Word* about the issue at hand. It expresses his will on the matter. Quote it aloud as the occasion demands. There is great empowerment when you do. This is precisely how Jesus dealt with the temptations laid before him by the devil (read Matt 4:1–11).

Second, *just say "no!"*. This isn't just an old tool from the war on drugs (which may date your writer!), it's a biblical principle (read Titus 2:12). Deny the validity of what's being offered.

Third, and if you can, simply *take a hike* from the situation. There's a reason that recovering alcoholics don't step into bars. And there's a stark, slow-motion picture in Proverbs 7 of someone being seduced by temptation. The guaranteed disaster would not have happened if he'd just walked away. "Take a hike" are words not found in the Bible, but the principle is; the New Testament word is "flee" (1 Cor 6:18; 10:14; 1 Tim 6:11; 2 Tim 2:22).

All three of these tools are just expressions of faith—in God, of course. You will discover that temptation becomes dicey only in proportion to the amount of faith you place in yourself to handle it.

The Essential of Confession. So, what if you happen to get tripped up? Or what if you stumble when there wasn't an apparent temptation— just an occasion where you unthinkingly lapsed into an old, habitual response? To put the question differently, what are you to do with personal sin *after* you've become a believer? The New Testament is plain that it's something that every believer faces, preferably with decreasing frequency. So, let's get after that, too.

First, know that Jesus died for your sins irrespective of when they were or would be committed. Any sins after the fact were also covered when you received Christ as your Savior. They will not cancel your salvation or keep you out of heaven. Paul says this: "Therefore, there is now no condemnation for those who are in Christ Jesus..." (Rom 8:1).

Well, that's a great start. But what to do with these failures? John tells us: "If we confess our sins, he is faithful and just and will forgive us our sins and purify us from all unrighteousness" (1 John 1:9). John is talking to believers here. Once again, to "confess" means (literally) "to say the same thing" about a matter as God does. It's agreeing with him on the issue of the particular sin at hand. Confession is just openly admitting to him that you fell short of what he expected.

There are two sources for his identifying just what classifies as sin: his word (another good reason to keep your nose in it) and your conscience. Of the two, God's word is the more dependable, but your conscience will begin to get in closer step with the Scriptures, the more you take them in.

The verse above says that if you will confess the occasional sin, your issue will be cleared and he will "cleanse" you from it. Practically speaking, he'll declare you "good to go". These acts on his part reflect both his faithfulness to you and his justice in light of Jesus's death for those sins. That doesn't mean that such sins won't have consequences, but it does mean that they won't be disqualifying. What he expects is that you'll learn something in the process.

Here's perhaps a poor illustration. Remember when you first learned to ride a two-wheeler? Even if you graduated from training wheels, you probably wiped out a few times before you got the hang of it. Someone probably encouraged you not to despair but to keep at it. And later, after you proudly pronounced yourself competent, you'd still eat some gravel from time to time. It just became more infrequent as you became more aware of the dangers under your wheels and of what good balance felt like. More knowledge of God's will, more obedience to it, more honest (and immediate) response to the slips is a good pattern toward holiness. It's what Bible teachers would call practical holiness or *progressive sanctification*.

Summarizing Practical Holiness. This matter of progressive sanctification is one of the primary, on-going processes of Christian living. In a number of ways, many of the other disciplines serve or support it. A great place to read about it is Romans 8 where Paul describes it as life ("walking") in the Spirit. Take a break here and read it—a couple of times. It's so important that it's discussed from all sorts of angles in the New Testament (as in Gal 5:19–24, Eph 4:17–32, 1 Pet 4:1–11, and 2 Pet 1:5–11). Read them, too. If not now, perhaps the *second* time you go through this chapter.

Now, before we move on to the next discipline, there's one more thing to say. The worse that things get before Jesus returns, the more challenging this process will probably become. There may be times when you're tempted to pack it in. Or you may be tempted to compromise in some way what you know is the right thing to do. Don't be surprised: remember that every person that comes to Christ has piled up years of experience in rationalizing and justifying questionable behavior. And don't be surprised if this gremlin pops up when he's least expected. If you catch yourself, do the right thing. If you don't, pick yourself up, admit it to God, appropriate his forgiveness, and move ahead.

Chapter 9

Basic Christian Disciplines – III

Service (Ministry and Giving) and Self-Sufficiency

<u>The Bare Bones</u>

- Service and ministry are an expression of your having become the hands and the heart of Christ. Giving is just an extension of the same—by means of your stuff. They are all carried out through the enablement of the Holy Spirit and by the employment of special, spiritual gifts. These gifts are exercised in a love that seeks another's benefit over one's own.

- Self-sufficiency is really not *self*-sufficiency at all, but a reliance on God's all-sufficiency in every circumstance. It generates contentment regardless of situation. Self-sufficiency creates the capacity to meet not just one's own needs, but those of others. It will be increasingly indispensable as the Tribulation proceeds.

The Essence of Service and Ministry. When you believed in him, you became the hands and the heart of Christ to the world around you. It was a part of the package. You can be a fragrance of him (2 Cor 2:14–16) wherever you are, not just by your character and what you say, but by what you do. Jesus was lavish in his service to everybody, whether they were his followers or not. He addressed needs that were spiritual, social, and physical. You can do the same.

The Lord's outreach wasn't just an invitation for folks to consider his claims as the Messiah, but a reflection of God's generosity to the just and the unjust alike (Matt 5:43–48). He urged his disciples to display it in the same way (Matt 10:40–42). As his follower, you get to shower his graces on those that you meet, even on those you'd be inclined to consider as enemies (Rom 12:14, 17–21).

The Capacities for Service and Ministry. But start with this: God doesn't leave you to help others simply out of your own internal resources (though he might tap some of them in the process). No, he provides two magnificent divine means for the task. The first is his grace, the second is a spiritual gift.

Grace: Let's talk about grace first. Earlier, we spoke of God's grace as his freely providing what we don't deserve, particularly in salvation (see Rom 3:24; Eph 2:8; Titus 3:7; etc.). But there's another way that grace is used in the New Testament. It's used for the *enablement* to serve. Paul gives a great example while speaking of giving: "And God is able to make all grace overflow to you, so that, always having all sufficiency in everything, you may have an abundance for every good deed;" (2 Cor 9:8).

And here's this same use in more general terms: "But by the grace of God I am what I am, and his grace to me was not without effect. No, I worked harder than all of them - yet not I, but the grace of God that was with me" (1 Cor 15:10).

Look at how Paul speaks of grace in the last sentence of this second example. He directly related grace to work that he was doing for Christ. That's where grace is enablement. And enablement speaks of power, the capacity to accomplish something.

But even though grace addresses the capacity to do something, it must be joined by the will to employ it. You express that will by laying hold of the power of the Holy Spirit when you put your hands and heart to the task. Grace was the enablement that Paul used to conduct his ministry. It's how real service for God is accomplished (see Acts 4:33; 6:8; Rom 12:3, 6; 15:15–16; 1 Cor 3:10; Eph 3:2, 7–8; etc.). And it will be the same for you. What you will accomplish will be done by reliance on his strength, not your own.

Gifts: Now, let's talk about God's *gifts* for service. They are many:

> For just as each of us has one body with many members, and these members do not all have the same function, so in Christ we, though many, form one body and each member belongs to all the others. We have different gifts, according to the grace given to each of us. If your gift is prophesying, then prophesy in accordance with your faith; if it is serving, then serve; if it is teaching, then teach; if it is to encourage, then give encouragement; if it is giving, then give generously; if it is to lead, do it diligently; if it is to show mercy, do it cheerfully. (Rom 12:4–8)

There's a lot to bite off here. But the central core is this: "we have different gifts, according to the grace given to each of us". All of these things are either restated or amplified in other places (1 Cor 12:1–31; Eph 4:7–12; 1 Pet 4:10–11). 1 Corinthians 12:7 says that the gifts are "manifestations of the (Holy) Spirit". Four verses later, Paul says that the same Spirit is the one who sovereignly distributes these gifts to each believer. That's why they are commonly called *spiritual* gifts. You were given at least one when you received Christ as your Savior and Lord. Yours will come to the surface and be recognizable in the process of your getting busy for him. Don't be surprised if others begin to notice this gifting before you do.

Like the various parts of the physical body, some gifts are more "visible" than others. Because of this, they can easily draw attention to the person that's exercising them. You can probably guess where this can lead. It could be the selfish desire to have been given flashier gifts, or a false notion that less showy gifts are relatively unimportant. Paul wrote that selfish perspectives about them created disorder among early believers. The Holy Spirit directed Paul to address each of these issues and more. That required ten times as much teaching as it took for him to mention them in the first place (1 Cor 12:12—14:40)! But there is one overriding corrective for any fleshly approach to the gifts and their use. It's love.

Love: A biblical understanding of love gets really hammered by the secular culture. Not because it seeks to trash it directly, it's more that the world system has corrupted its meaning. Today's "love" is heavily oriented toward feelings. And therefore, it takes on selfish aspects. But the primary form of love in the New Testament is just the opposite: it constantly seeks the betterment of the person that's on the other end. Generally, at the personal expense of the person offering it. It's totally others-oriented.

Paul teaches that it's this kind of love that must always accompany the exercise of any spiritual gift. There are no exceptions! That's the whole message of 1 Corinthians 13. Take another break right here and read that chapter. It will be familiar; if only from hearing much of it recited at weddings or from seeing some framed needlepoint of its snippets. Now you know what it's *really* talking about. Take it to heart. Put it to use. Lavishly.

As we've said, in serving the Lord Jesus you're following his example (Matt 20:28; Luke 22:27; John 13:3–5, 12–15). In many ways, you're his direct manifestation, not just to other believers, or to a dying world generally, but particularly to those in it that he'll be calling to himself. As you give of yourself to the saints, it contributes to their own growing into his likeness. As you give of yourself to the lost, it becomes a major means toward their redemption.

Service and Ministry Through Giving. There's the giving of yourself in service, and then there's the giving of your stuff. In fact, the second can be a barometer on your commitment to the first. That's why it's natural to bring up the sharing of material resources in connection with service.

We believe the Tribulation will be a time of diminishing resources for almost everybody. If only because of world-wide cataclysms and other disruptions. But this will hit believers especially hard, particularly following the mid-point of the Tribulation. At that time the Antichrist will demand to be worshipped as God (Rev 13). But to leverage that worship, he'll institute a system that will require everyone everywhere to have a "mark" to proceed with normal commerce. You will get the mark only if you're willing to worship him. No mark, no power to buy— or do much else, at least legally (Rev 13:16–18). We'll talk about this in more detail later. But for now, think of its effect on what you'll be able to acquire. And therefore, on what you'll have available to give away.

But here's an amazing principle: normal standards for what you have available to help others isn't an issue with Jesus. After all, he demonstrated his capacity to multiply the minimal to meet the maximum need at hand (Matt 14:15ff; 15:32ff). And then there's the example of early but very poor churches, who begged Paul to be able to contribute to other poor saints they'd never even met (Rom 15:26; 2 Cor 8:1—9:2). At the proper time, God saw to it that they were able.

Which leads us to...

Self-Sufficiency

Its Basis: Self-sufficiency might seem a rather odd discipline, but especially for believers. To call it this appears to be inconsistent with reliance upon God. But let's consider some other factors.

First, one of the marks of maturity in Christ is moving away from material dependency upon others (Acts 20:34–35; 1 Cor 4:12; 1 Thess 4:11–12). The chief means of God providing our basic needs is through *our* work, not someone else's. Unless we're unemployed, unemployable, or terrible managers of our bucks, we're able to adjust to this without too much difficulty.

Second, and perhaps more importantly, self-sufficiency only becomes a problem went we get confused about where it comes from. Most folks presume that it comes from their own talents, willpower, and effort. But the Bible makes it plain that our capacity to produce is a gift from God himself (Deut 8:17–18). It turns out that if you're thinking biblically, self-sufficiency really *is* relying on God! In this sense, "self-" has nothing at all to do with the source of the capability, but speaks only of the person in which that capability's been invested. You're not the power, just the vessel that holds it. Nothing to get big-headed about at all!

Its Purpose: God intends that our labor not just satisfy our own needs, but those of our families (1 Tim 5:8), and others beyond (Eph 4:28; 1 John 3:17). In the Bible, welfare is not a function of the government, it's the responsibility of those who are able to work. And it's a responsibility that God addresses to each person's conscience as a moral obligation. It cannot be shuffled off by passively allowing government to tap your resources and care for it on your behalf. It's a heartless and degenerating world that allows folks to pass off the challenge of their moral obligations. And particularly by allowing the government to become both master and conscience in the matter.

Its Perspective: "It's far more comfortable to move up, than it is to move down." That's a principle that won't get much argument. The first half of the statement is the source of TV comedies, the second half of TV dramas. As you're not likely to be moving up during the Tribulation, let's look at the moving down.

Significant loss of material resources is a major hurdle for just about everybody. Believers included. Loss and lack are a direct threat against our natural sense of security and well-being. They breed anxiety, and they strangle concern for others. The greater the loss, the greater the effect. And if that weren't enough, contentment quickly gives us a kiss good-bye.

During the Tribulation, believers should expect the loss of resources to pay unwelcome and repeated visits. But the New Testament provides a principle that is astounding in both its practicality and its comfort. Like many others, it's displayed out of the experiences of the apostle Paul:

> Whatever you have learned or received, or heard from me, or seen in me—put it into practice. And the God of peace will be with you. I rejoiced greatly in the Lord that at last you renewed your concern for me. Indeed, you were concerned, but you had no opportunity to show it. I am not saying this because I am in need, for I have learned to be content whatever the circumstances. I know what it is to be in need, and I know what it is to have plenty. I have learned the secret of being content in any and every situation, whether well fed or hungry, whether living in plenty or in want. I can do all this through him who gives me strength. (Phil 4:9–13)

We're being a bit free here by including that first verse about God's peace. It's technically more attached to the preceding verse, one that lists the things that are worth thinking about. But it's also a great introduction to what Paul says here about having and not having.

He'd just received a financial gift from the folks he's writing to. They'd finally been able to send him some funds for his ministry. And he's thankful. But according to habit, he also takes the occasion to do some teaching about circumstances. And what he says about circumstances may have never had any world-wide application for the saints greater than right here at the end of the age.

Its Essential Compliment—Contentment: Look carefully at those last three sentences. Paul knew how to "move up" or "move down" with equal ease. Because he'd learned the "secret" of contentment: he could do all things the One who gave him strength. That's Christ Jesus. And that word "content"? It's the Greek term for—are you ready?—*self-sufficiency!* A self-sufficiency that rests on the active presence with and in you of the very Lord of Glory. Here's the principle: Whatever a believer has at hand, whether from his own labors or as given to him by others, whether it's little or lot, it's from God. *And if it's from God, it's adequate for the moment, regardless of its nature, regardless of its size.*

Okay, that should give a good New Testament foundation for the issues of service and self-sufficiency. But in view of the circumstances pounding on your front door, it's necessary also to get to...

Some Practical Matters

1) Lifestyle Adjustments. The more advanced a society becomes, the more interdependent are the people in it. Put a bit differently for Americans, very few folks directly produce any of their own essentials. Instead, virtually all of their labor is exchanged for purchase power. The net result is that most peoples' capacity to fend for themselves on a subsistence level has largely been lost.

As Americans, we're captive to levels of availability. Of food, of goods, of services. The inertia of daily living keeps us from realizing this inherent liability, and also keeps us from doing much about it. We don't have the necessity of learning to make things, fix things, grow things. Even trade things. Now, we'll give farmers, hunters, and fishermen a break here, but only if they still have seed, ammo, and bait! Transitioning from normal ways to get what you need-will be a tremendous task. With not a lot of time to learn.

This difficulty will be greatest in urban settings, where farming or "living off the land" is not only a lost art, but a virtual impossibility. And in cities and towns, the closeness of those with whom you can barter also means a greater exposure to someone who might betray you. The factors of faith, discretion, and contentment therefore become all the more important.

If you grew up on a farm, you'll probably have a real "leg up" on dealing with this crunch. The capacity to work with your hands in building and repairing things of all sorts will also be a great asset. Not just for you, but for believers around you. Regardless, be prepared for a radical reduction in "creature comfort" and standard of living.

You're probably now starting to take stock of what you have, where you are, and what you can do. It's probably pretty sobering. But take a breath and don't despair or fret, at least excessively. Think of the millions in history who had no experience with war. But when its privations suddenly hit, they discovered unexpected adaptabilities—and endurance.

But more importantly, think of who you are as a believer. The Lord Jesus has an uncanny capacity to draw people together in crunch time, but particularly with the proper mix of capacities and resources to get them through. It's evident through the pages of the Bible and the history of the true church over the previous 2000 years. Isn't easy by any stretch, but it's always been done. Even so, if you can, it might be good to stock up on really critical essentials. Like meds, if you can. Like chocolate, if you must.

2) Expectations. "Lifestyle adjustments" leads to another matter: expectations. When it comes to these, folks lie on a spectrum. You may be a person with few or with many. But the ones you do have are applied to just about everything around you: people and their behaviors, the durability of your washing machine, what you get for customer service from your wireless provider, the alertness of people driving (and walking) in parking lots – the list is virtually endless. And if you're rather unaware of the level of your expectations, just ask your family members and close friends; they'll give you an interesting read!

Let's add some cultural factors to the mix. We'd venture that the expectations regarding a whole range of items are higher for those in developed countries that for those in what we call the "third world". Shortages and inefficiencies abound there, and folks are more attuned to dealing with them without pulling out their hair.

Apply all this to the extra load that will come with the Tribulation to those who carry high expectations of—whatever. Not only will the availability of products and services become volatile, but the Scriptures portend dramatic social and environmental upheaval as never before. Except for the sun's rising and setting, very little will have its former stability. If you're a person that has cultivated a high level of expectations, the challenges to your contentment will be all the greater.

From one perspective, one's expectations are a character quality. And the Tribulation will be nothing, if not a constant test of one's character. Perhaps all the more so for new Christians. But you will have the most powerful partner in the process, the abiding presence within of God's Spirit. Be aware and be willing to make the adjustments and you'll move in the right direction.

3) Effects of the Mark of the Beast. The capacities for you to manage normally will diminish greatly as persecution becomes more systematic. This difficulty will reach its peak with the implementation of the Mark of the Beast, half way through the seven years of the Tribulation (Rev 13:16–18). The Mark is directly tied to a willingness to worship the Antichrist, and it's the only means by which anyone will be authorized to do business or make purchases—world-wide. In some senses, the Mark is more important even than money itself.

It's almost certain that under this policy a *whole range* of transactions that aren't even direct purchases or sales of goods will also be prohibited. Things like health care services, public transportation, payment of benefits, banking services, permits and licenses. The probable list is extensive; just think of all the transactions you've taken for granted in the past. Trying to secure them through alternate means will be just as prohibited and subject to harsh penalty or imprisonment as buying a loaf of bread.

Only true believers will refuse to receive the Mark of the Beast. This means that they will be limited to barter or what we would otherwise describe as "black-market" transactions—if they can be arranged at all.

4) The Challenge of Moral Conflicts. Here's the rub: folks committed to God's standards of morality will face ever-increasing ethical conflicts when the means of basic living become illegal. But continuing to live isn't just an instinct, it's a moral priority. Wow, it's a pretty perverse world where what's moral becomes illegal. Well, considering how things have degenerated in recent decades, we can't say we didn't see *this* coming! But when it arrives, what's a person to do who wants to be obedient to God?

5) Moral Conflict Resolution. Thankfully, an issue from the early church gives some direction. It's found in the third and fourth chapters of the Book of Acts. You should take a break here and read it—it's a great story anyway. But before you do, here's the necessary summary. Peter and John had been preaching Jesus as the Messiah on the Temple grounds in Jerusalem. As an object lesson, God providentially had them come across a lame beggar, who they promptly healed in Jesus's name. This had given the Gospel a whole lot of clout with the people, but it also put the Jewish religious leaders on the spot. Shooting first and asking questions later, they arrested the apostles and brought them before the chief court of the Jews. The Council issued an edict forbidding the preaching of the Gospel. It was the best they could come up with—and they hoped it would work. Sorry, guys: "Peter and John answered and said to them, 'Whether it is right in the sight of God to listen to you rather than to God, make your *own* judgment; for we cannot stop speaking about what we have seen and heard'" (Acts 4:19–20 (NASB)).

The authorities had imposed a ruling that directly contradicted the will of God. Peter and John rightly stood their ground in this *apparent* moral conflict. Though there were potentially grave consequences (no pun intended), they chose to obey God. And they did so with a clear conscience.

This principle has always applied to God's servants. You can read of two additional examples in Daniel 3:8–30 (Daniel and his three friends in the fiery furnace) and 6:3–24 (Daniel in the lion's den). God has always stood with his own. It won't be any different for you.

6) Moral Conflict and Government. Consider also what Jesus taught when the Pharisees attempted to face him with a moral dilemma. They asked him whether it was lawful to pay a poll-tax to Caesar. Instead of dithering as they'd hoped, he pointed out the emperor's image on a coin, saying: "So give back to Caesar what is Caesar's, and to God what is God's" (Matt 22:21).

Even during the Tribulation, the principle of government will still exist. Perverse and corrupt as never before? Yup. But still the last vestiges of God's order for society. And therefore, still existing under the will of God (Rom 13:1–7), regardless of its condition. But though governments have divine authority to manage society for good (Rom 13:4)—a real stretch during the Tribulation—they will *never* have the right to order or coerce individual behavior that's in violation of God's revealed will.

Jesus's statement cuts to the core of the issue: the maintenance of life and good ultimately belong to God, not to the State. And certainly not to the chief emissary of Satan himself, the Antichrist. Every Tribulation believer will have to distinguish a proper course when government forbids the pursuit of life and a good conscience. There will be many hefty moral dilemmas. But we believe there won't be any that can't be resolved and handled, if only by refusal to compromise, whatever the cost. Knowledge of the Scriptures and the guidance of the Holy Spirit will be the means of doing so, just like they've always been.

We could easily add a few more disciplines to those we've discussed here. Your unique circumstances and journey through the Scriptures will likely disclose some that you can develop on your own. But there's one more discipline that needs to be addressed. It's related to the nature of the unseen war that will reach its height in your days. And about the weapons that God has provided to be victorious in it.

Read on, friend.

Chapter 10

Basic Christian Disciplines – IV

Spiritual Warfare

Bill was busy assembling some patterns to his new life in Christ. Thinking of them as "disciplines" made a lot of sense to him. It was a perspective aided by his approach to so much else. He was still an engineer, after all.

Regarding fellowship, he still hadn't been able to develop any relationships with other new believers. But there were a handful of folks he ran into that he thought might be. One was Art Watkins, one of his CAD drafters, a single guy whose fiancée had disappeared also. That was Carolyn Jones, his company's receptionist.

Every now and then he would run into people who claimed to be followers of some supposed messiah. They were generally pretty bold—street corner preaching, and such. But in the snippets he'd overheard, there was rarely any reference to the Scriptures. Something he was now devouring. He thought their failure to quote the Bible was both odd and suspicious.

There was one exception among these preachers. A guy who, oddly enough, claimed to be Jewish! He was a real firebrand, waving a Bible in his hand and saying this and that from this book and that, many of which Bill now recognized as in the Old Testament. He had been drawing rather large numbers of listeners and he was constantly referring, not just to Jesus being the Messiah, but to the world-wide judgements of the "Day of Yahweh". Unlike the others, Bill had been instantly attracted to what he was saying. But he noted that he hadn't seen him in a couple of weeks. Probably an itinerant.

Except for that Jewish guy, the only ones he thought might be real believers seemed to be cautious in what they said, flirting on the fringes of spiritual subjects but not, or at least not yet, making statements that might tip their hand on the subject of Jesus. Actually, Bill realized that he was acting much the same. Why, he was even being somewhat guarded with Thomas on all of this, even though his son was well aware of Bill's new faith. Thomas had certainly seen his dad giving Susan's Bible a workover, and noted that Bill's paperback on the Rapture now had a bent spine (in two places) and had a half-dozen, colored tabs stuffed between its pages. Bill was honest enough admit that his own tip-toeing was leaving him a little conflicted.

This wasn't the only thing that was bugging him. Another was the increasing frequency of bizarre public behavior he'd begun to notice. Everywhere. On the street, at the pump, in the aisles at the local Aldi's. This was a little more than what he'd come to expect from the miserable folks that lived in the encampments along the Hickman Trail or behind the Industrial Park. Some of the folks behaving oddly were well-dressed or driving nicer cars, not beaters.

This wasn't all. Even though he'd largely weaned himself away from TV, and particularly the cable news networks, he'd still catch the national and local news on occasion. Two things struck him from these reports. First was the uptick in wanton, unprovoked public violence. It was no longer a "big city" distinctive. And then there were the sound-bites of national leaders and personalities from entertainment, sports, and industry. Some of their statements were becoming startling in the way they vilified traditional values and American history and institutions.

It was far more extreme than what he recalled hearing before the Rapture (Bill had chucked calling it "The Disappearance" weeks ago). There was discussion of suspending the Constitution altogether, not just certain amendments. There was talk of turning over national sovereignty to the UN or some other potential international entity. There was a lot of buzz about some upstart Hungarian named Khoshek who was making waves in Europe with huge rallies and captivating proposals. The old "normal", which had left the Earth even before the China Virus, must certainly now be well beyond Neptune.

Bill was gaining a good grasp of what the book had described as the conflict between a biblical worldview and its secular substitutes. But all of this recent stuff seemed beyond that dispute, in a way that he couldn't quite pin down. He wondered if the tipping point in his mind had been reached when Thomas had brought home a School Board notice that it would be implementing a new curriculum for the coming year throughout the District. The letter was bold enough to acknowledge the six principles upon which the new program was based. It was the third of them that really had raised his hackles. It was the proposition that the family and parenthood were now obsolete as fundamental social structures. The community was supreme in moulding the personalities and potentialities of the nation's children. Its implications chilled him. He'd been aware that schools around the country had been instituting strange social programs for years. But this one was more than he could bear.

Bill couldn't shake the thought that the entire world was now littered with wars of various sizes. Even countries long thought of a "neutral" were getting involved. It was becoming bizarre. He sensed that it was becoming something never seen before in history.

And there was one other thing. Nice as the Cabermans seemed to be, Thomas had recently started to give him some sort of "look" when he come back from their place. And particularly when he found Bill reading from the Bible or the Rapture book. A couple of times there had been a somewhat snarky comment that followed. What was that about? This was a bit more than just Thomas' despair over the loss of his mom and his little sister. He was now becoming, well, angry. Was it something that he'd picked up at his friend's house?

Chapter 10

Basic Christian Disciplines – IV

Spiritual Warfare

The Bare Bones

- The chaos in the world is derivative of an angelic rebellion against God. That rebellion was instituted by Satan before mankind's fall into sin. There is a vast and organized structure of angelic beings (demons) that assist him in his chaotic purposes.

- An angelic hierarchy, whether by God or by Satan, for good or for ill, is assigned even to the protection or domination of nations and governments (Daniel 10 and 12).

- The whole of the world system lies in the power of the evil one (1 John 5:19). The nations and their rulers are bent on a parallel rebellion against God (Psalm 2) and the principles under which he has ordained them to operate.

- Satan's schemes are consistent with his nature as an intelligent, artful, and now fallen being. He is arrogant, deceitful, and destructive of the divine order. His strategies and devices are many, highly refined, and particularly effective against the weaknesses of human character.

- Apart from their rebirth and renewal in Christ, men and women are darkened in their understanding and easy prey for the deceptions and schemes of the devil. They are constantly subject to becoming the unwitting objects of his intentions and schemes. The net result is a world of moral chaos and disorder, the effects of which extend even to the physical creation.

- Demonic activity among mankind appears to be heightened and intensified by the imminent coming or presence of Jesus and the vigorous advance of the Gospel. Accordingly, it will see a notable increase prior to and during the Tribulation.

- This increase in activity will be most dramatic following the expulsion of Satan and his angels from the heavenly realms at the mid-point of the Tribulation (Rev 12:7–9). This coincides with the Antichrist's breaking his covenant with Israel and his demand (as Satan's ultimate representative) to be worshipped as God (2 Thess 2:4, 9; cf. Isa 14:13–14).

- Believers are uniquely strengthened against and shielded from the ultimate intentions of the evil one (1 John 5:18), but are still subject to his attacks and his deceptions. They become most vulnerable when they are ignorant of God's word and under the effects of unconfessed sin.

- Resistance against him and his forces is essential for the Christian. Believers are capable of successful struggle with the devil and his demons, even to the possession of authority over certain of their works. Believers should have confidence in their capabilities in spiritual warfare because "greater is he who is within (them), that he who is in the world" (1 John 4:4).

The Conflict of the Ages

Let's go back to some previous quotes about what the end of the age will look like. The first is by Jesus:

> Watch out that no one deceives you. For many will come in my name, claiming, 'I am the Messiah,' and will deceive many. You will hear of wars and rumors of wars, but see to it that you are not alarmed. Such things must happen, but the end is still to come. Nation will rise against nation, and kingdom against kingdom. There will be famines and earthquakes in various places. All these are the beginning of birth pains. Then you will be handed over to be persecuted and put to death, and you will be hated by all nations because of me. At that time many will turn away from the faith and will betray and hate each other, and many false prophets will appear and deceive many people. Because of the increase of wickedness, the love of most will grow cold,... (Matt 24:4–12)

And, the next, by Paul:

> People will be lovers of themselves, lovers of money, boastful, proud, abusive, disobedient to their parents, ungrateful, unholy, without love, unforgiving, slanderous, without self-control, brutal, not lovers of the good, treacherous, rash, conceited, lovers of pleasure rather than lovers of God... (2 Tim 3:2–4)

These descriptions are not exceptions, but the general behavior of mankind during the final years before the Second Coming of Christ. The obvious question arises: "How did things get this way?"

Major players in politics and the press will offer up all sorts of explanations: the rich victimizing both the less fortunate and the environment because of their greed, disputing political parties failing to work together for the common good, "systemic" this, that or the other, Critical Whatever Theory, degeneration of infrastructure, not enough work, too much work, not enough tech, too much tech. Rationalizations without end. All of these people will be competing for followers—and failing to touch the real issue. Because they'll all ignore the spiritual source behind it.

Then, there will be the folks who offer that all this degeneration is not really new, but has existed for thousands of years. "History and societies have always been littered with it. When has there not been out-and-out war or revolution somewhere?", they'll say, adding on oppression and injustice. Just for starters, of course. What they won't be able to explain, though, is how pervasive it's become across the globe and irrespective of cultures and economies.

Believers could answer by offering that it's all traceable to sin. Of course, that's a biblical answer, not one to be offered by anyone you'll be hearing or reading in the media, entertainment, education, or politics. Before the Rapture, you'd have heard this in Bible-oriented churches and from Christians on the street or over some back fence. And yet, even as a biblical answer, it would fall a bit short, if the person from whom you heard it was speaking of sin from simply a human perspective.

The Source of the Struggle

The main root of the current darkness goes much deeper than the fallen nature of mankind. It lies in a realm beyond that of mere human existence. Its foundation lies in a long-running conflict in the spiritual realm. For starters, here's some words from the prophet Ezekiel:

"...You were the seal of perfection,
full of wisdom and perfect in beauty.

You were in Eden,
    the garden of God;...
You were anointed as a guardian cherub,
    for so I ordained you....
You were blameless in your ways
    from the day you were created
    till wickedness was found in you.
Through your widespread trade
    you were filled with violence,
    and you sinned.
So I drove you in disgrace from the mount of God,
    and I expelled you, guardian cherub,
    from among the fiery stones.
Your heart became proud
    on account of your beauty,
    and you corrupted your wisdom
    because of your splendor.
So I threw you to the earth;
    I made a spectacle of you before kings."
(Ezek 28:12b, 13a, 14a, 15–17)

Before we identify who the "you" is here, we need to provide a little background. By inspiration, Ezekiel was tasked to take up a prophetic lamentation against the king of Tyre, a small but powerful city-state on the Mediterranean coast. But in his words, the prophet included a number of things that go beyond symbolic overstatement. What we've quoted above steps beyond human description.

Like referring to the subject as being a "guardian cherub". Don't picture a chubby baby angel here, shooting arrows into hearts on valentine cards. This is a word for a highly elevated order of angels. And it's one that's never used anywhere else in the Old Testament for a human. The king of Tyre had never been an angel, and he'd certainly never been in Eden. This other being was perfection in every respect. Until his vanity corrupted his character and wisdom. Let's see from another text the extent to which that character was distorted.

Isaiah also includes a passage that steps beyond human description in a number of places. It's in a taunt against the king of Babylon:

"How you have fallen from heaven,
   morning star, son of the dawn!
You said in your heart,
   'I will ascend to the heavens;
I will raise my throne
above the stars of God;
I will ascend above the tops of the clouds;
I will make myself like the Most High.'"
(Isa 14:12a, 13, 14b)

"Star" is sometimes a poetic figure for an angelic being (Job 38:7; Rev 1:20). And Isaiah speaks of one who has fallen, not just because he wishes to rule ("raise my throne") over the other angels, but because he's proud enough to imagine himself as God's equal. This conceit is what's at the heart of this rebellion in the heavens.

Both Isaiah and Ezekiel are speaking of Satan himself.

The One Becomes the Many

But Satan's not alone in this revolt, nor in what will become of its fallout among humanity. He's gathered his own troops from among the rest of the angels (Rev 12:7–9; 1 Cor 15:24–25). Before he drew mankind into sin, he seduced as many as a third of them (Rev 12:4). And, as the Bible says that the angels are beyond count (Dan 7:10; Rev 5:11), Satan's also can't be numbered. These are his demonic forces. Some are so perverse that they've been locked up even before their final judgment (2 Pet 2:4). It's not out of place here to mention that hell itself was created for the devil and his angels (Matt 25:41).

Paul refers to this Satanic horde by multiple terms: "For our struggle is not against flesh and blood, but against the *rulers*, against the *authorities*, against the *powers* of this dark world and against the *spiritual forces of evil* in the heavenly realms" (Eph 6:12, italics ours).

These terms also occur in Rom 8:38, 1 Cor 15:24, and Col 2:15. We can see from these passages that they are organized in a sophisticated, cosmic hierarchy beneath Satan, eagerly carrying out his schemes (Eph 6:11) and deceptions (1 Tim 4:1).

It's both by his servants and by his devices that the evil one has taken captive the world's philosophies and principles (Col 2:8; Eph 4:14). It's in this sense that Satan is the "god of this world" (2 Cor 4:4), its "ruler" (John 12:31), and that the whole world currently lies in his power (1 John 5:19).

Not only does he master the current world's operating principles, he can deceive, direct, and coerce specific nations to accomplish his destructive goals. He does this by assigning significant angelic beings to them. Daniel 10:10–21 references a struggle between Michael, and the "prince" of Persia. Michael, an archangel, is the chief angelic guardian of Israel. It's obvious that Persia's prince opposes the rule of God as one of Satan's chief servants. And once Michael overcomes him, there's a prince of Greece in the wings. Talk about a cosmic struggle that's spilled over onto the earth!

It isn't unreasonable to conclude that many of human history's major powers (or their rulers) have been assigned an evil angel, especially where these nations have had a direct bearing upon the history of Israel. Didn't you ever wonder who was assigned in the spiritual realm to pull the levers in the regimes of Hitler and Stalin? Or of Idi Amin and Pol Pot? Of Genghis Khan and a spectrum of nations and their leaders who've rewritten the boundaries of violence and oppression everywhere?

Haven't you ever wondered just who is behind the descent of America from its former position of world excellence and influence? We'd offer that, ultimately, it's not its politicians and other human power brokers. Little wonder, then, that the nations and their rulers are seen in the Scriptures as pawns in Satan's attempted overthrow of God, of his restraints, and of his Messiah (Psa 2:1–3).

The Status of Satan and His Forces, and Their Understanding of Their Own End

As we've mentioned already, Satan and his forces have already been placed under judgment, particularly in connection with the death and resurrection of Christ (John 16:11; Col 2:15; Heb 2:14; 1 John 3:8). And some of these angels have already been confined in the abyss (a prison for spirit-beings), so terrible were their past spiritual crimes (2 Pet 2:4; Jude 6). It's apparent that the demons are fully aware of their final judgment (Matt 8:29; Luke 8:28, 31), and yet they continue without repentance in their service to Satan.

And the devil himself is also aware of it, condemned already by the Lord Jesus Christ (John 16:11). He's aware of the teaching of the Scriptures on the end of the age, not to mention the preaching of the believing church. He's not ignorant of what the Bible describes as his participation in the world's collapse. No, he's delighted to finally be unrestrained (see 2 Thess 2:7-9) against Christ and his people. We shouldn't be surprised, then, that he'll be all the more filled with rage when he's cast down to the earth (Rev 12:12).

Demonic Activity: Past, Present, and Future

You need to be aware of the kind of opposition that the devil and his demons can exhibit toward both mankind and Christ. Here's a prime example from the gospels:

> When he arrived at the other side in the region of the Gadarenes, two demon-possessed men coming from the tombs met him (Jesus). They were so violent that no one could pass that way. "What do you want with

us, Son of God?" they shouted. "Have you come here to torture us before the appointed time?" (Matt 8:28)

It's interesting to note that these men—under demonic influence—had no difficulty at all recognizing Jesus's divinity. But Matthew's summary of them as "violent" is almost a bit tame. Here's how Mark describes the demons' effect on at least one of these men:

> ...and no one could bind him anymore, not even with a chain. For he had often been chained hand and foot, but he tore the chains apart and broke the irons on his feet. No one was strong enough to subdue him. Night and day among the tombs and in the hills he would cry out and cut himself with stones. (Mark 5:3b–5)

Now, let's add this particular item: in this incident it wasn't the effect of just a single demon or two within him, but of a *legion* of them (Luke 8:30).

There are at least sixteen other occasions where Jesus or his followers dealt with people who were "demonized" (Matt 4:24; 8:16; 9:32; 12:22ff; 15:21ff; 17:14; Mark 1:23ff; 1:39; 16:9; Luke 6:18; 7:21; Acts 5:16; 8:7; 16:16–18; 19:12, 15–16). It's reasonable to conclude that the frequency of these scenes had something to do with the presence of the Christ among the people and, shortly thereafter, the potent activities of the early church. One thing is certain: prior to Jesus's appearance, no one was able to deal with demonic activity effectively (Matt 9:33).

All this raises the question of whether similar demonic activities occurred in the run-up to the Tribulation. Well, at least until the Rapture occurred, they didn't *seem* to be common in America. But it may not have been as uncommon as it seemed. That's because media has had a long history mishandling or to dismissing anything in the spiritual realm. Unless, of course, it was something horrific that might be pinned on Jesus. But how else can much of the increased wanton and perverse violence of the of the years even *before* the Rapture be explained, except by the work of these dark spiritual forces?

We're of the opinion that, just as it was common in connection with the first coming of Christ, it will again be amplified prior to his return in power and glory at the conclusion of the Tribulation. This will be covered in greater (and rather horrific) detail in Chapter 16. Even so, let's deal with some preliminary information.

Increased demonic activity will be traceable to at least three specific factors: 1) an increasing indulgence in "gateway" behaviors, 2) the wholesale casting to the earth of the forces of evil, and 3) the release of demonic hordes from their present imprisonment.

First, demonic activity is tied in the Bible with involvement in a boatload of occult practices (Deut 18:9–14; Rev 21:8; etc.), including astrology (Isa 47:13–15; Dan 2:2). These generally have had connections with false religions and their associated moral corruptions. Why, the word for sorcery in the New Testament (Gal 5:20; Rev 9:21; 18:23; 22:15) is the same Greek term from which we get *pharmacy*! Even apart from their use in false religion, illicit drugs are a direct gateway to these terrible experiences. Strangely, the progress of history and its reliance on science and technology hasn't seen a decrease of interest in the occult and drugs, but an increase instead. The reason why is plain: the behaviors described in the Bible as abominations to God are demonstrations of the world's spiritual rebellion against him.

The second factor will be the effect of the devil and his angels taking up residence on the earth after their being evicted from the heavenly realms (Rev 12:7–9). If the rise in demonic activity leading up to and during the first half off the Tribulation was notable, how much more once the planet has become the only place for the activities of the devil and his servants? This will happen at the mid-point of the Tribulation, when the Antichrist suspends his covenant with Israel, raises an image to himself in a rebuilt Temple in Jerusalem, and requires the world's worship. Demonic activities will no longer be occasional but commonplace. And they'll be dramatic. Resistance to anything and anyone related to Christ will be vigorous, even violent.

The third is the direct implication that the spirits released from past confinement are demonic in nature (Rev 9:1-11; see also Luke 8:27-31; 2 Pet 2:4) and serve not only to afflict mankind but to draw the nations together for the Battle of Armageddon (Rev 16:12-16).

Your Part in the Struggle

What's your place in these circumstances? Well, just as the early believers, you'll be found in the midst of this colossal conflict. And just like them, you've been called to be an active part in it (Eph 6:10–12; Jas 4:7; 1 Pet 5:8–10). The critical issue is how you will manage. Jesus Christ does not intend that you be "cannon fodder" or collateral damage in the war. Nor does he intend that you merely take up a defensive stand. You will be faced with appropriate opportunities to take the initiative according to the depth of your faith. Don't faint at the prospect: along with your faith, you've been given divine protections to appreciate, and divine resources to employ.

The Protections of the Believer

The perfect way to recruit an army is to be able to guarantee their life. God does that from an eternal perspective. You can't be separated from Christ. Paul says that your life is now "hidden with Christ in God" (Col 3:3), using a verb form there that emphasized its permanence. Here are two other passages for you to read: John 10:27–29 and Romans 8:33–39. Take a break here and look them up.

Finally, in a context of a Christian's relation to sin, John said this: "We know that anyone born of God does not continue to sin; the One who was born of God keeps them safe, *and the evil one cannot harm them*" (1 John 5:18). We've italicized an important principle at the end of this verse. It's that the devil can't bring you to grief *by his own accord.*

By God's allowance Satan may sift you through his fingers (see Luke 22:31 and Job 1:8ff; 2:3ff), but he can't touch your person without divine permission. And he can't lay hold of your soul at all.

The Armor and Arms of the Believer

Here's how Paul introduces you to a Christian's role in this conflict:

> The weapons we fight with are not the weapons of the world. On the contrary, they have divine power to demolish strongholds. We demolish arguments and every pretension that sets itself up against the knowledge of God, and we take captive every thought to make it obedient to Christ. (2 Cor 10:4–5)

But he gets more specific here:

> Therefore, put on the full armor of God, so that when the day of evil comes, you may be able to stand your ground, and after you have done everything, to stand. Stand firm then, with the belt of truth buckled around your waist, with the breastplate of righteousness in place, and with your feet fitted with the readiness that comes from the gospel of peace. In addition to all this, take up the shield of faith, with which you can extinguish all the flaming arrows of the evil one. Take the helmet of salvation and the sword of the Spirit, which is the word of God. And pray in the Spirit on all occasions with all kinds of prayers and requests. With this in mind, be alert and always keep on praying for all the Lord's people. (Eph 6:13–18)

It's pretty easy to imagine Paul visualizing a Roman soldier that was fully decked out. And then using all of his gear as analogies of what's required by the believer to turn away the forces and strategies of evil. Let's go through these items in terms of their practical effects.

The nature of the battle is reflected in both the armor and the armament that God provides for it:

1.   The belt of **truth**: Bible teachers have offered differing views of why truth is associated with a belt. Let's consider it simply as the attachment point for the sword and lower edge of the breastplate. And something that keeps other critical items both secure and orderly.

But here's the substance: truth comes up first because it has great power against the "father of lies" (John 8:44). He has corrupted the truth from the beginning (Gen 3:1–7), and in so doing he's manipulated all of humanity through the ages. By half-truths, plausible substitutes, blatant falsehoods. "Bait and switch" arguments on moral and ethical questions. High sounding theories that subtly contradict God's truth. He's the consummate wolf in sheep's clothing, appearing as an angel of light (2 Cor 11:14) when he's really the personification of darkness.

In order to thwart his redemptive mission, he even attempted to foist these devices on Jesus (Matt 4:1–11). But our Lord parried each of his deceptive offers with the truth of the Scriptures. Little wonder that the devil's servants do the same as their master. And that you should do the same as *your* Master.

2.   The breastplate of **righteousness**: This piece of equipment is a little more obvious in its importance—a protection of the vital organs against the weapons of the enemy.

You ask about the value of righteousness in a battle? Consider this: one of the chief ways that Satan uses to remove God's servants from the fray is to charge them with being unfit for duty. He does this by slandering either their character or their deeds ("devil" means "slanderer", by the way). In this sense he's also the accuser of believers (Rev 12:10;

see also Job 1:9–11; 2:5; Zech 3:1ff). What is your protection? When you believed, God immediately categorized you as righteous. That is, in Christ he applied to you his own righteousness (Rom 3:21–22; 4:5, 21–25; 2 Cor 5:21). That is your standing before him. You've been justified, classed by God as fit to serve (Rom 3:26).

But the practical side of righteousness may also be in view here. That's because what you accomplish that pleases God is a reflection of both your obedience and your faith. Neither of which can be demonstrated by Satan and his angels. From this other perspective, our godly behavior gives him no opportunity for challenge. It actually becomes his silent rebuke. Think of your character as a vital protection. The righteousness with which you've been fitted by Christ has got you covered.

3. Feet fitted with the **readiness of the gospel of peace**: Historians of ancient military forces would list any advance in equipment as a major edge against the enemy. This extends even to an army's footwear. The Romans had the best, giving them a decided advantage, even before the fur began to fly. What's on *your* feet?

For spiritual conflict, Paul says "readiness of the gospel of peace". "Readiness" (or preparation) speaks of something brought to a point of usefulness. The Gospel is, of course, the "good news" and all that it promises both now and for eternity. Peace is the settled confidence that arises from what we've been promised (see Chapter Five).

But the question may not so much be what these words mean as how they fit together in this verse. Perhaps the best view is not one about how you whip up a Gospel message for others. Instead, it's about your readiness for spiritual conflict because of the peace *produced in you* by the Gospel. But let's not split hairs here; Paul might say it applies to both. Let's just remind you that the certainty of your future in Christ, and the divine resources at your disposal, should instill real confidence when you have to take on the forces of the devil. Let that peace be sufficient. Just make sure that it doesn't become the occasion for presumption or self-confidence.

4.   The shield of **faith**: Paul uses the term here for the big shield, about 30 by 50 inches in size, not the garbage can lid that the gladiators held in one hand. This was the one you could get your whole body behind. Review your recollection of sweeping scenes in old movies, please. This larger shield was especially effective in both stopping *and dousing* the flaming arrows that used to be launched in massive volleys against advancing troops. As Paul notes, the evil one has plenty of these at hand.

What will the devil and his forces launch against you? Accusations? Temptations? False narratives? Doubts? Threats of destruction? All these and more. But consider the Christ in whom you stand. Consider what he's promised. Consider both the truth *that he is by his very nature* and the truth that he fits you with from his word. They're all more than sufficient to snuff out the enemy's missiles. Your trust in them is what overcomes the world (1 John 5:8).

Do you doggedly maintain your reliance on your Savior's nature, on his promises, on his presence? Or do you get a little wimpy when the heat gets turned up? Review what you know. Say it out loud. First to yourself. Then to the devil. And move ahead. The shield is large, but it's still plenty portable. "Your adversary the devil prowls around like a roaring lion, seeking someone to devour. Resist him, firm in your faith..." (1 Pet 5:8b–9a (ESV)).

5.   The helmet of **salvation**: Here's another one to think about. Don't imagine the polished, shiny one with the red bristles that remind you of a punk-rocker's hairdo. Those spiffy ones that you've seen on centurions were for parades and government business (and movies). Haven't you noticed that they never sport any dents? We'll bet the soldier donned something well-worn (and maybe more functional) when the enemy was closing in. Something of bronze, with rugged leather attachments. You know what it's *really* for, after all. And it certainly isn't for show. It's representative of salvation.

Salvation. One of those words that we sometimes take too narrowly when we first hear them. Yes, it does have to do with being saved by Christ from sin and from the hell that it promised. But let's drop back twenty feet for a broader perspective. Salvation in the Bible is very comprehensive in its meanings. It's really helpful to see where it starts: *deliverance* from something. In the Bible those "somethings" are off a long list: people, situations, conditions, armies, diseases, thoughts, desires; yes, and sins. It's quite amazing to consider all the things that assail us. We need a salvation that's just as comprehensive. Something that doesn't just cover all our circumstances but something that can look back, work in the present, and supply something in the future— all in one, fell swoop.

So, let's tie salvation to an issue that's just as comprehensive: hope. That applies here because Paul speaks in 1 Thessalonians 5:8 of the helmet as the "*hope* of salvation", that which salvation produces. Comparatively, hope looks back because you had none before you were saved (Eph 2:12). Hope looks forward because salvation's full effects (in heaven) are yet to be realized (Rom 8:23–25; 1 Pet 1:5). But in the present battle, the hope of salvation is our motivator for endurance (Heb 6:9–12), an anchor for the soul (Heb 6:18–20) when the fur flies. Salvation is the divinely preserved possession you've been granted through Christ Jesus. Stand in it. Use it.

6. The sword of the spirit, **the word of God**: Two terms are used in the New Testament for swords. One's the huge, double-edged hacker that you'd heft with two hands, like the medieval era's broadsword. The other was maybe half that length, a one-hander that could be used in close combat. To be really effective, it required a quick eye, a fast hand, and an arm that wouldn't run out of gas. It's the smaller sword that Paul speaks of here. It wasn't much of a brute-force weapon, it was more surgical. Rather radical surgery, of course.

As they're spirits, it's plain that you won't be able to physically cut up the Devil or his demons. But you can use what's in the Bible to confront and disassemble their lies and schemes. The writer of the book of Hebrews speaks about the capacity of God's word to even dissect the motives and intentions of the heart (Heb 4:12). And so, like any weapon, this spiritual sword has inherent and unique capabilities.

But what makes it really effective is the proficiency of the hand that it's in. And that, friend, is the product of two things: knowledge and practice. Your knowledge and your practice. Swordsman or pianist, mathematician or mechanic, natural talent won't hold a candle in the end to knowledge and practice. You will get out of it what you put in. The time and the effort are your part of the equation. Now, God's Spirit will certainly join the process (see John 16:13–14). And because of the shortness of time, he may do so in an unusual way. But in large measure, your capacity will reflect what you invest in the process, the process of learning what's in your Bible. Learn and practice, learn and practice...

7. **Prayer**: Some commentators on this passage dismiss this as part of the "full armor" (v. 13) because it's not visualized by Paul as a piece of military equipment. We'll grant that the analogy is missing. However, not everything a soldier brings to the fight is something that's parked on his body or carried in his hand. Indeed, most of the things that are the essence of what Paul has talked about here have a decided *mental* aspect. And so does prayer. Not only that, prayer is unique in seizing God's direct assistance and power in the conflict.

Prayer doesn't simply request his assistance, as though we're doing most of the work, but just need a little extra to finish the job. It begs his involvement in every aspect of the struggle. And it does so from before the action starts right on through the mop-up. Without his involvement, no, without his very *intervention*, victory isn't just in question, it's altogether unattainable. His is the only power that will prevail.

Prayer, then, is the indispensable ingredient in all spiritual warfare. It accesses not only God's power, but his sovereignty over circumstance, his wisdom, his perfect knowledge of the enemy and his artful devices and cruel strategies. Prayer uniquely reflects your willingness to serve as his vehicle in this conflict with the forces of darkness.

But it's people, both saved and unsaved, that are caught up in the conflict. Paul says, "be alert and always keep on praying for all the Lord's people." He gives prayer for other believers the priority. They're your comrades in arms. To use a military expression, you're the one that "has their back" through your prayers on their behalf. And you can expect the same in return. How important is this? Well, note for starters that Paul uses the word "all" four times in verse 18.

Of course, Paul would not discount the power of prayer on behalf of the lost, either. For he says elsewhere:

> I urge, then, first of all, that petitions, prayers, interces-
> sion and thanksgiving be made for all people—for kings
> and all those in authority, that we may live peaceful and
> quiet lives in all godliness and holiness. This is good,
> and pleases God our Savior, who wants all people to
> be saved and to come to a knowledge of the truth. (1
> Tim 2:1–4)

Verse two (about kings and other authorities) gets lots of attention, but we can't ignore the "all people" in verses 1 and 4. Join this with what Isaiah prophetically places on the lips of the Messiah:

> "The Spirit of the Sovereign LORD is on me,
> because the LORD has anointed me
> to proclaim good news to the poor.
> He has sent me to bind up the brokenhearted,
> to proclaim freedom for the captives
> and release from darkness for the prisoners..."
> (Isa 61:1)

Doesn't this especially describe the lost during the Tribulation? And look how Jesus passes on this commission to his disciples, regardless of when they live: "Peace be with you! As the Father has sent me,

I am sending you" (John 20:21). Of all the things that we could offer the lost, the Gospel is the most important. And who we'd speak to, we ought to pray for.

The Warfare of the Believer

Sooner or later, you will come across the kind of demonic oppressions illustrated in the Gospels and Acts. When you do, the resources and power of Christ will be sufficiently present both to be unaffected personally and to accomplish his purposes. But we can say with certainty that you'll be faced with other manifestations of this spiritual war. Three of them immediately come to mind:

- Deception—not just in what you hear (at every conceivable level), but in circumstances that could lead you or others into bad choices. You can find refuge in the truth (John 8:31–32), the truth of God's word (John 17:17). Which leads us to...

- Temptation—expect it to increase and be even more artful. But the essence of these temptations will be the same as it's always been; and you'll find a way of escape (1 Cor 10:13), first, by saying "No!" to sin and "Yes!" to God (Titus 2:11–14). Additional necessary steps will appear as you're willing to take them.

- Persecution—which won't so much be a matter of escaping it as being given what to say in response (Matt 10:19; cf. Dan 3:8ff!).

Regardless of what comes down the road, we offer this observation: take each circumstance as a new one. Don't presume that just because you handled the last one is a guarantee that you'll handle the next. Jesus's disciples learned this the hard way. Jesus had given them authority over demonic forces when he sent them out in pairs (Mark

6:7). And yet, on a later occasion they failed in dealing with a spirit that was producing epileptic seizures in a boy (Mark 9:17ff). Jesus laid this failure to their inadequacy in prayer (vv. 28–29). They had either failed in their intensity or had forgotten to pray at all. Don't get caught just going through the motions.

On every new occasion, you'll be asked to exercise humility, faith, and earnestness in prayer in every facet of the task at hand. Recall your past victories as an encouragement. But don't let them become some mechanical formula for success in the conflict of the moment. The bigger battle will not be lost, of course, but your pride or presumption could take a licking. Rejoice not in the authority that you've been gifted (Mark 16:17), but that your name is recorded in heaven (Luke 10:20). Rejoice and move on.

The Reward of the Believer

Spiritual accomplishment in the End Times will require overcoming the dark forces of Satan. And there are particular promises made by the Lord of Glory to such folks. To him (or her) who overcomes:

> ...I will grant to eat from the tree of life, which is in the Paradise of God. (Rev 2:7)

> ...(they) will not be hurt by the second death. (Rev 2:11)

> ...I will give some of the hidden manna, and I will give him a white stone, and a new name written on the stone which no one knows except the one who receives it. (Rev 2:17)

> ...and the one who keeps My deeds until the end, I will give him authority over the nations. (Rev 2:26)

...will be clothed... in white garments; and I will not erase his name from the book of life, and I will confess his name before My Father and before His angels. (Rev 3:5)

...I will make him a pillar in the temple of My God, and he will not go out from it anymore; and I will write on him the name of My God, and the name of the city of My God, the new Jerusalem, which comes down out of heaven from My God, and My new name. (Rev 3:12)

...I will grant to him to sit with Me on My throne, as I also overcame and sat with My Father on His throne. (Rev 3:21; all above references NASB)

And,

The one who overcomes will inherit these things, and I will be his God and he will be My son. (Rev 21:7)

We've piled up these references for impact; there are never too many encouragements from the Lord Jesus. As with every success in living for Christ, you will overcome the forces and effects of the evil one by your faith (1 John 5:4). It will be fully rewarded. Finally, to these promises of the risen Savior, we add Paul's own confidence:

I have fought the good fight, I have finished the race, I have kept the faith. Now there is in store for me the crown of righteousness, which the Lord, the righteous Judge, will award to me on that day - and not only to me, but also to all who have longed for his appearing (2 Tim 4:7–8)

We trust that what we've said to this point has given you a solid grasp of what the Rapture was, of the necessity of your own trust in Christ, and of what new life in him is all about. If you have placed your faith in Jesus and are committed to exercising the perspectives and disciplines that we've laid out, you have every resources in hand to navigate the turmoil that lies ahead. And, in the process, you will bring satisfaction to your soul, blessing to others, and glory to Christ. It won't be easy. But what of real value ever is?

Chapter 11

Two Foundational Christian Observances

Baptism and the Lord's Supper (Communion)

Bill was becoming convinced that he needed to be more vocal about his new faith in Christ. He'd already read through the Book of Acts (twice), and was impressed by the fearlessness shown in its characters' willingness to speak about Jesus— pretty much to anything that moved. But he seemed to be caught in a struggle between two voices. While one was encouraging him to be more vocal, the other was telling him that he didn't know enough yet to be persuasive. And that he needed to be careful in view of potential betrayal. That had been one of the alerts contained in Chapter Ten of his now second-favorite book. He just was not sure how far to take it at this point.

As if on cue, Bill thought about Keith Melville, one of the other engineers at his business. He'd recently noticed on several occasions that Keith seemed to be on the verge of speaking to him about something important, but not work-related. Surely, he would have coughed it up if it was. No, these were moments when they found themselves in relative privacy. Keith's hesitancy to speak had only been matched by Bill's hesitancy to ask what was on his friend's mind. It was becoming a rather strange dance between the two, kind of reminiscent of halting, guarded conversations between himself and a few young ladies he was fond of back in junior high.

And sure enough, another thought dropped by for a visit. Bill had now become accustomed to his mind hop-scotching between initially unrelated items. At first, it has an unwelcome intrusion into the mental orderliness he'd cultivated for years. But now, it was becoming an amusing curiosity, one of observing how God seemed to integrate otherwise unconnected matters in constructing new designs for his life. And this new process generally produced something fairly quickly.

This next thought was of baptism. Of all things. Where did that come from*? Perhaps it was just another item from Acts that he'd noticed. Something that had followed people's response to the preaching of the Gospel. And it seemed to follow rapidly at that. Why, there was even some guy who'd heard about Jesus while travelling. It must have made quite an impression—he'd asked one of the disciples why he couldn't be baptized right there by the road! Wow. These new Christians didn't seem to mess around with things before getting down to business. Had he missed something?*

And here came the next link in this chain. Bill recalled an occasion three years ago when Susan had invited him to a special evening service at her church. It wasn't a holiday, and she was mum about its nature. As she was careful not to pester him about coming to church, he found himself curious and decided to humor her interest. He'd hoped it wasn't going to be the appearance of some flaming evangelist!

They'd arrived to find the auditorium fairly well-packed. What was more interesting, though, was that the platform had been pretty well cleared of its expected piano, pulpit, music stands and potted shrubbery. Instead, the center of the platform had an opening in it about the size of his small back patio. He couldn't see what lay below the edge. The church's pastor came out in fairly casual clothes, made some opening comments about the potency of the Gospel, and turned to welcome a guy in his early 30s who was coming on stage. Shoeless, jeans and t-shirt. Oooh-kay. They both descended unseen stairs and Bill could hear water splashing.

Pastor Jacobsen faced the audience and said, "Friends, let me introduce Tim Bennett." Then he turned to his guest and asked Tim to tell everybody his story. It was plain that Tim was not your normal church-goer. Not just from the way he talked, but from his experiences. Life was a mess for him but Jesus had turned it around. He spoke for only two minutes. It was concise. Bit it had real impact. The Pastor had then asked a couple of quick questions that each got a one-word, affirmative response. He then assisted Tim going over backward and under the water, after which he climbed out soaking wet to—what's this?—applause.

Seven more followed, each with their own stories about how Christ was in the process of changing them and how they were committing themselves publicly to be his disciples. A waitress, a financial planner, a former atheist, a police officer, an 82-year-old retired college professor with a heavy

*German accent, an auto mechanic, and last, a disabled vet-
eran, who'd descended the stairs artificial legs and all.*

*The stories were all different. Some longer, some shorter.
Some dramatic, some not quite. But they all had a common
thread: Jesus Christ had broken into their lives. In a couple
of them he had walked in a front door recently shattered by
the vandals of life. In others he'd walked in a back door that
the owner had left ajar, taking a chair at the kitchen table
while someone worked on dinner. In all cases, in short time
or long, Jesus had made himself welcome.*

*Bill also recalled how he'd quietly begun to squirm as the
testimonies continued. On one hand, he'd been surprised
that Susan had been so obvious in inviting him to this service – and yet silent on the subject after it was over. On the
other, he recognized that to get through it after Tim Bennett
had spoken, he'd adopted the attitude that, though this was
where Jesus had brought these people, Bill Archer wasn't
ready yet to have a deep conversation with him.*

*And now here he was. Like a chess master, the Holy Spirit
had again brought together the events and recollections of
Bill's life to face an important decision in the moment. He
was amazed at how artfully it had been done, how unaware
he'd been of the importance of each move at the time, and
how inescapable they'd now become.*

*Chapter Ten had been sobering, to say the least. He recalled
that when he'd finished it, he'd glanced ahead to see what
the next chapter was about, if only for possible relief. And
now Bill understood. It was the final domino to fall. Bill
walked into the den, picked up the book, and began to read.*

Chapter 11

Two Foundational Christian Observances

Baptism and the Lord's Supper (Communion)

The Bare Bones

- Baptism is a one-time observance by a new believer that's an early declaration of their faith in Christ. It signals a commitment to discipleship and visually pictures God's regeneration of them as a new person.

- The Lord's Supper (communion) is a recurring observance for gathered believers that remembers both the costliness of their redemption and Jesus's commitment to its certainty. It is a reminder that this covenant will be fully realized upon his return.

Since the beginning of the church, there have been two formal practices that the saints have observed everywhere. Both are symbolic in nature. One of them looks back (but usually not far), one looks forward (and in your case, not far either). One focuses on what happened to you when you were saved, the other focuses on the cost of our redemption and the promise of Jesus's return. The first is baptism, the second is communion, or what many believers call the Lord's Supper (from 1 Cor 11:25).

In most Bible-oriented churches these two observances have been called "ordinances", which pretty much implies something of an obligation. One is an obligation to testify, the other is an obligation to remember. On the other hand, some branches of Christianity have called them "sacraments", which casts a different view of them.

Technically, a sacrament is a ceremony that confers upon its participants a special "grace" or spiritual status. It's much more than just a remembrance of something; the act itself places the person in a new condition. In some traditions, the baptism of children and infants (generally by sprinkling or pouring, not by immersion) brings them into the spiritual company of the church—even though they aren't yet capable of making a conscious, knowledgeable commitment to Christ. In some traditions, the bread and wine of the communion service actually become the body and blood of Jesus, to enable John 6:53 to be taken literally, rather than figuratively *as the larger context requires*. We believe that the New Testament does not support these views and that, in the end, this sacramental approach to baptism and communion lessens or destroys their original function.

And some believers would be of the opinion that neither baptism or the Lord's Supper are appropriate for folks who come to Christ after the Rapture. Their argument would be that these two observances were given to the Church, and the term for "church" does not appear in any of the Bible texts that speak of the Tribulation. In other words, if the true Church is gone, so are its ordinances.

We believe that this last opinion takes an unnecessarily narrow approach. First of all, the lack of reference to the Church during the Tribulation is at the very least an argument from silence. But more to the point are the aspects of each observance that easily transcend historical or local church contexts.

We will establish shortly that Christian baptism is fundamentally a testimony to faith in Jesus as Savior and Lord. Is this not also important during the Tribulation? Are not people responding to the Gospel and committing themselves to discipleship and obedience to Christ? And we would also note that one of the earliest recorded examples of baptism occurred by a roadside following a response to the Gospel by a travelling Ethiopian (Acts 8:26ff). Surely, this occurred outside of the context and presence of a local church body.

As for communion, it certainly was a commemoration that was handed over for observance by local churches (1 Cor 11:23ff). But we would also note that in teaching about it, Paul says that it represents a proclamation of the Lord's death *"until he comes"* (v. 26). Here you are as a Tribulation believer, also awaiting his return in power and great glory (Matt 24:30). Are you not also a citizen of heaven, anticipating the fulfilment of all those things he secured for you upon the cross (Phil 3:20; 1 Thess 1:10)?

On Baptism

Baptism has been a ceremony from the very first days of the church. It was the appropriate successor to those carried out by John the Baptist. Under John, they were visual statements made by Jews who were repentant in light of the imminent appearance of Messiah (Acts 13:24–25; 19:4). The water baptism of new believers in Jesus rendered John's baptisms obsolete.

Christian baptism appears on nine occasions in the Book of Acts and is referred to at least six times in the letters of Paul and Peter. The early church doesn't seem to have dithered regarding the ceremony. When folks believed in Christ, they were baptized immediately (Acts 2:38–39). The longest recorded delay in a person's baptism was three days—for Paul's (Acts 9:9–18). From its earliest days, water baptism appears to have been the rule in the churches. Put another way, the concept of a believer in Jesus remaining *un*baptized was treated as an oddity, something that needed to be remedied immediately (see Acts

19:5). In some respects, an unbaptized believer in the early church was kind of a walking contraction in terms.

This raises the question of why baptism was (and is) so important. At least two reasons immediately present themselves. First, baptism was the first occasion for most believers to give a public testimony to their new faith. And it served as a message not only to onlookers, but to the person being baptized: he or she was taking a first and firm step on the road of discipleship. The spiritual and social implications were conscious and significant. That's remained unchanged for 2000 years, but particularly where Christianity has been a target of persecution. Take a lesson, friend.

But there's a second reason, as well. It's because of the spiritual truths that it pictures of being born again in Jesus. The primary place where this is discussed is in the Book of Romans. Here's how Paul explains it:

> What shall we say, then? Shall we go on sinning so that grace may increase? By no means! We are those who have died to sin; how can we live in it any longer? Or don't you know that all of us who were baptized into Christ Jesus were baptized into his death? We were therefore buried with him through baptism into death in order that, just as Christ was raised from the dead through the glory of the Father, we too may live a new life. For if we have been united with him in a death like his, we will certainly also be united with him in a resurrection like his. For we know that our old self was crucified with him so that the body ruled by sin might be done away with, that we should no longer be slaves to sin – because anyone who has died has been set free from sin. Now if we died with Christ, we believe that we will also live with him. For we know that since Christ was raised from the dead, he cannot die again; death

no longer has mastery over him. The death he died, he
died to sin once for all; but the life he lives, he lives to
God. (Rom 6:1–10)

This is a heavy passage. So, here's the bottom line. Paul has been
talking about God's grace to sinners that comes when they respond
to the Gospel. When he gets to this point, he theorizes that someone
might say, "Hey, let's get even more grace from God by continuing
to lead a life of sin as Christians!" Paul says, "Hold up there, buddy.
You've missed the point of what's happened to you. Jesus died not only
to pay the penalty for your sin, but also to eliminate sin's dominating
reign over you!" Paul is referring here to something we mentioned in
Chapter Three; when you trusted in Christ, you became a *new person*
(2 Cor 5:17). And right here is where he makes a tremendous analogy.

The analogy has to do with death, burial and resurrection. Just with
these three. Not with sin, because although humans are riddled with it
outside of Christ, Jesus had none whatsoever. No, Paul is only directing
us to consider, first, that when Jesus died on the cross, he was buried
and then came alive! Well, when a person trusts Christ as his or her
Savior, the New Testament treats it as a "death to sin". Obviously, Paul
switches to a figurative use of death at this point. But this death to sin
is not just the believer's choice, it's a work of God.

Paul's analogy is this: you can't be raised to new life without being
dead and buried. Paul establishes an identity here between Jesus Christ
and all of those who place their faith in him (he also covers this same
material in 2 Cor 5:14ff and Colossians 3:1–7). And it's here that Paul
adds the matter of baptism. Baptism is all about identity, both spiritually and visually. Water baptism *pictures the spiritual truths* of our unity
with Jesus in death, burial, and resurrection. Our confession of faith
speaks to our death to our former lives apart from him. Going under
the water pictures being buried. Coming up out of it corresponds to
being raised to newness of life: resurrection. For most early believers it
was their first "sermon", in deed. Truly, a sermon indeed!

Now, you may be in an interesting situation. You could well have come to Christ solely by the work of God's Spirit through reading this book. Or by some other means that didn't didn't directly involve another Christian. Those who may have contributed to this process along the way could well be gone. Well, who's left behind to baptize *you*? As it never appears in the New Testament that a person baptized themselves, this is a fair question. Finding deep enough water in which to be immersed (see John 3:23) is probably not an issue. Instead, it may be finding another believer to join in the process. Perhaps you will find someone who also is unbaptized and you can swap roles with them. You may even lead someone to Christ yourself. Don't count that out as a possibility as the Holy Spirit will be doing some amazing things in your day!

The New Testament doesn't prescribe a technique (other than implying total immersion). Nor does it formally prescribe what's to be said on the occasion. But we'd suggest the following as an appropriate "script" when you can find a fitting partner and adequate location. Note that it reflects the essentials of the Gospel from Chapter Two:

The person doing the baptizing: "Do you believe that Jesus Christ died for your sins?"

You: "Yes."

The other person: "Do you believe that Jesus rose from the grave?"

You: "Yes."

The other person: "Is it your intention to follow Christ by faith as the Lord of your life?"

You: "Yes."

Anything else you wish to say consistent with these responses is also appropriate. Remember, a baptism is an unusually powerful witness. Remember to pinch your nose and hold your breath. Down you go, up you come. You won't need to do it again. Ever.

On the Lord's Supper

The communion service or observance of the Lord's Supper is the second ceremony conducted over the generations by believers. It allows believers of all ages to participate indirectly in the Last Supper, Jesus's last meal with the twelve disciples. Toward the end of their dinner (read Matt 26:26ff), Jesus's words over the bread and the cup established it as a memorial. Here is how Paul passed it on to us at Jesus's direction:

> For I received from the Lord what I also passed on to you: The Lord Jesus, on the night he was betrayed, took bread, and when he had given thanks, he broke it and said, 'This is my body, which is for you; do this in remembrance of me.' In the same way, after supper he took the cup, saying, 'This cup is the new covenant in my blood; do this, whenever you drink it, in remembrance of me.' For whenever you eat this bread and drink this cup, you proclaim the Lord's death until he comes. (1 Cor 11:23–26)

Jesus indicated that the bread represented his body. It's being broken indicated the costliness of our redemption. The contents of the cup represented his blood, the shedding of which secured a new covenant established with those he redeemed by it. Again, a reminder of costliness. But also, a reminder of the unconditional nature of the pledge of eternal life.

Remembering your Savior in this ceremony is a regular and sober reminder of the price that was paid to buy you out from under sin. And it's a reminder, by your observance, that he has promised to return for you. Finally, it is a continuing reminder of the unity of all believers in Christ (1 Cor 10:15–17).

You can see why the Lord's Supper (as with baptism) is a key aid to discipleship. Little wonder, then, that participation in this simple ceremony should never be taken lightly. Paul particularly noted that illness and even death fell upon some folks in the church at Corinth because they treated the occasion without due respect and self-examination (1 Cor 11:20–22, 27–30).

Beyond these things, the New Testament says relatively little about how this memorial was conducted in the early church. Was the bread without leaven? It certainly was at the Last Supper, as that was required for the Passover meal. Was it wine? Again, almost a certainty, even though Jesus described it rather generically as the "fruit of the vine" (Matt 26:29). But no strict requirement exists for the particular elements. The focus remains on the symbolism, not on the materials.

We might also ask how often early believers observed it. Well, it appears that it was customarily observed on a weekly basis (Acts 20:7, 11). It may have been more frequent among some (Acts 2:42, 46). But again, no strict requirement regarding frequency was established.

One thing is evident by the nature of the service: it was observed only by those who had placed their faith in Christ for salvation. Participation in it becomes irrelevant for those who are not believers, if not an outright self-deception or self-condemnation.

Owing to the nature of the times upon which you have embarked, you may ask if the Lord's Supper can be observed in private. As a formal ritual, it has always been held by believers gathered together for the purpose. "Communion", of course, is all about having something in common with others in Christ. On the other hand, the essence of its meaning *begins* with one's redemption and communion with Christ himself. If circumstances in the last days isolate you from other believers for some period, you are free as conscience directs to remember in private the Lord's death and imminent return for you. Bless whatever

183

appropriate materials may be at hand and use them. It is a symbolic observance, after all.

We'd now like to present in more detail what you will see during your journey toward the day when Jesus will return to establish his earthly kingdom. James De Young, an accomplished biblical scholar for decades, will expose from both the book of Daniel and the New Testament the events and personalities that will soon play out before you. Sometimes the better part of being prepared is knowing ahead of time what will happen. That's why it's been laid out in God's word all these many centuries.

Be ready for a shift in style, but not in urgency.

PART 2

ANTICHRIST'S REIGN OF TERROR AND GOD'S REVENGE

Chapter 12

The Antichrist Rises to Destroy Israel

When Thomas turned on his father and betrayed him as a Christian to the authorities, Bill was devastated. He didn't know how soon it would be before he would hear a knock on his door. Almost in desperation for knowing what to do, he reached for the book his wife had left behind for him to read after the Rapture. "Perhaps Sue's book for surviving the Great Tribulation will help me somehow survive this terrible betrayal," he thought. He picked up the copy and sat down in his big, easy chair. He began to read. Suddenly the news on his cell phone blared out the headline: "The Leader has been assassinated."

Bill opened the screen and followed the live reporting. Shot at the Wailing Wall, the Leader had been rushed off to the emergency room of Jerusalem's Sinai hospital. But try as they may, the surgeons could not save the life of the Leader. The bullet wounds were fatal. "How could this happen?" Bill uttered out loud. The Israeli authorities quickly discovered that the Jewish secret society known as the Maccabean Brigade was responsible. They had left behind their symbol of anarchy—the four letters of the holy name of Yahweh.

The Leader had the name Benjamin Christos. But for the last three years he had endeared himself to all the world and the title, "the Leader," became commonplace.

This terrible act was but one in a series of acts of terrorism. When Muslim terrorists blew up the Dead Sea Scrolls Museum, and demolished the Golden Gate, a reign of terrorism had begun. The Brigade retaliated. On Yom Kippur four years ago they placed explosive devices at all eight sides of the Dome of the Rock and destroyed it.

The Leader had quickly marshalled the power of the ten nations to prevent a war between the Muslim world and the Jewish nation. No doubt his quick action stopped a world war. The great powers of Europe, the USA, and China were compelled to fall in line behind the Leader.

When the Leader brokered the peace treaty between Israel and the Palestinians the world rejoiced. After years of strife between the two claimants over the land of Israel, now at last there was peace. Both sides had compromised. Israel gave up its claims to half of the west bank and half of old Jerusalem, while the Palestinians had finally recognized Israel's right to exist. The Leader guaranteed Israel's preservation by signing a treaty with them guaranteeing absolute protection and peace.

Now that the land was clear on the Mount, Orthodox Jews had begun construction of the Temple. It was almost complete.

But the Maccabean Brigade had criticized the fragile peace. For the last three and a half years the Brigade had been openly defying the Leader's overtures to the Jewish nation.

They believed that Israel's leaders had made a covenant with the devil. So they went after the one who was responsible for all of the compromise and destroyed him.

With the Leader's assassination there was a flurry of guessing what would happen next. Every country's capital was abuzz with wild speculations. Would the peace between Israel and the Arab world collapse? Who could now hold the fragile peace together? What would the companions of the Leader do? Who would take control of his armies? Who could possibly fill the vacuum? But the whole world was unified in its condemnation of the Maccabean Brigade.

Bill's phone then quickly covered the convening of the ten nations which were meeting in emergency session. They laid out a plan for handling the crisis. But there was not unanimity. Three of the nations, which had been a continual thorn in the side of the Leader, posed objection after objection. They had even gone so far as to challenge the power of the Leader himself. The remaining nations could hardly believe the statements of insurrection and sabotage. Surely if the Leader were alive he would never have tolerated such thoughts.

Bill noticed that the news overload could hardly keep up with the unfolding events. Crowds had gathered in all of the world's major cities to mourn the death of the Leader. The local and international police had hunted down the assassins and dragged them through the streets of old Jerusalem. Surely, they would never get a trial: they didn't deserve it.

All of a sudden there was a live stream coming in from the Mount of Olives back in Jerusalem. Huge crowds were screaming "He's alive! He's alive! He is the Messiah! Christ has come!"

Bill could hardly believe his eyes. There on the screen was the Leader dressed in white and holding up both of his hands to accept the adulation of the people. He stood in the portal where the Golden Gate once stood. The crowd on the Temple Mount soon swelled to fifty thousand or more.

The Leader took control of the video stream. Up close his face was aglow and his suit reflected the sun. His resurrection held the news outlets of the world spellbound. A great hush fell over the crowds as he opened his mouth to speak. What possible words could he speak? Words of triumph? Of condemnation for his enemies? Of peace to his friends?

Chapter 12

The Antichrist Rises to Destroy Israel

With this chapter we arrive at one of the most central characters of the time after the Rapture—the Antichrist. He will rise to absolute power to control the events of the Great Tribulation under God's allowance. He is the person identified as the "Leader" in the preceding vignette.

In this chapter and the next we answer these questions about the identity of the Antichrist:

- Who or What is the Antichrist?

- When will he arise? How will you recognize him? What will he do?

- Whom will he target for destruction? How bad will the suffering get?

- Why and how will he seek first to court the nation of Israel, then turn against the Jewish people and seek to destroy them?

- How will he gain world-wide control? What means will he use?

- How will he on earth try to attack God in heaven?

- How is he related to the ancient Roman Empire and the present world powers?

- What is his relationship to Jesus Christ? What does Jesus say about him?

- What are the various titles of the Antichrist?

The Contemporary "Signs of the Times"

The 2020–2022 pandemic was used to push the idea that the whole world needs revolutionary change in government and economics.

- In 2021 and 2022 the World Economic Forum met to "reset" the world's economies to help the third world and spread the wealth of the West to them.

- These so-called "leaders" believe that it is immoral, even racist, for such a wealthy nation as the USA to have so much without sharing its wealth with the rest of the world.

- The Joe Biden presidency is taking steps toward globalism and open borders which will aid the rise of the Antichrist.

- National borders are evil; all people are international citizens of the world.

- America's past is filled with racism and inequality and needs to be cancelled.

The world-wide dominion of the Antichrist is what secular people call Orwellian—the world wide upset Orwell described that would take place in 1984. But steps are now being formulated to curb freedom of speech and other freedoms that will far out-strip what Orwell imagined.

But our resource is not Orwell or other human speculations of the future. We go to the Bible. It is the only book in all the world's literature that outlines what the future and its end will be like, including the Battle of Armageddon. In fact, the Bible gives more space to the Antichrist than any other person or event except for the person of Jesus Christ. At times the Bible speaks of the Antichrist as a person and at other times as a kingdom or a government.

How to Read This Chapter

There are two ways to read this and the next chapters. If you have the time you can profit from every paragraph. If your time is short, read just the topics in bold print: they summarize the essential points for identifying the Antichrist and what will happen in the time of the end.

This format of the chapters intends to make it easy to read and scan them, if necessary.

Why It Is Relevant to Discuss the Antichrist As Revealed in the Book of Daniel

Why is it necessary to spend time in the Old Testament to discuss the rise of a world ruler to come at a time still future to us? There are several reasons. Without the prophecies of the Bible there is **_NO_**—

- explanation for the world's obsession to destroy the nation of Israel;

- explanation for the world's obsession to give one person control of the world's economic, military and social power;

- understanding how the rise of precursors in past and present history (for example, Hitler) point to the Antichrist;

- explanation for the darkest time of world history and why it is happening;

- hope that the time of the world's greatest suffering and economic collapse has an end;

- hope how people may be delivered from this time of suffering;

- explanation why great nations, including the USA, fall into anarchy and become instruments of enslavement and bondage rather than freedom;

- understanding of what the New Testament says about the Antichrist since information derives from what is said about him in the book of Daniel.

The Antichrist Is First Revealed in the Book of Daniel

While the Antichrist is best known by the title, the Antichrist, the Bible uses this title in only three places (1 John 2 and 4; and 2 John 7—two very brief letters of the New Testament). Otherwise, the Bible gives us sufficient information about the Antichrist that you will be able to identify him by a plethora of titles and descriptions.

An Overview of the Antichrist in the Book of Daniel

- Daniel is the first book of the Bible to reveal the Antichrist.

- The Antichrist is one of the ten toes on the feet of the great image that belongs to the dream of Nebuchadnezzar and its interpretation about the course of world history (Dan 2).

- He is the little "horn" (symbolic of a ruler or king) among the ten horns on the terrifying beast in the dream of Daniel (Dan 7). He slanders God (7:7, 11, 20, 25). He overcomes three of the ten horns (7:24), wages war with the saints (7:25), and prevails in power for 3 and ½ times (years; 7:25). But he will be destroyed (7:11, 26).

- Antichrist is symbolized or typified by Antiochus IV, persecutor and desolator of Israel during 168–165 BC (described in Dan 8). We learn from Israel's greatest tormentor of the past how the future Antichrist will exceed his evil toward Israel at the end of history.

- Antichrist is the ruler to come who will make a covenant with Israel for seven years (Dan 9:27).

- He is entangled in the struggle between good and bad angels for the control of the empires of Media-Persia and Greece (Dan 10) and all nations (including Rome and the USA).

- He will cause the "abomination of desolations" (8:11; 9:27; 11:31; 12:11) to destroy Israel.

- During his dictatorial, absolute rule the world will experience the worst suffering in human history (Dan 12:1).

Does any political leader today meet this description? Is there anyone who slanders the God of the Bible and Christians?

The Antichrist Will Arise to Head the Fifth, and Final, World Empire

The visions and dreams of Daniel first introduce the Antichrist to the world's literature and to world history. The book of Daniel is the key to biblical prophecy about the time of the end. What we will learn from the next chapter of this book is solidly dependent on what we learn in this chapter.

Prophecies about the Antichrist and the Great Tribulation occur in chapters 2, 7, and 8–12—the bulk of the book of Daniel. While the book begins with Daniel as a young man of about 16–18 years, in the year of 605 BC, it ends with Daniel about the age of 85 or more years in the year of 535 BC. While the book begins under the second year of the rule of Nebuchadnezzar (Dan 2:1) ruler of Babylon (605 BC), it concludes under the third year of the rule of Cyrus king of Persia (536–535 BC) (10:1). Babylon and Media-Persia are two of the five empires revealed in chapters 2 and 7.

Daniel Was Highly Educated to Be an Interpreter of Dreams

In 606–605 BC Nebuchadnezzar II brought neo-Babylonia to empirical power by his great victory over the Assyrians and Egyptians, and Greek mercenaries, at Carchemish (about 600 miles north of Jerusalem). Then Nebuchadnezzar went on to conquer Jerusalem, the capital of Judah, of the Southern tribes of Israel. In three separate attacks (605, 597, and 586 BC) he took much of the great treasures of the temple to Babylon. He also captured about 10,000 Jews, including Daniel and his three friends, and took them to Babylon. He reigned from 605–562 BC.

- Daniel was of royal lineage.

- Daniel and his three friends refused to compromise Jewish customs by eating and drinking the Babylonian food and drink. The Lord honored this commitment by giving the four youth "knowledge and understanding of all kinds of literature and learning. And Daniel could understand visions and dreams of all kinds" (Dan 1:17; NIV).

- Daniel was probably the most educated and informed person of his day, knowing the Scriptures and secular history.

- Daniel was most qualified to receive the prophecies of the course of history to the end of time.

God Revealed a "Mystery" to Daniel That Included Nebuchadnezzar's Dream of a Great Image and Its Interpretation

It Predicted the Whole Course of Human History

In chapter 2 we learn that God revealed to Daniel both the content of the dream that Nebuchadnezzar had of a huge image, and the interpretation of the dream. The content and interpretation are couched in the terms of a "mystery." In the Bible mystery is not something "mysterious." Rather, it is new, unrivalled revelation from God about his plans for the course of all history to the end of time. "Mystery" occurs for the first time in Daniel (2:18–19, 27–30, 47; 4:9). Mystery encompasses four empires that will come and go. In the end times a fifth will arise— that of the Antichrist. He will be destroyed at the second coming of the Lord Jesus Christ. Christ will come as the Son of Man in triumph over the Gentile nations to set up his everlasting kingdom on earth (2:34–35, 44–45; 7:13–14).

Humans cannot discover such truth ensconced in "mystery." It is necessary for God to reveal it. It is actually breath-taking in its scope and detail. See the Introduction in my book, *The Apocalypse Is Coming* (2020).

Daniel acknowledges that God gave to him both the content of Nebuchadnezzar's dream and its interpretation (2:22). "I thank and praise you, O God of my fathers: You have given me wisdom and power, you have made known to me what we asked of you, you have made known to us the dream of the king."

The Great Statue Depicts Five Kingdoms Conquered by the "Stone"

The Antichrist Is One of the Ten Toes on the Feet

The mystery entails the entire *future* course of five empires in world history. They are symbolized in Nebuchadnezzar's dream by a giant, awesome statue of a man with five parts, each represented by a different metal (Dan 2:3–35). These empires will come to their end by the "stone."

History and Biblical Prophecy Meet Together to Validate Five Great Empires:

Four Are Past; One Is Future

- The gold head of the statue is Babylon (2:36–38); the silver chest and arms represent Media-Persia (2:39a); the bronze belly and thighs represent Greece (2:39b), and the two legs of iron represent Rome (2:40).

- The feet of ten toes made of iron mixed with clay represent the future ten kingdoms of the Antichrist (as clarified in 7:19–27).

- Four empires have come and gone dating from the time of Daniel: Babylon (625–539 BC); Media-Persia (539–331); Greece (331–63); and Rome (65 BC to AD 476 [the fall of the West part of the empire] or AD 1453 [the fall of the East part to Islam]).

- The fifth empire, that of the Antichrist, is yet future. It arises during the Great Tribulation and lasts for 7 years, with special suffering during the last 3 ½ years. While short lived, his empire will exceed all previous empires in extent (it will rule virtually the entire world) and in evil (*all* who will not receive his mark of 666 and worship him as God will be put to death; so Rev 13).

Thus, the Antichrist first appears as symbolized by one of ten toes on the feet of the statue of Nebuchadnezzar's dream. He is the *final* world ruler of a fifth empire. He is yet future.

Jesus Christ Appears in Daniel 2 As the "Stone" Who Destroys the Previous Empires

The surprising feature is that Daniel reveals that there is a "stone cut out of the mountain without hands" that will follow the fifth kingdom of the ten toes.

- It strikes the toes and destroys them, bringing an end to the entire great statue (2:34–35, 44).

- The stone symbolizes a great kingdom that God will establish to demolish the preceding five kingdoms that have culminated in the empire of the Antichrist.

- It will "endure forever" (2:44–45).

- Clearly the stone symbolizes the Lord Jesus Christ who will violently bring God's rule in heaven to earth for an everlasting reign (as Jesus describes his coming in Matt 24:27–31).

In the Next Vision the Antichrist Is One of the Ten Horns on the Head of the Fourth Beast, the Greatest Empire

About fifty years later (553 BC), when he is about sixty–eight or seventy years old, Daniel has his own dream about the course of history to its end. The dream reveals four beasts (7:3ff) that represent the five kingdoms that parallel the five kingdoms of chapter 2. How do the five kingdoms come out of four beasts?

- The first beast is a lion with the wings of an eagle (7:4); it symbolizes Babylon.

- The second beast is a bear raised on one side with three ribs in its mouth (7:5); it symbolizes Media-Persia.

- The third beast is a leopard with four wings and four heads (7:6). It is Greece.

- The fourth beast is unlike any beast in the creation. It is indescribable. Daniel writes that it was "dreadful and terrible, and extremely strong, with large iron teeth...it was different from all the beasts that were before it, and it had ten horns" (7:7). It is Rome—plus a following kingdom of ten parts.

- The ten horns (kings) represent a fifth empire (Antichrist's). From the ten a little horn came up and crushed three of the ten horns. The little horn had human eyes and a mouth uttering great boasts (7:8). Clearly the little horn is a human being—the Antichrist.

This dream parallels the dream of chapter 2 and has a similar meaning. But here the fourth beast, the supra-creature, and especially its little horn, captures Daniel's attention. The text gives greater detail about the Antichrist.

God Is the "Ancient of Days" Who Gives the Son of Man (Jesus Christ) an Everlasting Kingdom after the Destruction of the Antichrist

After his dream of the four creatures and the little horn, Daniel "sees" the "Ancient of Days" (representing God the Father) sitting on his throne in heaven with myriads of angels worshipping him (7:9–10; cf Revelation 4). Then Daniel's dream is interrupted with a vision of the end of the kings and their kingdoms: Antichrist and the other beasts are destroyed.

On the clouds of heaven appears "one like a son of man" who approaches the Ancient of Days. The latter person gives the son of man "dominion, honor, and a kingdom" and universal worship and a kingdom that is everlasting (7:13-14).

This is a very crucial passage. It means that the words in the "son of man" should be capitalized.

- In the New Testament Jesus Christ claims to be the Son of Man, both during his ministry and at his trial. Jesus even quotes this text (Dan 7:13).

- It is an implicit claim to deity. For this claim Jesus was crucified (Matt 26:63–66; cf Mark 14:61–64; Luke 22:69–71).

- Jesus described himself again as the Son of Man when he returns in "power and great glory" at the end of the Great Tribulation (Matt 24:29–31).

The Interpretation of the Dream:

Antichrist Is the "Little Horn" Who Will Oppose God and Destroy His People Israel

In just one verse we are told that the four beasts are four kings who will arise from the earth (7:15) to be followed by the saints who will receive an everlasting kingdom (7:18). The next ten verses (the interpretation in 7:19-28) enlarge on the fourth beast and the ten horns and the little horn, who represents the Antichrist.

The fourth beast is Rome. The ten horns on the head of the strange beast represent ten kings (v 24). The little horn/king (v 8) is "different" from the other horns/kings and will humble (destroy) three of the ten horns/kings (v 24). Then his (the Antichrist's) deeds are recorded in two verses.

Daniel Reveals the Evil Deeds and Final End of the Antichrist

From this paragraph we first learn of the evil deeds of the person to come at the end of the age.

- He will "speak against the Most High (God) and wear down the saints of the Highest One" (v 25). This means that the Antichrist will attack God and his people on earth.

- He will "make alterations in times and in law; and they will be handed over to him for a time, times, and half a time" (v 25). This crucial verse means that he will make world-wide changes that will affect history and will be successful for 3 ½ years.

- Yet he will be judged, lose his dominion, and be destroyed (v 26).

- Then all the world's kingdoms will be given to the saints who will serve God in his everlasting kingdom (v 27).

Other texts will make it clear that these verses are describing the Antichrist.

The Most Important Question for Modern Times

What/Where/When Are the Ten Nations *Today*?

But one more important point needs to be made to help identify the Antichrist at the end of the age, at the end of history. Verses 24–25 tell the reader that the ten horns/kings come out of the fourth kingdom/empire—the strange, terrifying fourth beast (= Rome). The ten horns parallel the ten toes on the feet of the great image from Daniel 2; and the feet are on the two iron legs of the fourth kingdom (which is Rome).

Thus the future, fifth kingdom/empire of ten kingdoms at the time of the Antichrist will be an extension, a continuation, a rebirth, a renewal (all the terms seem appropriate) of the fourth (Rome) empire that ceased in both AD 476 (in the West) and AD 1453 (in the East). *What does this have to do with contemporary history?*

- Will the ten nations occupy the same land/territory as ancient Rome did (from the western Mediterranean to India in the East)?

- How does this prophecy correspond to the European Union today?

- What does Brexit mean in light of these matters?

- What of the USA? Where does it fit in?

- How do Muslim nations in the Middle East fit this prophecy, since some of them today occupy lands once part of the Roman Empire?

As the months and years unfold during the Great Tribulation it will become more and more clear what this ten-nation configuration means, what geography will be involved, and how the Antichrist takes control.

Yet we are dependent on the Holy Spirit to teach us the "things to come" (John 16:13).

The Vision About Antiochus IV of Ancient Greece Helps Us Identify the Antichrist

How is it that Daniel's prophecy (chap 8) of the historical rise of Antiochus IV in the 2ⁿᵈ century BC gives details about the future Antichrist? It is an amazing prediction.

In Daniel 8 there is a partial retelling of the world's future when Daniel has a vision of two animals. The setting is the third year of King Belshazzar (about 548 BC; about five years after the dream of ch 7), about 55 years after Daniel 2. The chronological order of the chapters, as indicated by the first verses of the chapters, is 1–4, 7–8, 5–6, 9–12. The text explicitly asserts that the ram with two horns symbolizes the empire of Media-Persia (v 20); the shaggy goat with a large horn symbolizes Greece (v 21). The text asserts that the large horn is the first king of Greece, which means Alexander the Great. The ram attacks toward the West and encounters the goat heading toward the East. The goat (Greece) defeats the ram (Media-Persia). But at the peak of its power the large horn of the goat is broken off and four "prominent horns (Alexander's four generals) grew up toward the four winds of heaven" (v 8). But in the latter part of their reign (v 23) another horn will arise, which will start small but grow exceedingly powerful (v 9).

Now chapter 8 easily falls into two parts: the vision of Daniel (vv 1–14) and its interpretation by an angel under the authority of the angel Gabriel (vv 15–27). As shown above the two animals are interpreted as kingdoms in the second half of the chapter.

The Amazing "Small" Horn

The big interpretive question is this: Who or what is the "small horn" that becomes predominant? Reflecting on Daniel 7 it is clear that this is the same king/kingdom as the "little horn" of that chapter. There he is identified as the Antichrist who will arise out of ten kings who form the last kingdom that comes *after the Roman Empire*. While Rome has come and gone, this last kingdom belongs to the future, the end of the age. As pointed out above, we can identify the Antichrist as one of the ten toes of chapter 2.

Yet chapter 8 tells us that the "little horn" comes out of the *Greek Empire* (the third empire of Dan 7). He arises out of one of the four successors of Alexander: Cassander, Lysimachus, Seleucus, and Ptolemy. So far this is an amazing prophecy given to Daniel, living in the 6th century BC, of events that occur in the fourth century BC (the time of Alexander the Great) and later.

Antiochus IV Is the "Little Horn" of the 2nd Century BC Who Tries to Destroy Israel

Who is this "little horn"? The Books of the Maccabees give us the answer.

- The Books of the Maccabees (historical Jewish documents outside the Bible) describe this Greek King as Antiochus IV, known as Epiphanes, who reigned 175–164 BC.

- He arose as a descendant of Seleucus, the king to the north of Israel.

- He is one of the most evil kings that the Jews have ever encountered.

- Beginning in 167 BC, he sought to make Israel a Greek state. He desecrated the temple by sacrificing a pig on its altar which had been dedicated to the god Zeus.

- He tried to destroy Israel and Judaism by outlawing the law, circumcision, the temple service with its sacrificial system, and more.

But the family of Mattathias, including his five sons, one of whom was named Judas Maccabeus, sparked a rebellion. Against overwhelming odds, the Jewish rebels prevailed. In 165 BC, the temple was restored to its biblical form and to the worship of the God of the Bible. To this day this occasion is marked as one of the great feasts of Israel, the Feast of Hanukah celebrated near the time of Christmas.

By Typology, Antiochus IV Predicts What the Antichrist Will Do

Now here is the big question: What does Daniel's prophecy of the rise of Antiochus IV in the 2ⁿᵈ century BC with his evil attack on Israel have to do with the Antichrist to arise in the end times? Just this: Antiochus is an indirect prophecy of the Antichrist. This kind of prophecy is typology. A type is a person, event, or thing that in history and in the Bible points to, portends, its later, greater fulfilment in the Bible and in history.

But why should the Bible illustrate the future Antichrist by describing a past historical evil king?

- History and the Bible correspond; they agree.

- History shows the patterns of the 2nd century BC which repeat in the end times.

- Historical Antiochus IV with his lesser evil provides a pattern for the greater evil of the Antichrist. There is an escalation from the type to its fulfillment, the antitype.

- Such patterns witness to God's sovereignty over all events of history and the Bible.

- Good people learn techniques for survival from past examples of triumph.

- Evil people learn techniques for conquering people from past examples of despotism.

- In this way God prepares his people for the time of the end.

The proof that the text is making Antiochus IV a type of the Antichrist is in the text of chapter 8 itself that finds parallels with chapter 7.

- The "little horn" grew up to "the heavenly host" and "trampled some of the stars" (v 10).

- It set itself up to be as great as the Prince (= Jesus Christ) of the host (=great group); it took away the daily sacrifice from him, and the place of his sanctuary was brought low.

- The host of the saints and the daily sacrifice were given over to it. It prospered in everything it did, and truth was thrown to the ground.

- It will take "2300 evenings and mornings" (v 14) before the sanctuary will be reconsecrated (which corresponds probably to the "time, times, and half a time" of Daniel 7:25).

Antiochus IV Predicts the Antichrist Belonging to the End Times

The interpretation of the dream (vv 15–27) clearly points to the future Antichrist by pointing to "the end." From Antiochus IV we learn additional evil deeds that the Antichrist will do.

- In three ways the angel Gabriel refers to the end times, the time of the Antichrist. He tells a terrified Daniel (v 17) "that the vision concerns the *time of the end...in the time of wrath*, because the vision concerns the appointed *time of the end*" (v 19) (NIV).

- He will cause terrible desolation.

- He will destroy the mighty men and the holy people (v 24).

- He will cause deceit to prosper, and he will consider himself superior.

- He will destroy many and take his stand against the Prince (Jesus Christ) of princes (v 26).

- Yet he will be destroyed, but not by human power.

A repeated characteristic of the Antichrist is deceit—something that other Scripture makes a major trait. In a time of a false peace he will oppose even God himself in the person of Jesus Christ (as revealed in 1 John). But he is destroyed "not by human power." We can infer that it is by God's power.

Only Daniel 9 Reveals That the Antichrist Makes a Seven-Year Covenant with Israel, then Betrays Her

In one of the most powerful prophecies in the Bible, Daniel 9 reveals the first coming of Jesus as the Messiah (Christ) and his death. This chapter also reveals for the first time in the Bible that the Antichrist will arise to try to destroy Israel during a time of seven years.

How will this happen? The Antichrist will make a covenant, a binding agreement, with Israel for a period of seven years. Then in the midst of the years (after 3 ½ years) he will betray Israel, break the covenant, and seek to destroy Israel.

> *This event reveals the great hatred that the Antichrist will have toward Israel at the end.*

The Seven-Year Period Belonging to the Antichrist Arises from Daniel's Reading Jeremiah

Daniel 9 begins with Daniel's great prayer of repentance and petition. He confesses the sins of his people Israel, then petitions God to keep his promise that he would end the Babylonian Captivity after 70 years. The exile of Israel would only last this long, as Jeremiah the prophet had predicted twice (Jer 25:11–13; 29:10–14).

Daniel spoke his prayer in the first year of Darius, son of Xerxes (539–538 BC). Daniel was over eighty years old. He had experienced the entire seventy years of Captivity (605–538 BC). The seventy years were almost completed.

The angel Gabriel brings God's spectacular answer to Daniel's prayer. What does it involve?

Gabriel Reveals That 490 Years Cover All History up to the Antichrist

The Seventy Weeks Include the Work of Messiah as Both Savior and King

Gabriel declares that during this time of 490 years Messiah would bring *six* world-wide achievements to Daniel's people and the holy city (v 24)—but not just to the Jews and Jerusalem but to all humanity.

Verse 24 reveals that Messiah will accomplish *six* marvelous deeds on the cross by his atoning death. He died to pay the price for the sins of all humanity, not just the Jews, so that all who believe and receive him as Savior may have sins forgiven and receive everlasting life (so John 3:16; Rom 3:21–26).

- Three of these world-transforming events have been actualized or realized. By his death, Jesus dealt finally with transgression, with sin, and made atonement for wickedness.

- Three events await fulfillment. By his death Jesus also secured the basis for everlasting righteousness, the sealing (completing) of vision and prophecy, and the anointing of the most holy—the holy of holies in the temple. But these have not yet been actualized, i.e., fulfilled in history, but will be accomplished when Jesus Christ returns. These matters had been prophesied by other prophets prior to Daniel (cf. Isaiah chs 2; 4; 9; and 53).

- These six accomplishments directly oppose the plan and work of Satan to promote evil, destroy Israel, and to enslave the world under his stooge, the Antichrist.

Gabriel Reveals That the 490 Years Are Divided into Three Parts

Verse 25 reveals that God has made a simple plan/pattern whereby to accomplish his care of Israel and to bring Messiah's future rule over all kingdoms. He has marvelously plotted the time from Daniel for the next 2500 years by the pattern revealed (v 24) as "seventy sevens." It is a play on the words of the "seventy years" of the Babylonian Captivity (v 2). These seventy years become the type pointing to a greater period—"seventy weeks of years." The calculation is 7 x 70 = 490; but these are not days but years. Hence the text means 490 years. (See also Lev 25:8; 26:18; 2 Chr 36:21 where "sevens" refers to years).

God Has Fulfilled 69 Weeks of Years to Restore Israel Prior to the First Coming of Christ

Verses 25–26 twice mention the coming of the "Anointed One" [the Messiah], who is Jesus Christ. Verse 25 reveals that "from the command to restore and rebuild Jerusalem until the Messiah the Prince there will be 7 weeks and 62 weeks." The time indicated is a total of 69 weeks of years, or 483 (69 x 7) years. The first 49 years are spent rebuilding Jerusalem "in times of trouble."

In God's plan, several Persian kings issued decrees to restore Jerusalem: Cyrus (Ezra 1); Darius (Ezra 6); Artaxerxes (Ezra 7); and Artaxerxes again (Neh 2). The best view is that this is King Artaxerxes of Nehemiah 2 who issued his decree in 445 BC. Calculating 483 years (the 69 weeks of years) from the time of Nehemiah coincides with the crucifixion of Jesus Christ about AD 33. This calculation results from adjusting for the 360-day year (not 365 days) used then. Allowance is also made for the later adjustment of calendars that place the birth of Christ about BC 5–6, not AD 1.

The words of verse 26 assert that "after the 62 weeks the Messiah will be cut off and have nothing," These words clearly mean that he will be killed or destroyed. The words fit the crucifixion of Jesus Christ. And the crucifixion occurs after the 62 weeks which are after the first 7 weeks (for a total of 69 weeks of years). They are prior to the last week of 7 years.

The Last Seven Years Belong to the Antichrist and His Seven-Year Reign of Terror in the End Times

The rest of verse 26 refers to the deeds of the Antichrist at the end—during the last 7 years.

- He is the "prince who is to come" whose people will destroy the city (Jerusalem) and the sanctuary (the temple). The next words reveal that this will occur at "the end."

- War will continue until the end, and desolations *have been "decreed"* (they come by the permissive will of God). Jesus will repeat the emphasis on war, as recorded in Matthew 24.

Verse 27 uniquely reveals that the Great Tribulation will last seven years.

Then he will confirm a covenant with many for one seven ("week" of years), but in the middle of that seven ("week" of years) he will put an end to sacrifice and offering; and on the wing of abominations [will come] the one who makes desolations, until the end (or, consummation) that is decreed is poured out on the one who makes desolate.

- "After" the crucifixion of Jesus Christ the Antichrist arises.

- During the first half of the seven years the Antichrist will court Israel's favor, going so far as to make a covenant with them.

- Then after three and a half years the Antichrist will betray Israel (and the world: note the "many" in the verse). Elsewhere this period is identified as "3 ½ times" (7:25; 12:7).

- As Daniel says elsewhere: the Antichrist will seek to destroy Israel by desecrating the temple and ending their sacrificial system and committing other abominations (8:13; 9:27; 11:31; 12:11).

Now it is clear why we could say above that in chapter 8 the evil Greek king, Antiochus IV, is a type, prefiguring the Antichrist to come at the end of the age. They do similar horrendous acts against Israel, yet, in keeping with a type, the Antichrist does worse.

Note the reference to the "consummation" or "end" pointing to the end of the age (which was referred to three times in chapter 8).

So now all 70 weeks of years (490 years) have been described.

The Big Question

So the big question is: What has happened to the many years that have transpired since the death of Jesus Christ until now? The 69 weeks of years from Daniel 9:26 led up to the death of Christ. Then the prophecy speaks of the final 7 years of the future Antichrist and his fake covenant with Israel which he severs after 3 ½ years.

A 2000-Year Gap Occurs between the 69th Week and the 70th Week and Includes Today

The answer is obvious. There is a hiatus, an interregnum, a gap, a span of time that goes undescribed in these verses but is obviously necessary.

- In the middle of verse 26 comes a gap of 2000 years.

- Such gaps allowing the present era between the first and second comings of Christ are frequent in the Bible: Zechariah 9:9–10; Isaiah 53 and 52; Isaiah 61:1–2a and 2b.

- In the New Testament Jesus himself separates his first from his second coming. In Luke 24:25–26 he says to his disciples after his resurrection: "How foolish you are, and how slow of heart to believe all that the prophets have spoken! (26) Did not the Christ (Messiah) have to suffer these things and *then* enter his glory?"

Verse 27 is all about the Antichrist, but the last words remind us that he exercises his terrible deeds by the "decree" of God, under God's permissive will (as also said in v 26). Thus the words of God, the Scripture, are intended to encourage his people during their darkest times, the Great Tribulation.

How amazing is this prophecy! It predicts not only the coming and death of Jesus Christ to happen within 483 years soon after Daniel but also the coming, reign, and evil deeds of the Antichrist within seven years in the time of the end.

Why the Gap?

Why does Daniel 9 predict only 490 years and not 2500 years? Because the chapter is concerned with Israel's history/future. During the present hiatus of 2000 years, since AD 70 until now, Israel as a nation has been virtually non-existent. It is the time of Gentile predominance. The 490 years belong to Israel's time and power. Significantly, Jesus said (Luke 21:24) that "Jerusalem would be trodden down by the Gentiles (now for 2000 years) until the times of the Gentiles are fulfilled."

During the 70ᵗʰ Week the Antichrist Will Seek to Destroy the Nation of Israel. Why?

- The Antichrist is inspired by Satan to accomplish his evil plan to stop Jesus Christ and have the world worship him. In Matthew 4 Satan tempts Jesus to do this very thing.

- Satan's attempt to destroy Israel is part of his larger agenda to rule the world.

- Jesus is the Savior of Israel, the true Messiah, who offers deliverance for all the world.

- Israel's existence is absolutely essential to God's plan both to present Jesus Christ as the Savior of the world and to enable him to reign on earth in the line of David.

The Liberal "Daniel Deniers" Fail in Their Attempts to Destroy Daniel's Prophecy

By the way, the prophecy of the rise of the Antichrist during the 70 weeks of years makes it impossible that Daniel could have been written in the 2ⁿᵈ century BC, as liberal interpreters of the Bible assert. There are not 69 weeks of years from about 165 BC till the death of Jesus Christ (unless all the numbers are figurative/symbolic). The same people reject the Rapture, the Great Tribulation, the Battle of Armageddon, and the return of Jesus Christ in "power and great glory."

If you have followed and swallowed these lies of liberal pastors and theologians, you need to come to repentance and believe the truth. With the coming of the Antichrist, the GT, and the end, there is no longer any way to deny these prophecies of the Bible. See The Apocalypse Is Coming, *chapter 2.*

The Antichrist Is Allied with Demonic Beings Who Seek to Influence Nations against Israel and against God

Daniel has more to tell us. More than any other book of the Old Testament, Daniel reveals much about angels, both good and bad. The Antichrist is allied with fallen angels (demons) and with the archangel of evil, Satan himself.

The last vision of Daniel (chs 10–12) occurs in the third year of Cyrus king of Persia (536 BC) (10:1). It is Daniel's fourth and final vision that will conclude with a direct address to Daniel's rise in resurrection at the end of this age, after the Antichrist's demise (ch 12). It occurs about two years after the vision of chapter 9; Daniel is now about eighty-four years or older.

A Summary of Daniel's Prophecies

Here is a summary of the life and visions/dreams that Daniel relates:

- Chapter 2: 605 BC; Nebuchadnezzar's dream of a great statue. Daniel is about 18–20.

- Ch 7: 553 BC; Daniel's first dream/vision of 4 beasts + the little horn. Daniel is about 70.

- Ch 8: 548 BC; Daniel's second dream/vision of a little horn (Antiochus IV as a type). Daniel is about 75.

- Ch 9: 538 BC; Daniel's third dream of 70 weeks of years: Christ & Antichrist. Daniel is about 85.

- Chs 10–12: 536 BC; Daniel's fourth dream/vision of angels and GT. Daniel is about 87+.

This section adds further, valuable information about the Antichrist.

- There is an unseen world of good and bad angels, including the protector of Israel, Michael

- Antiochus IV appears again as a type of the Antichrist.

- Antichrist rules for "three and a half years" (note how this time builds on 7:25).

- The righteous are promised resurrection in the end but the wicked will have everlasting suffering.

- The destination of the wicked, those without God, is unchangeable.

- Prophecy is sealed up (kept unclear) till the end times.

- The Great Tribulation (GT) is truly "great."

The most important details in this section concern a description of the GT that Jesus Christ and John the Apostle will utilize. The contributions of Daniel to understanding the end times continue to amaze us.

Daniel Sees the Preincarnate Christ

Chapter 10 reveals amazing details about the unseen world of reality. It emphasizes the spiritual battle between the Antichrist, inspired by Satan (Rev 13), and Jesus Christ and his people.

- Daniel encounters a theophany (a "manifestation of God") of the preincarnate Jesus Christ (before he was born as a human; vv 5–9). Why such a vision? It counters the fake Christ, the Antichrist.

- In the Revelation of the New Testament John the Apostle has a similar encounter, and there the person reveals himself as the resurrected Jesus Christ (Rev 1:12–18).

The Angel Reveals the Future of Israel

- An angel reveals that he has been sent to Daniel to "explain what will happen to your people in the future, for the vision concerns a time yet to come" (v 14).

- An evil angel, the "prince of Persia," sought to prevent the good angel's mission.

- Michael, one of God's "chief princes," helped the angel succeed (vv 12–14).

- The good angel has come to reveal to Daniel "what is written in the Book of Truth" (v 21), which is the content of the next two chapters (11–12).

- After this revelation the angel will encounter another hostile angel, the prince of Greece.

- These verses teach us that behind all Gentile nations are evil angels seeking to dominate them for evil ends (as Paul reminds us of the "spiritual forces of evil in the heavenly realms" belonging to the devil (Eph 6:11–12)).

- Our only access to this realm is prayer (so Paul affirms in 1 Tim 2:1–2).

Daniel Sees All History Revealing the Kings from His Time in the 6th Century BC to the Antichrist of the The Times of the End

At this point, the angel reveals the whole course of human history beginning with the last days of the kingdom of Persia (which is Daniel's year) and the rise of the Greek kingdom (11:1–2).

- After a "mighty king" (Alexander the Great, v 3) four kings will succeed him (v 4). It is amazing that the revelation shows what will happen two hundred years in the future from Daniel's time.

- Chapter 11 goes on to predict the ongoing conflict between two of Alexander's successors, the line of Seleucid in the North, including Syria, and the line of Ptolemy in the South, controlling Egypt.

- History concurs with the accuracy of this revelation that stretches from the 4th century of Alexander to the 2nd century BC (11:5–20).

As in chapter 8, the Seleucid king, Antiochus IV, arises and works his treachery upon Israel (vv 21–35).

- He is noted for his deceit and intrigue (vv 21–23, 27).

- When he is rebuffed in Egypt by forces from "ships of kittim" (=Rome; the western coastlands), he will "vent his fury against the holy covenant" (Israel) (v 30).

- Antiochus will "set up the abomination that causes desolation" (v 31)—the ultimate evil act in his attempt to make Israel into a pagan, Greek nation.

The Antichrist in the End Times Will Exalt Himself As God and Be an Invincible Conqueror

At this point, as in chapter 8, Antiochus becomes a type of the Antichrist. Verse 35 points to the transition to the end: "Some of the wise will stumble, so that they may be refined, purified, and made spotless until *the time of the end*, for it will still come at the appointed time" (v 35). The words of verses 36-45 were not fulfilled by Antiochus IV.

- The Antichrist will "exalt and magnify himself above every god and will say unheard of things against the God of gods" (v 36a).

- He will "be successful until the [time] of wrath is completed, for what has been determined must take place" (v 36b; NIV).

- At the "time of the end" he will war with *both* the king of the North and the king of the South.

- He will "invade many countries" and capture them (vv 40–43).

- He will "pitch his royal tents between the seas at the beautiful holy mountain" (=Israel) (v 45a).

- Yet "he will come to his end, and no one will help him" (v 45b).

Just a perusal of this passage shows remarkable parallels to what Daniel 7, 8, and 9 tell us about the Antichrist. But new material reveals his special focus on the land of Israel. This is in keeping with what the Prophet Zechariah (ch 14) and the Book of Revelation tell us.

The Angel Michael Is the Protector of Israel

He Will Prevent Her Being Annihilated by the Antichrist

The first four verses of chapter 12 continue chapters 10–11 and bring them to conclusion. New points for understanding who the Antichrist is and what he does are revealed in these verses and the conclusion of the book (vv 5–13). "At that time Michael, the great prince who protects your people will arise." Clearly the time is the same as that of 11:35–45: the time of the end. Michael also appeared in 10:13, 21.

For the First Time the Tribulation Is Introduced As the *Great Tribulation*

The first new feature of chapter 12 is then revealed. A "time of distress" that is *unique* in history will arise, but Israel—"everyone whose name is written in the book [of life]—will be delivered."

- This is the first time in biblical literature that these words are used to describe what Jesus will call the "Great Tribulation" (Matt 24:21), followed by John (Rev 7:14).

- Through this time of unprecedented distress God will preserve his people.

- The book of life is also expanded in the Revelation (20:12, 15).

The rest of verses 1–4 reveal special things about the end times.

- There will be a resurrection of the multitudes: those written in the book will rise to everlasting life, others will rise to everlasting judgment ("shame and contempt").

221

- The wise and those who lead many to righteousness will "shine" like the stars and the heavens for ever and ever (vv 2–3).

- An angel commands Daniel to "close up and seal the words of the scroll until the time of the end. Many will go here and there to increase knowledge" (v 4). This is the fourth reference since 11:35 to the time of the end when the Antichrist arises.

- In light of the first part of the verse, the increase of knowledge points to the growing understanding of prophecy.

Two Critical Questions Surround the Antichrist:

When **Does He Exercise Power and** *What* **Is the Outcome of All This?**

Two questions consume the rest of chapter 12.

- The first takes place between two angels. One *asks*: "How long will it be until the end of these astonishing things"? The *answer* is: "It will be for time, times, and half a time. When the power of the holy people has been finally broken, all these things will be completed" (v 7).

  (1) This same time frame was first given regarding the activity of the Antichrist in Daniel 7:25. The New Testament will make it clear that this is the last 3 ½ years of the GT.

  (2) Note that the Antichrist will almost destroy Israel—a point also made and repeated in Daniel 7, 8, 9, 10–11. Again we are told of the special, Satanic inspired, hostility that the Antichrist has for Israel.

- The second question is raised by Daniel because he does not understand what the answer to the first means. He asks: "What will be the outcome of these events?" (v 8).

The reply is not helpful (v 9). He is told to "go his way" without having an answer, "because the words are closed up and sealed until the time of the end." No further revelation about the actions of the Antichrist will be given now.

But the next verses disclose some startling features of what will happen in the meantime.

The Opportunity for the Wicked, Including the Antichrist, to Repent and Believe the Gospel Comes to an End

- First, the GT is a time of testing which will purify the godly but the wicked will "continue to be wicked." These words teach the doctrine of the perseverance of the saints and the confirmation of all, the righteous and the wicked, in the choices they make whether to obey God or not.

- The Antichrist is the chief example of the wicked. *This verse means that he cannot repent and turn from his evil.* He is destined for "destruction"—spiritual death (prophesied several times: Dan 7:6, 26; 8:25; 9:27; 11:45). He is hardened in his evil choice.

- The angel continues that the wicked will not understand the prophecy of Daniel but the wise will understand. Clearly the wise are those who are true followers of God.

- Another time indicator is given regarding the work of the Antichrist. The angel reports that there will be 1290 days "from the time that the daily sacrifice is abolished and the abomination that causes desolation is set up" (v 11). He adds: "Blessed is the one who waits for and reaches the end of the 1335 days" (v 12). These days go beyond the 1260 days of the 3 ½ years to allow apparently for the Battle of Armageddon and the judgments of death.

The Antichrist's Most Evil Act, His Desolation of Israel's Temple, Is Cited Again

This is now the last reference to the Antichrist's work of desolating the temple of Jerusalem, the most horrific irreligious act against the Jews (and God). This act was identified in 8:11–12; 9:27; 11:31, 36ff. We note that verse 12 makes another reference to the end.

With so much attention devoted to this act in Daniel, the desolation of the temple must be a chief defining trait of the Antichrist. Jesus's citation of 9:27 (in Matt 24:15) confirms this observation.

After the Antichrist Is Destroyed at the End, Daniel Will Be Resurrected to Eternal Life

- Finally, attention focuses on Daniel again and his own future resurrection. It is a wonderful promise given to an elderly statesman through whom God has revealed the most far-reaching prophecies of the Old Testament. The angel tells him that he will go his way "till the end. You will rest, and then at the end of the days you will rise to receive your allotted inheritance" (v 13).

- With these words Daniel is assured that his "sleep" (see v 2) in death will come to an end in his resurrection at the end times when he will be rewarded for his faithfulness (which began in chap 1).

- His resurrection is one of the clearest references to resurrection in the entire Old Testament. It provides the words for Martha to use at Jesus's raising of Lazarus (see John 11:24). It also leads to Paul's writing about the resurrection of believers at the Rapture, another aspect of "mystery" from Daniel 2 (cited in 1 Cor 15:51–58; 1 Thess 4:13–18).

The impact of the life and sleeping of Daniel lives on in every Christian's being assured of everlasting life (12:2). Daniel is a type for every believer who trusts Jesus Christ as one's Savior. But those who follow the Antichrist will have "everlasting shame and contempt" (12:2) just like their leader.

The Antichrist in Daniel

From the book of Daniel we have learned many startling and far-reaching features about the coming Antichrist that make his identity unmistakable. It is also the essential foundation for what we discover in the New Testament in the next chapter.

Chapter 13

The Antichrist Targets Jesus Christ and Christians for Annihilation

The Leader rose to the podium and addressed the crowds. For ninety minutes all the world hung on his every word. He wrapped up his great oratory with several promises: "I will end the pandemic; I will institute universal peace; I will bring economic hope to all those distressed; and I will control the world's militaries including the stockpiles of nuclear and biological weapons. I will control all governments in order to assure law and order. My resurrection validates me as the one person, who can save the world in its time of distress. I am God."

Suddenly another figure appeared with him who led the people in their chants and praise. On the world's screens the Leader introduced his companion as Sudo Nabi. He compared himself to Aaron who assisted Moses to lead the Israelites out of Egypt during the Exodus of the OT. "This is a new Exodus," Nabi proclaimed. "The Leader is the Messiah. Let's rejoice that God has raised him up to save us. A new world order has come."

Nabi acted quickly. Like Aaron before him, Nabi led the people to make an idol of the Leader. Every major city was to build a temple, a sacred place, for the Leader and enshrine his image by means of a hologram for all to worship. Nabi began making the images via the holograms to come alive. Nabi also healed blind people, crippled people, people with cancer and other deadly diseases. It seemed that there was no end to what he could do in the name of the Leader. Miracle after miracle drew world-wide wonder and amazement.

The resurrected Leader also took quick action. He demanded total power—over the vast collected armies of the world. He erased all religions: he alone was to be worshipped. Those who called themselves Christians worshipped him as the resurrected and returned Christ. Muslims heralded him as the Madhi arriving at the end of the age. Jews hailed him as the Messiah of their nation. Hindus abandoned their many deities to exalt the Leader.

The Leader destroyed the code of immoral behavior inherited from Babylon and replaced it with his own code. He redefined morality. He alone would rule government. He quickly annihilated three of his ten-nation confederacy and exalted seven nations which yielded total power to him. He took control of the arsenals of atomic weapons and the more sophisticated wmds.

The Leader's vast holdings in big tech enabled him to control all communications. No news would inform the billions of cell phones except what he approved. Everything else was blocked and banned.

Finally, with his prophet, he devised how to control all the world's economies. The algorithms that scientists had been building to identify and classify the behavior of every person in the world were now complete. Video cameras in personal computers and on every street and building constantly updated the algorithms. By using extreme AI he was able to take total control of all individuals and companies and place them under the various commanders under his control. He took up headquarters at the UN.

There would be no private property or private enterprise, no freedom of religion, speech, assembly or the press. All had to receive his brand, 666, by tattoo or embedded by microchip in people's brains or under the skin on their arms. This code could be scanned by every computer or cell phone. Those who refused his code would be destroyed. In their adulation the people of the world thought that such absolute control from their Savior was entirely appropriate. "All who refuse his code should be branded as ungrateful obstacles to his rule and a threat to the world's stability," they reasoned.

To cement his control over all economies, and in league with the seven nations, the Leader seized control of all the choke points of all the major shipping lanes: the Bosporus, Gibraltar, the Suez Canal, the Panama Canal, the Mandeb Strait, the Straits of Hormuz and Malacca, the St. Lawrence Sea Way, and the English Channel. All were seized to give absolute, world-wide control over the shipment of all produce and manufactured goods. The nations gladly relinquished such control to the Leader to prevent world-wide conflict and starvation.

The world was convinced that the Leader was the world's Savior who was on the verge of bringing in the millennial kingdom, as the Bible foretold. The prophet at his side used miracle after miracle to show that the Leader had supernatural powers. There was no escape from his persona and his power. There were no exceptions.

In addition to Evangelicals, the Leader vowed to destroy the Jews and their homeland. The Leader proclaimed: "I hold the Jews responsible for killing me and sparking world-wide turmoil. They are an existential threat to everything I envision to do." The Leader went into the newly constructed Temple in Jerusalem and there implemented the holographic image of himself. He would not allow worship of anyone other than himself. He demonstrated his superior power over the two troublesome witnesses sent by God. "For over three years these two have been invincible and an inspiration to Christians, but now I'm putting them to death." He began making preparations to bring the world's military might, including the use of WMD's and biological weapons, against Israel and Christians. "There will be no restraint; unconditional destruction is the only fair retribution."

Suddenly Bill was awakened from his nightmare. The Leader's troops were pounding on his door. They had tracked him down. As a Christian Bill had refused the identifying code of the Antichrist, 666. Bill was in rebellion against the Leader. He spoke with a muffled voice: "I haven't been dreaming after all. I wonder how I'll survive this?"

The commander yelled: "Open your door or we'll smash it down."

Chapter 13

The Antichrist Targets Jesus Christ and Christians for Annihilation

The New Testament brings to completion what we can know about the Antichrist and the end times. It builds on the essential foundation from the book of Daniel in the preceding chapter. This chapter will expose what we learn from Jesus himself, and the Apostles Paul and John.

Jesus Predicts the Time of the Antichrist's Arrival by Citing Daniel

Before he is tried and crucified, in his final discourse from the Mount of Olives, Jesus Christ warns of the Antichrist and the end times. Jesus has just warned of the destruction of the Jerusalem temple. The disciples ask him two questions (Matt 24:3) similar to the two in Daniel 12: "When shall these things be? What is the sign of your coming and the end of the age?" The following verses give Jesus's answers. The destruction of the Temple pertains both to the near future and to the time of the end.

The singular "sign" combines Jesus's coming with the "end of the age." They happen at the same time. In fact, Jesus brings about the end of the age, the end of Gentile power (Luke 21:24: "Jerusalem shall be trodden down by the Gentiles until the time of the Gentiles comes to an end").

First, Jesus gives a brief description of the course of the age until the end (4–14). When the Gospel has been preached in all the world then "the end will come" (v 14). Then he surprisingly cites Daniel about the Antichrist. He warns about the "abomination of desolation which was spoken of through Daniel the prophet, standing in the holy place—" (Matt 24:15). Jesus is the only one in the New Testament to use Daniel's name. For Jesus, Daniel is the authority for understanding the end most clearly.

Jesus is quoting Daniel's prediction of the Antichrist given in Daniel 9:27. As we learned from Daniel in the preceding chapter this act of desecrating the temple occurs in the midpoint (at 3 ½ years) of the Great Tribulation (GT). It is at this point that the Antichrist strikes out against Israel and seeks to exterminate her.

Jesus Warns of the Deceit Surrounding His Coming

The chief concern of Jesus is to prepare his followers for the great deceit that the Antichrist will practice at the end. He warns of deceit at least four times (vv 4, 5, 11, 24). He warns that even the elect, his faithful believing followers, are susceptible to such deceit (v 24). Jesus is the true Messiah; the Antichrist is the false Messiah. Antichrist's false prophets will try to lead Christians astray by claiming that Jesus could be found in a particular place, out of doors or inside (24:24–26). But Jesus says that his return will be seen by the whole world. It will be like lightning, stretching from the East to the West (v 27). He will come "with power and great glory" (Matt 24:30).

Jesus's words about the temple require, of course, that a temple must be existing in Israel at the time. We must know what Daniel has said (the previous chapter) to fully grasp the weight of Jesus's words about both the Antichrist and his own glorious coming.

Paul Identifies the Antichrist As the Satan-Inspired "Man of Lawlessness" Who Performs Miracles

Paul describes the Antichrist in both unique ways and familiar ways (2 Thess 2).

- His appearance and the "apostasy" are the signs that the "day of the Lord" (= the GT) has begun.

- He is the "man of lawlessness and son of perdition" (= "destruction"; 2:2ff).

- He will take his seat in the temple of God and display himself as God (2:4).

- The removal of the restrainer (the rule of government and law) allows him to appear (6–7).

- He is the lawless one (2:8).

- He will be destroyed by Jesus Christ at his coming (2:8).

- He will be empowered by Satan to do "powers, signs, and wonders" (2:9).

- His chief work is deceiving those who rejected the truth (2:10). Clearly Paul draws upon both Daniel and the Lord's words in Matthew 24.

- God will add to the deception by sending the "working of delusion so that people believe the lie" of the Antichrist (v 11).

- Christians will not be deceived but will be singled out for punishment and death.

We learn here for the first time about the special, present role of the restrainer. Also, the Antichrist will have special powers to do miracles, the same things that Jesus and the Apostles did. He will be empowered by Satan—as part of his deception. John will attribute this same power of deception to the Antichrist (Rev 13:2).

John Is the First to Use the term "Antichrist"

In his Epistles John the Apostle is the only one to use the title, "the Antichrist" (1 John 2:18). The word means that he is a substitute for ("instead of") Jesus Christ (implicitly pointing to deceit). Yet the word also means one who is "against" Christ. Thus the Antichrist aims to replace Jesus Christ.

- He is "a liar" and will deny both that Jesus Christ is the Messiah and that he is deity (2:22–123). He will also deny that Jesus Christ has come in a real human body (4:1–3; 2 John 7).

- Thus the Antichrist denies both the true humanity of Jesus Christ and his deity (as one of the Trinity).

John Writes of "the Antichrist" and "Many Antichrists": A Puzzle?

- Another unique contribution is John's assertion that many antichrists have already come, and that this is an indicator of the "last hour" (1 John 2:18). The last terms point to the arrival of the end times. But John knew of many "antichrists" who had already come by his time near the end of the first century AD. What does he mean?

- He means the same thing that Daniel does who pointed to the rise of the Greek wicked king, Antiochus IV, whose actions and character in the 2nd century BC would *typify* those of the Antichrist at the end of history (Dan chs 8, 11).

- John declares that false teachers and leaders of his day were in the same league as the Antichrist of the end time because of their denial of the deity and humanity of Christ. They had left the circle of true believers headed by the Apostles and anointed with the truth by the Holy Spirit (2:19–21, 26–27).

- The many antichrists are types, portents, adumbrations, of the final Antichrist.

Take note: you who live during the GT will witness the Antichrist. His chief aim is to replace Jesus Christ. He is not the antibuddha; he is not the antimuhammad; he is not the antichrishna; he is not the anticonfuscius. He is not even the antiatheist. Indeed, at the beginning he will no doubt employ all the world's religions (what the Bible calls "Mystery Babylon"). Then he destroys them in order to exalt himself. Yet this desperate act fulfills God's plan (see Rev 17:16–18). But the main focus of the Antichrist, and that of Satan, is the destruction of the saints and their God and their Savior (as also in Daniel 7:25; 8:9–11, 23–25; 11:36–39; 12:10).

The Antichrist on Earth Attacks God in Heaven

By Attacking Jesus Christ on Earth and His People

How does the Antichrist on earth seek to destroy God in heaven, as Daniel predicts?

- By seeking to destroy the incarnate Christ who is both divine and human. Jesus Christ became a real human being. In this way Satan seeks to destroy him, his work, and the saints in whom Christ by his Holy Spirit dwells. Paul asserts that "Christ lives in me" (Gal 2:20); that "Christ be formed in you" (4:19); that Christ is "in you, the hope of glory" (Col 1:27); and that believers are the "temple of the Holy Spirit" (1 Cor 6:19).

- Why is the title, the "Antichrist," ever employed? "Anti*christ*" is an explicit biblical defense that Christianity is the only true faith. Satan seeks to destroy Christianity, the true way to God. He actually employs the other world religions as his vehicles to deceive the world to pursue a false way apart from God and the truth who is Jesus Christ. He said: "I am the way, the truth, and the life" (John 14:6). In this regard all other religions are false and satanic.

The Revelation Reveals Many Astounding Descriptions of the Antichrist

In the last book of the Bible, the Revelation, John the Apostle gives us more information about the Antichrist than anywhere else in the Bible. He describes the Antichrist in many ways.

- He is the "beast" who arises from the abyss (Rev 11:7), the abode of demons. Such a description suggests that he is either demonic-like in behavior or he is supernatural in being (he has recovered from death; see below).

- He is demonic and kills God's two witnesses who for 3 ½ years give warning of impending doom (Rev 11).

- He is the "red beast (17:3) who arises out of the sea" having seven heads and ten horns with ten crowns on them (13:1; this is explained in Rev 17, discussed below).

- The beast is "like a leopard" and having feet "like a bear" and a mouth "like the mouth of a lion" (13:2). This description recalls three of the beasts depicted in Daniel 7.

- The Antichrist is empowered by Satan (13:2).

- He suffers a "mortal wound" but is healed, drawing all the world's amazement (13:3) to the point of worshipping him (13:4) as God (13:8).

- For forty-two months he exercises authority over the world (13:4–5, 7); he slanders God and his name and his people (13:6); and he makes war with the saints and overcomes them (13:7). The forty-two months equals 3 ½ "times" as in Daniel 7:25; 12:7.

Some of these descriptions have parallels in Daniel and in Paul. But all the preceding are new features except the fourth one.

The Antichrist Has a Special Companion, The False Prophet

The Antichrist will have a companion who will lead the world to worship him (Rev 13:11). He is the "false prophet" (19:20) who is described as a beast that has "two horns like a lamb" and speaks "like a dragon" (13:11). This description makes him into an imitation of Jesus Christ, the Lamb of God revealed in Revelation 5. He is actually satanic.

- The false prophet has all the authority of the Antichrist and performs miracles (13:12–13).

- He deceives all humanity to make an image of the Antichrist which speaks and causes all who do not worship the image to be killed (13:14–15).

- He causes all to receive the mark of the Antichrist, namely 666. Without 666 on a person's forehead or hand no one will be able to buy or sell (13:16–18). No one will be able to live without the mark.

While much speculation through the centuries has surrounded the meaning of the number 666, it is obvious that only those living contemporaneously with him will know the meaning. To their chagrin, those living in the Great Tribulation will know what this number means.

At First the Antichrist Embraces the Prostitute of False World Religion

There is more from the visions of John in the Revelation. In chapter 17 the Antichrist bears, i.e., gives support to and empowers, all false religion in the world. The latter is symbolized by a woman dressed like a queen who bears the title, "Mystery Babylon the Great, the Mother of Prostitutes and of the Abominations of the Earth" (17:5).

- These verses show the close relationship that the Antichrist has with all false religion and its accompanying great immorality and iniquity that began at Babel.

- At the Tower of Babel God confused all humanity with languages that became the basis for different nations (Gen 10–11).

- "Mystery Babylon" connects her to the mystery revealed to Daniel in Daniel 2 during the empire of Babylon under Nebuchadnezzar.

- She is drunk with the blood of the saints (17:6).

- False religion lies behind all false political power (in the sense that it seeks to destroy God's kingdom and his people on earth). It is the internal compulsion to please and obey false deities that compels the political power to conquer.

- Thus, John writes at the end of the chapter: "The woman whom you saw is the great city (=Babylon), which reigns over the kings of the earth" (17:18).

While there are many false religions in the world (such as Islam, Buddhism, Hinduism, and others) they are here conceived as one, large entity. They are all opposed to the worship of the one true God revealed by the Bible in the person of his one and only Son, the Lord Jesus Christ (John 1:18). God is uniquely revealed to Israel, and his law has been uniquely given to Israel, which is to be a beacon of light to the Gentile nations (Deut 4:6–8; Isa 49:6).

What does it mean to live during the Great Tribulation?

- The Antichrist will court all religions and be the universal uniter. He will welcome the support that religion will give him in his rise to absolute power.

- Around the midpoint of the Tribulation he will destroy all claimants to religious devotion and demand, upon penalty of death, that all worship him alone.

- It will be the most fantastic demonstration of idolatry because the false prophet will make an image of the Antichrist and cause it to speak as though it were alive!

Is the Antichrist Supernatural?

John adds further, strange descriptions of the seven-headed Antichrist.

- He is the beast "who was and is not, and is about to come up out of the abyss and go to destruction" (17:8). This four-fold description points to the Antichrist's history and involves a supernatural nature, including a resurrection, it seems (although this may be fake, since the false prophet has special powers to deceive the world's people, as seen above from chapter 13).

- The four-fold history is reduced at the end of the verse to three points: "he was, and is not, and will come" (17:8).

- This description appears to be a parody, an imitation, of the identity of God and of Jesus Christ as given in Revelation 1:4, 8, 18.

- The career of the Antichrist will spark wonder among earth's unsaved inhabitants (17:8). The angel notes that these people are those whose names are not "written in the (Lamb's) book of life from the foundation of the world."

- That the career of the Antichrist may involve supernatural elements should not be surprising since the dragon (=Satan; 12:9) has given the Antichrist his "power, throne, and great authority" (13:2).

- As Daniel prophesied (7:8, 20), and the angel reveals in this text, the Antichrist assumes total authority over the ten-nation confederacy (17:13, 17).

The Symbolism Describing the Beast Means That He Is the Antichrist With Seven Heads

We need not stumble at the symbolism of these verses. The angel gives to John the interpretation of all this symbolism. "Here is the mind which has wisdom," the angel says (v 9). Such words recall the promise given to Daniel in his last vision that the words of his prophecy were to be kept secret and the book sealed till the end when knowledge will increase (Dan 12:4, 9). "None of the wicked will understand, but those who have insight will understand" (Dan 12:10). The time for understanding has finally arrived.

- The angel says (vv 9–10) that "the seven heads are seven mountains... which are seven kings: five have fallen, one is, the other has not yet come; and when he comes, he must remain a little while" (11).

- "The beast which was, and is not, is himself an eighth and is one of the seven, and he goes to destruction."

What do these puzzling words mean?

• Many interpreters take the seven kings to be seven emperors of Rome—the empire existing at the time of the writing of the Revelation. But there is no consensus as to which emperors these are.

• Others take the words as a reference to the actual, physical hills upon which Rome was built—a common description of Rome. But why this would have special meaning for the future of the Antichrist makes no sense.

The Seven Heads Represent Seven Empires

To discover John's meaning, it is best to follow John's lead throughout the Revelation. His source is constantly the Old Testament, especially the book of Daniel. The seven heads are seven empires already revealed.

• Thus, this text must be connected with the disclosure of the four kings and empires, plus that of the Antichrist, to exist from Daniel's time to the end of history.

• To these five we must add the two empires that preceded Daniel's time but are known to us from other prophetic literature: Egypt (16th century BC; and Assyria (1420–609 BC). The prophets Isaiah and Ezekiel identify the first three empires as Egypt, Assyria, and Babylon (Isa 52:4; Ezek 16:26–29). The third, Babylon, overlaps with Daniel's five empires that begin with Babylon.

The Ten Horns Are Ten Future Kings from Whom the Antichrist Will Come

The ten horns of the beast, John writes, are ten kings and their kingdoms (17:12). Daniel 7 first revealed this meaning.

- They exercise power for a limited time.

- They have one purpose: to serve the Antichrist (v 13).

- Together they will attack the prostitute (world religion) and destroy her (v 16).

- This fulfills God's purpose, namely, that he has put it into the hearts of the Antichrist and the ten kings to destroy religion so that "the words of God will be fulfilled" (v 17).

God's Purpose Clarified

We know that all the horrific events that take place during the Great Tribulation are fulfilling God's purpose. What is God's purpose?

- Daniel has already revealed it (chs 2, 7). God is bringing to an end all Gentile, idolatrous, wicked powers, and bringing his kingdom from heaven to this earth so that a time of universal peace might prevail under the rule of God's Son, the Lord Jesus Christ.

- The prophets proclaimed this kingdom (e.g., Isa 2; 4; 9; Zech 9:9–10; and many more).

- It will be fulfilled in the millennial kingdom described in Revelation 20.

The False Religions of "Mystery Babylon" Are Totally Destroyed: Revelation 18

Our pursuit of the complete story of the Antichrist is almost done. We've traced him through Revelation 17.

Revelation 18 clarifies the destruction of Babylon the Great, the Mother of Prostitutes and of the Abominations of the Earth (identified in 17:5).

- She is "fallen, fallen" declares an angel (18:2).

- She has become the habitation of demons and unclean spirits (v 2).

- Coincidentally all the nations have fallen also because they have committed "sexual immorality" with her and become wealthy because of her (v 3). These verses expand on the brief statements of 17:15–18. (This statement suggests that the 10 kings are symbolic of all pagan kings).

- Verses 4-8 expand on the extent of her great sins. She will be paid back double according to her wicked deeds (v 6). Consequently, in one day plagues, mourning, and famine will come on her, and she will be destroyed in the fiery judgment of God (v 8).

- The rest of chapter 18 expands on how the kings (vv 9–10), the merchants (vv 11–17), and ship masters will lament Babylon's sudden destruction (vv 18–20). The economies of the world will collapse.

In the conclusion (vv 21–24) Babylon's sudden destruction is illustrated by a mighty angel casting a great millstone into the sea, declaring that Babylon will be cast down with violence and never exist again.

- All the dynamics that make up a city (music, craftsmanship, manufacturing, civic affairs, and more) will never exist again in her.

- By her witchcraft she deceived all the nations (v 23).

- She is guilty for the murder of the prophets, the saints, and of all those killed on the earth (v 24).

For you living near the end of the Tribulation, these words should strike terror in the hearts of all who observe these events.

The Antichrist Meets His End at Armageddon

The rest of this chapter concentrates on the Battle of Armageddon. Revelation 19 is the final chapter that brings all discussion of the Antichrist to an end. His career terminates in the Battle of Armageddon. When people popularly talk about Armageddon they rarely think of the "why" of such a battle. In summary, the battle occurs because the Antichrist has stirred up the nations to engage in a great war (the conflict is described in Ps 2) to destroy once and for all the nation of Israel and God's people, both Jews and Gentiles.

More specifically, chapter 14 reveals how great God's wrath is against the Antichrist and why.

The Person Causing the Greatest Evil Deserves the Greatest Wrath

One of the greatest expressions of the depth of God's anger occurs in Revelation 14. And God's wrath is focused on the Antichrist and his followers.

- It provides insight into how great is the evil of the Antichrist and his followers that should call forth such anger. It reads (14:9–11):

A third angel followed them and said in a loud voice: "If anyone worships the beast and his image and receives his mark on his forehead or on his hand, (10) he, too, will drink of the wine of God's wrath, which has been poured full strength (with added spices) and undiluted (by water) into the cup of his anger. He will be tormented with burning sulfur in the presence of the holy angels and in the presence of the Lamb. (11) And the smoke of their torment arises forever and ever. There is no rest day or night for those who worship the beast and his image, or for anyone who receives the mark of his name" (my translation).

- Note how the doublets emphasize the soberness of the judgment: the two objects of worship; the two places where the mark occurs; God's disposition as both "wrath" and "anger"; the undiluted form of the wine; the double mention of "torment"; the double mention of presence (before angels and before the Lamb); the double mention of future "time" (forever and ever); "day or night"; the two indictments: they "who worship" or who "receive the mark of his name."

- All the bowl judgments—the final series that bring the GT to conclusion—are specifically focused on destroying the Antichrist and his authority and his followers (Rev 16).

- *With this sense of the enormity of evil we can appreciate why the defeat and end of the Antichrist at the Battle of Armageddon makes the Battle worthy of its distinction as the greatest of all battles in history.*

The Combatants at the Battle of Armageddon Are the Antichrist and the Genuine Christ

So, what are the details? Even before the Battle is engaged the Bible reveals that there is no doubt about the outcome.

- Jesus Christ will triumph.

- Four anthems of praise, of "Hallelujah" ("praise to Yahweh") are sung from heaven. The first two (19:1–3) praise God's judgments of the "great prostitute" (of ch 18) as "true and just," and this is echoed by "Amen, Hallelujah" (v 4). Then God's servants are exhorted to praise God (v 5). The final Hallelujah anticipates the victory of Christ at Armageddon and proclaims that God reigns and the wedding of the Lamb with his bride has arrived (vv 6–9). The latter words refer symbolically to the joining of Jesus Christ with his people (note Hos 2:19–20; Eph 5:23, 32). They are the faithful followers of the Lamb (Matt 22:1–14; Rev 13:9–10).

- Following the four anthems of praise, the angel instructs John that only God, not an angel, is worthy of worship.

- The words conclude with the centrality of the person of Jesus Christ in prophecy: "the testimony of Jesus is the spirit of prophecy" (v 10). What does this statement mean?

Jesus Christ Is the Center of All Prophecy

It means that we should look for Jesus Christ throughout the Old Testament, as Jesus himself taught after his resurrection. He tells his followers to find him in Moses (the Torah, or Law) and in all the prophets (Luke 24:25–27). He fulfills them all (Matt 5:17). This is a primary principle for interpreting the Bible (the practice of hermeneutics).

This principle is certainly true in our pursuit of the identity of the Antichrist in the Old and New Testaments.

- From Daniel onward Jesus Christ is constantly opposed throughout history by the Antichrist.

- He is revealed both in direct prophecy and in indirect prophecy (typology; chs 8, 10–11).

- He has also revealed himself in direct encounter as a theophany (ch 10).

The Battle of Armageddon Brings the Antichrist to His End

But Not His Death

Revelation 19:11–21 describes the Battle of Armageddon. The focus of attention is on Jesus Christ as the Warrior from heaven; it is not on the Antichrist. The Battle signals the second coming of Jesus Christ. He promised that he would return (John 14:1–3) in "power and great glory" (Matt 24:30).

The glorious coming of Jesus Christ from heaven is described with many symbols.

- He is on a white horse (the symbol of a victorious Roman commander) and accompanied by angels (and/or the saints) riding white horses (they, too, are victorious).

- His name is "Faithful and True."

- With justice he "judges and makes war" (19:11).

- His eyes are like "blazing fire" (=his piercing vision from which none can hide).

- His head bears many crowns (thus he is King of kings, v 16).

- His robe is covered with ("dipped in") blood. The Battle will be violent.

- From his mouth comes a large (spear like) sword (symbolizing that his word alone is sufficient to strike down his enemies).

- His scepter is made of iron (signifying his punishing, autocratic rule; and fulfilling what was prophesied of him in Psalm 2:9).

- He treads "the winepress of the wrath of the anger of God Almighty," which recall the words cited above from Revelation 14 describing the undiluted wrath of God poured out on the Antichrist and his followers. This reference to wrath anticipates the defeat of the Antichrist in the verses that follow.

Jesus Christ bears three names to signify his entire "history" before and with humanity.

- First, he has a name "which no one knows." This name sets him apart from humanity as the divine Son of God (v 12). It is his identity prior to all creation.

- His second name is the "word of God." This name points to his first coming as the Son of Man (so John 1:1–3).

- Finally, he is "King of kings, and Lord of lords." These titles signify his triumphant second coming here described.

The Humiliating End of All Armies: Eaten by Vultures

Verses 17–18 describe the invitation from an angel to the carrion eating birds. They come to the "great supper of God" where they will eat the flesh of all the participants (people and animals) of the fallen armies of the Antichrist. This invitation fulfills what Ezekiel prophesied to come at the end of the age (Ezek 38–39; esp 39:17–20). It also concurs with geography: the flyways of large birds over Israel every Spring and Fall.

The Defeated Antichrist Is Cast into the Everlasting Lake of Fire

The Battle of Armageddon is briefly rehearsed. Verse 19 says:

Then I saw the beast (the Antichrist; see chs 13, 17) and the kings of the earth and their armies gathered together to make war against the rider on the horse and his army. (20) But the beast was captured, and with him the false prophet who had performed the miraculous signs on his behalf...The two of them were thrown alive into the fiery lake of burning sulfur. (21) The rest of them were killed with the sword that came out of the mouth of the rider on the horse, and all the birds gorged themselves on their flesh.

While this record is amazingly brief, there are other texts that give fuller details of this Battle.

- Zechariah 14:2–15 predicts the horrendous features of earthquakes, changes in day and night, and a plague that will rot peoples' flesh, eyes, and tongues, and the flesh of all the war animals.

- Matthew 24:27–31 unfolds the great signs to occur in the heavens as Jesus comes in "power and great glory." The stars, sun, and moon are all affected. The heavens "are shaken."

- 2 Peter 3:1–13 compares it to the destruction of the universal flood of Noah's day.

- It will be a "unique day... a day known to the Lord" (Zech 14:7).

- All the descriptions of the "day of the Lord" (e.g., 1 Thess 5:1–9) belong here.

Armageddon in Popular Media Fades in Comparison to What the Bible Says

The media have made much of "Armageddon," and continue to do so. It stands for great conflicts and war. Yet all such portrayals fall miserably short. The reality is that it brings history and civilization to an end, just like the great flood of Noah (Gen 6).

- There is no tomorrow, no return to normalcy, no recovery, no hope, no living, no resurgence, no recovery.

- All human life having the mark of the beast, the Antichrist, dies.

- The old age ends; a new age dawns—the millennium kingdom in which Jesus Christ reigns as the consummate Prince of peace and King of kings.

- No rivals are permitted to exist.

- For a thousand years humanity and the earth itself enjoy the rest and peace and liberty and plenty it has sought in vain for millennia. It is a reign of righteousness (2 Pet 3:13).

Herein we arrive at the proper end of the Antichrist. Note that he does not die. With the false prophet he is cast alive into the lake of fire—the second death, the destination of all the wicked (Rev 20:14–15) and of Satan (Rev 20:10), "where they will be tormented day and night for ever and ever" (20:10).

- These words suggest that he is somewhat supernatural (see the discussion on 17:8–11), perhaps deceiving the world by his resurrected body, and thus he has already died once.

- Only the second, spiritual, death—eternal dying—is appropriate for him (20:14).

How to Recognize This Supreme Agent of Evil

The Summary of the Titles and Works of the Most Evil Person in History

Plus a Warning

In summary, the Antichrist has various titles; and the descriptions of him are exceedingly diverse and fearsome. He runs the gamut of political, cultural, and religious intrigue. The following descriptions will aid everyone living during the GT to recognize this agent of evil.

- In the end times he is one of the rulers of the ten-nation confederacy that succeeds the Roman Empire (one of the ten toes in Dan 2; the little horn among the ten horns of ch 7).

- Then he becomes the supreme ruler of this confederacy and controls the world.

- He is the desolator of the temple of Israel (Dan 8, 9, 12; Matt 24:15; 2 Thess 2; Rev 11).

- He is typified by Antiochus IV and by "many antichrists" from the past and even the present.

- He is the one who seeks to destroy Israel during the last half of the GT (the 3 ½ years) (Dan 7–8; 11–12). He makes a covenant for seven years with Israel; then breaks the covenant after 3 ½ years and commits the abomination of desolations (9:26–27; 12:7).

- He is entwined in the struggle between the good and evil angels to influence the direction and destiny of nations against Israel.

- He is the great deceiver, claiming to be Jesus Christ.

- He is the antichrist taking the place of Christ and opposing Christ.

- He is the man of lawlessness and the one destined to perdition. Anarchy and war will dominate.

- He is inspired by Satan.

- He arises from the abyss (the abode of demons) and kills the two witnesses sent by God.

- He kills all who do not worship him and bear his mark, 666.

- He is accompanied by a false prophet whose single role is to persuade people to worship the Antichrist.

- He is the red beast with seven heads and ten horns which have ten crowns.

- He initially supports all false religion and its accompanying immorality.

- He will destroy all religions and exalt himself as the only God.

- He "was, is not, arises from the abyss, and goes to perdition."

- He is both an individual and a government/power.

- Finally, he will not be able to turn from his wickedness (Dan 12:10); and he will experience everlasting judgment (12:2).

Now to the reader we say this. During the greatest suffering imaginable, that of the Great Tribulation, do not yield and give in to the pressure to accept the "mark of the beast" (666), of the Antichrist.

There is a day of unparalleled goodness coming and you will enter it if you persevere in your faith to the end of the GT. There is a special reward coming to those who stand fast and are martyred for doing so (Rev 20:1-6).

Secret Agents of the Antichrist Are Real

Now some who have read this chapter and the rest of this book are secret agents of the Antichrist seeking to betray and capture secret believers. The words of the Apostle Paul about apostates in his day are pertinent here. He warned his disciple Timothy that some have "suffered shipwreck with regard to the faith" and that he had "handed them over to Satan to be taught not to blaspheme" (1 Tim 1:19–20). To the Corinthians Paul wrote (2 Cor 11:13–15) about some people who were "false apostles, deceitful workers, masquerading as apostles of Christ. (14) And no wonder, for Satan himself masquerades as an angel of light. (15) It is not surprising, then, if his servants also masquerade as servants of righteousness. Their end will be what their actions deserve."

Chapter 14

Seven Years of Tribulation Decimate Israel

Bill stared at the news bulletin flashing on his damaged cell phone. The headline declared that the United Nations had just yielded to the Leader to take charge of the world's economic needs in order to resolve the pandemic and famine now ravaging the world from the war in Ukraine. He would also command the mightiest alignment of military forces in the world. Far more than one billion people were homeless and on the verge of starving. An equal number were infected. The Leader's troops began forcing everyone to quarantine to try to curb the raging epidemic. China, the USA, and much of Europe were stepping forward to fund the needed food and its distribution. Much of the famine and disease resulted from the huge earthquakes that had rocked different continents in the last several days, basically following the "ring of fire" along the coasts of the Western Hemisphere. But Central Asia and China had also suffered such quakes that tipped past 9 on the Richter Scale.

Bill's thoughts instantly wondered: "How can the world meet the needs of so many people? Even the West Coast of the US had been decimated. How can the government in Washington help us?" he wondered.

Living just a few miles out of the city, Bill and his family had enjoyed a comfortable life until recently. He had a good job and his kids enjoyed attending a good school. Last year had turned out to be the most difficult year for everyone in the country. The pandemic had forced many businesses, especially restaurants, into financial ruin. All the public schools had closed for the school year. But Bill had been able to work from home, and his wife, Susan, a Christian school teacher, had been able to teach at least part-time. His kids were able to attend school part of the day.

Three days ago, the great long-predicted earthquake hit the West Coast. A following tsunami struck along the coast and many coastal towns had been decimated. The news—whatever little there was—reported that up to one million people from California to Washington had been killed, either by drowning or by falling buildings.

Bill learned that downtown every one of the ten bridges over the river had collapsed into the water. The Interstate bridge fell almost 100 feet into the river. The three sky-scrapers had collapsed along with most of the buildings on the West side. Scores of people in their vehicles had been killed. The devastation and suffering was catastrophic. How will we ever recover from this? Bill wondered. He shuddered at the thought of what was yet to come.

The earthquake had shaken his house for almost two full minutes. But it remained standing. Everything inside was in shambles. Fearing aftershocks, Bill and his son slept outside for three nights. He was able to help his neighbors on either side, pulling one of them, bloodied, out of a pile of rubble. The fire department had finally come, along with an ambulance, but no one could be transported to the hospital. Roads were unsafe, bridges and overpasses on the Freeway were out, and emergency personnel from the city and county were nowhere to be seen. The hospital itself, though built according to earthquake standards, had been structurally damaged and was considered unsafe.

There was no electricity and no gas lines in the entire region. Fires were burning everywhere. Many cell towers had been toppled, making use of cell phones almost impossible. Only a few radio and TV stations were still broadcasting on the emergency frequency on battery powered sets, but news was intermittent.

Everyone was on his own to provide for his own needs. Only the next days and weeks would show just how extensive the devastation was. But at least it was a bright Spring day.

Ominously some neighbors walked by brandishing their fire-arms—both hand guns and semi-automatic rifles. It was quite clear that they were going to serve as "peace officers" in the absence of regular sheriff's deputies. But Bill wondered if some were out to "discover" resources for themselves.

Bill reflected: "Is this the end of the world?" He recalled that Susan had told him: "Jesus Christ is going to return to con-clude all history and to set up his kingdom. His return will be accompanied by a time of unprecedented suffering and calamities. Jesus had called it the Great Tribulation—so great that it would be unique in human history." Before she and Stephanie had disappeared, she had said that it was the time of God's anger toward rebellious, sinful mankind that had rejected God the Creator of heaven and earth. They had also spurned his Son who had given himself on a cross to pay for the sins of the world. But Bill, like most of his neighbors, had shown little interest in "spiritual things." His daughter shared her mother's faith, but his son had closely followed him. With these differences their marriage was challenged but had survived—at least till now.

Bill remembered that she had spoken of the last book of the Bible, the Revelation, that it predicted what would come in this Tribulation. "Earthquakes, famines, wars, and other calamities will all come," she said. Now they were here, it seemed. There had certainly never been a time before now when all these catastrophes were happening together.

If this was the predicted time of great suffering several questions flooded Bill's thoughts.

Chapter 14

Seven Years of Tribulation Decimate Israel

The previous chapters exposed the many features and actions of the Antichrist. In short, we found him to be the embodiment of evil who will rise to such power and prestige that his stooge, the false prophet, will demand that the world should worship him as divine. And the world will be eager to do so.

More significantly the Antichrist will deceive the nation of Israel, pretending to be her savior. But he will betray her and seek to destroy her. Because the world will be going through such dire challenges it will be looking for a savior. The deceit will be so convincing that the world will find no other one worthy of such adulation except the Antichrist.

Indeed, the most important characteristic of the age is deceit. The following pages will bear this out.

In general, the Antichrist belongs to the end of history. But the Bible has a special designation for this period of the end. It is the Great Tribulation (GT).

What Will Happen during the Great Tribulation?

In keeping with the purpose and tone of this book, to provide a manual for surviving the Great Tribulation, we have an obvious responsibility to tell what the GT is all about. In this chapter we aim to show just how hard it will be to survive the GT. Unspeakable suffering will be the lot of all—for believers suffering from the Antichrist and for unbelievers suffering from the wrath of God. In a real sense the GT is a contest between God and his people and Satan and his embodiment of evil, the Antichrist.

How to Read This Chapter

As with the preceding chapter, there are two ways to read this chapter. You can carefully read all the paragraphs and gain a comprehensive understanding of the Great Tribulation—as thorough as you can find anywhere, although somewhat abbreviated. On the other hand, if you lack the time and/or the occasion, you can read the bold type between the paragraphs and get a quick summary of the content of this chapter.

Startling Questions and Answers about the Great Tribulation

Here are some of the many questions that flooded Bill's mind as recounted above [with some short-hand answers]:

- What will the unfolding years of the GT be like? [Like hell on earth—as never before]

- Will living (if we can call this living) go from good to bad, and even get worse? [Yes]

- How long will it last? [Seven years]

- How extensive will it be? [World-wide]

- Why has the GT come about? [In short, it is God's judgment for the world-wide sin and rebellion of the nations and their peoples]

- Am I able to escape it, even by death? [NO]

- Is it part of God's plan? [Yes, God is in control]

- Can I become a Christian during it, and how? [Yes, if you believe the Good News about Jesus Christ who delivers from judgment for our sins and the coming wrath]

- In short, what is the GT? [The time in which the unbelieving world experiences the full anger of God]

- How is the GT associated with the Antichrist? [It is his time of unrivalled power and deceit]

- Will Christians suffer, and if so, how much? [They are protected from God's wrath but not from the anger of the Antichrist; many, perhaps most, will die]

- What marks the beginning of the GT? How will I know it has started? [Generally, it is the event of the Rapture]

- How will the GT end? [The Battle of Armageddon]

- Where in the Bible is the GT described? [In Daniel of the Old Testament and in several prophetic portions of the New Testament, especially the last book of the Bible, the Revelation]

- What is its significance for world history? [The GT brings world history to an end]

- How is it related to the five empires prophesied in Daniel 2 and 7? [It is the fifth empire yet to come]

- How much time does the world have? [Not much; with the Rapture, it has just begun!]

- What place does my country have in it? [The GT is universal]

During the course of this chapter we hope to answer all these questions, and even more. We will develop the short answers into long ones, and with clarity rather than obscurity.

The Antichrist and the Great Tribulation Go Together

Since the Antichrist rises to power during the GT, what we learned about the Antichrist in the previous chapters overlaps with our focus on the GT here. While we may necessarily revisit some of the material in the previous chapters, we will try to avoid duplication as much as possible.

As with the Antichrist, so there are many ways by which the Bible identifies the GT. The descriptions are noteworthy and alarming. There's never been a time like it.

The Great Tribulation Is First Revealed in the Book of Daniel

No other literature in the world besides the Bible tells us anything about the time of tribulation. And the Bible has much to say about it, as it did with the Antichrist (see the previous chapters).

As we first and specifically encountered the Antichrist in the Book of Daniel, so it is with the Great Tribulation (GT). We remind the reader that we give many details about that text and about history in the previous chapters of this book. Also see further details in my book, *The*

Apocalypse Is Coming! The Rise of the Antichrist, the Restrainer Removed, and Jesus Christ Victorious at Armageddon (2020).

Daniel Makes Unique Contributions for Understanding the GT

The book of Daniel makes several unique contributions to what the GT is: its length; its place in history; its connection with the Antichrist. Without this prophecy we would be impoverished in understanding this period. The New Testament itself is indebted to Daniel for the many features it discloses. So it isn't possible to know about the GT without first going to its first mention, in the Old Testament.

In the previous two chapters of this book we discovered what is involved in the "mystery" revealed to Daniel, chapter 2:

- It covers the entire course of world history under five empires to the end of time (Dan 2:18–19, 27–29, 45).

- It concludes with the fifth empire, that of the Antichrist (the ten toes of the statue), still future to us today. This is the Great Tribulation.

- The fifth empire will be destroyed by the "stone cut out of the mountain without hands" (it is supernatural; it is a symbol of Jesus Christ) which ushers in the everlasting kingdom of God on earth (Dan 2:34–35, 44–45). Yet here Daniel says nothing about how long the fifth kingdom will exist.

In **Daniel 7** we learned that four animals symbolize these same five empires. The little horn receives special attention. It is among the ten horns but becomes predominant over the other horns and actually conquers three of them. This little horn is a king of the end time, namely the Antichrist.

Daniel 7: Half the Length of the GT Is 3 ½ Years

Here we learn that the Antichrist rules during the fifth empire. The ten-horn configuration on the head of the fourth beast symbolizes the fifth empire after Rome. The fifth empire is an extension of Rome in some manner. It has not yet appeared on the stage of history. The Antichrist will arise during this time and will do various nefarious, slanderous, and supernatural deeds for a specific period: for "3 ½ times" (Dan 7:25; 12:7). As elsewhere in Daniel this number means 3 ½ years. The astute reader recognizes that this is half of seven years.

The GT Is Typified in History by Antiochus IV of the 2nd Century BC: Chapter 8

The next chapter, Daniel 8, builds on the previous chapter to give another indication about the length of the GT. Daniel predicts the coming of Antiochus IV of the 2nd century who will try to exterminate the Jews. Antiochus IV is a type of the Antichrist and points to the "time of the end"... the time of wrath... the time of the end" (vv 17, 19). "He will destroy many and take his stand against the Prince of princes" (v 25). Here the period of the GT, when "the rebellion that causes desolation" occurs, becomes 2300 "evenings and mornings" before the sanctuary is "reconsecrated" (v 14).

This time period is probably an approximation of the same period as that of chapter 7: three and a half years. Thus we have another clue as to the length of the GT. Yet we've already learned much of what will happen when the Antichrist rules (see the previous chapters of this book).

A question arises. Why is there typology at all—of both the Antichrist himself and of the time of the Great Tribulation. The answers are that typology shows that

- history correlates to the revelation of the Bible;

- God is in control of the events in history that fall into recurring patterns;

- biblical prophecy has a relevance for earlier generations before those living in the fulfillment of prophecy;

- there is a special urgency for holiness every time fulfillment seems about to happen.

The Actual Full Length of the GT Is A Week of Years: Daniel 9

Daniel is the first and only person in the Bible to tell us how long the whole GT actually is. In chapter 7 we have learned that the period is at least 3 ½ years. Now we learn that the GT is actually twice this long. It fulfills a "week of years."

Daniel 9 predicts the first coming of Jesus Christ and his death, the rise of the Antichrist and his covenant with the Jewish people and his breaking of it, the exact number of years when all this will take place, and the time in history when it begins. Truly amazing!!!

The History of the World from the time of Daniel Covers 490 Years +

The angel Gabriel (v 24) reveals that the whole future from Daniel's time until the end of history in the end is placed within the framework of just "seventy sevens" of years, that is, 490 years. The first 483 years extend from Daniel's time to the time of Jesus Christ, then comes a gap in time before the last seven years come to pass. During this time of 490 years God's great plan will complete six great events affecting the entire world and last forever. At the first coming of Christ he will end sin and wickedness by atonement on the cross (as Gabriel asserts in v 24). At his second coming Christ will bring in everlasting righteousness, seal up (fulfill) all vision and prophecy, and finally restore the temple during the millennium or in the everlasting era.

As God has planned it, the 490+ (note the +) years encompass all the following:

- the 483 years begin with a future Gentile king's decree that the Jews should return from Babylon to Israel to rebuild Jerusalem and the temple. This decree best begins with Artaxerxes who issues his decree favoring Israel in 445 BC (see Nehemiah 2:1–8).

- Then 483 years after the decree Jesus Christ dies by crucifixion about 30 AD (445-483 = AD 32, allowing for a calendar shift to place Jesus's birth about 5–6 BC; and adjusting for the 360-day year). The text describes Jesus's death: "the Anointed One [the Messiah] will be cut off and have nothing." [See various views of the 490 years discussed in *The Apocalypse Is Coming*, 149, 439-40.]

- Then comes an unreported gap of about 2000 years: from the time of the death of Christ until now.

- Then "the end will come like a flood: War will continue until the end, and desolations have been decreed" (9:26). These events concern the last seven years.

Now we come to the most important verse that gives us the length of the GT. We learn here for the first time in the Bible and in history that the GT will be *seven years* long. Here are the words of v 27:

He (the prince, "the ruler who is to come," v 26: the Antichrist) will confirm a covenant with many for one "seven" (for seven years), but in the middle of that "seven" he will put an end to sacrifice and offering. And one

who causes desolation will come on the wings of abominations until the end that is decreed is poured out on
him (= the Antichrist).

These words in v 27 cannot refer to Jesus Christ as the prince, since
he did not make a covenant with many for seven years, nor did he break
the covenant after 3 ½ years. Such periods have no correspondence
with Jesus's life (in spite of some biblical scholars to attempt to do this).

This last seven-year period is the last "seven" of the "seventy sevens"
(490 years).

All of Israel's History Occurs within "Seventy Sevens" (490 Years)

Why does Scripture summarize all of Israel's history as only 490
years? The most probable answer is that this is the length of Israel's time
back in the land from the time of Artaxerxes onward.

- Jesus Christ is crucified *"after"* the first 69 weeks of years,
  about AD 30.

- Then begins the period of extreme Gentile subjection of Israel.
  In AD 70 Rome stops Israel's rebellion against it by destroying
  Jerusalem and the temple. The Romans repeat these actions
  again in AD 135 after another rebellion under Bar Kokhba
  ("Son of the Star"). The Romans expunge all Jews from the
  land of Israel and make Jerusalem a pagan city, Aelia Capitolina.
  Until 1948 the Gentile nations scatter the Jews around the
  world and they have no homeland.

- Gentile domination fills the gap of about 2000 years when
  Israel has no homeland.

Here is what happens to Israel during the Great Tribulation.

- At the beginning of the GT the Antichrist will guarantee (by deception) a new homeland for the Jews in a seven-year (or, perhaps an open-ended) treaty.

- But 3 ½ years later he will break this covenant and begin his program to exterminate the Jews.

- The whole world will join in support of the Antichrist's evil design. They will believe the lies of the Antichrist, as the New Testament shows (2 Thess 2:3–12; see the next chapter of this book).

The Tribulation Escalates into the *Great* Tribulation

Daniel 10-12

We have not yet finished what Daniel adds to our understanding of a seven-year GT. Daniel has one more (fourth) vision that covers the rest of the book (chs 10–12). The year is 536 BC, the third year of Cyrus king of Persia. Daniel is about 90 years of age.

The first verse gives the occasion for writing down the vision. Daniel receives a troubling "revelation" that is "true and concerned a great war/conflict" (v 1). The vision then follows to enable him to understand the message/revelation. We are not told how the "revelation" came to Daniel but perhaps it was his greater understanding of what his earlier visions portended over fifty years before (in chaps 2, 7, 8, and 9).

Here is a possible sequence.

- Two years have passed since the prayer of chapter 9—requesting the end of the Babylonian Captivity—and the grand vision of the course of human history summed up in 490 years plus a great hiatus.

- Since then, Daniel has reflected on the meaning of his dreams and visions. He detects in them the revelations of several successive Gentile empires, the wars that are intrinsic to such successions, and, from chapter 9, the promise of a deliverer, the Messiah, who will not reign but be killed. Yet his death heralds the great redemptive accomplishments and everlasting peace and restoration which 9:24 gives.

- Then he reflects on the coming of the Antichrist and the repeated statements (7:25; 8:13, 24; 9:27) that he would desolate the temple of the Jews—meaning great suffering for his people.

- There is repeated emphasis on the time of the end (7:25; 8:17, 19, 26; 9:26–27).

- Chapter 9:26 predicted that war was to "continue until the end" (9:26) and in 10:1 Daniel's final vision concerned a "great warfare."

Thus, Daniel is greatly troubled about the future of his people Israel. After reflecting for two years, he seeks more understanding of how great this conflict/war will be. By the end of the present vision (ch 12) Daniel will quote an angel who asks: "How long will it be before these astonishing things are fulfilled?" (12:6). Daniel himself will ask: "What will the outcome of all this be?" (12:8). He is also concerned about the unseen agents, the angels, who have interpreted the future to him (in chs 7, 8, 9).

When he says that the revelation was "true and concerned a great war" he truly is alarmed and fearful (10:8–11, 15–19; as earlier: 7:15, 28; 8:27: illness) of what this "great war" means for his people.

- If the preceding conflicts (intrinsic to all the visions thus far) are serious and alarming for his people, will not the "end of the age" mean the worse conflict of all?

- How much suffering must his people endure prior to God's kingdom coming to earth (Dan 2:18–45)?

- The words, the "great conflict" (10:1), reflect back on what the words, "war will continue until the end" (9:26), signify.

- Daniel could never have imagined that a terrible dictator would arise in our times and try to conquer much of Europe and would try to destroy Israel by killing six million Jews.

- Daniel's words of "warfare" may here point to nuclear or other horrible forms of warfare that culminate in the Battle of Armageddon. Then all the world under the Antichrist will try to destroy all Israel once and for all.

- *No wonder Daniel is troubled and alarmed!*

But the purpose of the revelation and the vision is clear. The interpreting angel reports (10:14): "Now I have come to explain to you what will happen to your people in the latter days, because the vision pertains to the days yet future." The "latter days" links to the first vision (2:28) and has an eschatological reference throughout the Bible. There are twelve uses of the phrase in the Old Testament (Gen 49:1; Num 24:14; Deut 4:30; 31:29; Isa 2:2; Jer 23:20; 30:24; 48:47; 49:39; Ezek 38:16; Hos 3:5; Mic 4:1). There are twelve uses in the New Testament (Acts 2:17–21; John 6:39–40, 44, 54; 2 Tim 3:1; Heb 1:1–2; Jam 5:3; 1 Pet 1:5, 20; 2 Pet 3:3; 1 John 2:18; Jude 18). In Daniel 2:28 and 10:14 the words are "the end of the days."

Now, dear people of God, note how your present place in the suffering at the hands of the Antichrist has been all forecast in the book of Daniel. You need to know that God has planned it all for greater purposes which he will reveal at the end of the age: the end of Gentile nations and the restoration of the nation of Israel to everlasting blessing in the kingdom of Jesus Christ.

Daniel Has a Special Encounter with Jesus Christ 500 Years before Bethlehem

The vision of chapter 10 begins with Daniel's encounter with the pre-existent Christ, a theophany (literally, "an appearance of God"). He is the "Anointed One" in 9:25-26, who "will be cut off and have nothing"—a description of the incarnate Messiah. Here in chapter 10 he appears as divine more than 500 years before he is born as a human child in Bethlehem.

What is the point of this theophany?

- It emphasizes the personal acquaintance that God in the person of Jesus Christ has with Daniel. Twice an interpreting angel tells Daniel that he is "highly esteemed" (vv 10, 19).

- It emphasizes the serious nature of the meaning of this last vision.

- It serves to assure Daniel's special place, as a very old man, in the resurrection coming at the end (12:2, 3, 13).

- It exalts the person of Jesus Christ to the preeminent place in the book of Daniel.

- It provides a link to a similar experience that the Apostle Paul will have with the risen Christ (Acts 9).

- If forms a point of connection with the Book of Revelation. John the Apostle will have a similar vision at the beginning of the Revelation (1:10ff). The vision here serves to validate that vision then (and vice-versa).

- This vision is consistent with the reality that people in the Bible often have visions and dreams (just as people living in the Middle East today have dreams/visions that lead them to faith in Christ).

Spirit Beings (Angels) Seek to Capture Nations for Satan As Portents of the End

After the theophany, the interpreting angel reveals why he has come to Daniel (v 14; stated just above). Then Daniel learns much about the spirit world of unseen beings. Indeed, *Daniel contributes more to our understanding of angels than any other Old Testament book.*

- In the unseen realm of spirit beings, there is a conflict going on between good and bad (evil) angels to possess and control the human leaders of nations.

- Here we are told that the "princes" (bad angels) of Persia and Greece act to obstruct God's interpreting angels from delivering their messages to Daniel about the future course of nations.

- Michael, God's angel, overcomes the evil angels (v 21).

This special revelation about the reality of the realm of angels, good and bad, is important and unique to Daniel and underscores the spiritual dimension of the Antichrist during the GT.

- The "spirit of Antichrist" will deny the deity and humanity of Jesus Christ (1 John 2; 4).

- The Antichrist will employ false spiritual demonstrations of power to deceive many (2 Thess 2).

    (1) Satan will inspire him to perform miracles (2 Thess 2; Rev 13:2).

    (2) He will benefit from the demons who draw the nations to Armageddon (Rev 16).

    (3) He comes out of (or, is linked to) the abyss, the place of demons (Rev 11:7).

    (4) He himself may have conquered death and thus cannot be killed (Rev 17; 19).

The significant place of angels in Daniel finds its counterpart only in Revelation.

The Supremacy of Demons Reveals the Nature of the GT

The attention to angels is *key* to realizing that the nature of the GT is not just natural, physical suffering. Rather it involves the spiritual world where angels, good and bad (demons) are contesting for the lives of human beings. Indeed, the book of Revelation expands on this terror in almost incomprehensible ways. In the next chapter we elaborate on these judgments.

The Reign of Terror under Antiochus IV (Dan 11–12) Typifies the GT

Like chapter 8, chapter 11 serves to show how God's people can learn from history what the future will be like. Both in history and in the Bible God gives types, portents, or adumbrations of the end times to enable his people to understand the fulfillment of prophecy when it arrives. Thus, adumbrations of both the Antichrist and his rule in the GT have occurred throughout history.

All of chapter 11 traces the rise of two lines of the successors to Alexander the Great, who conquers Persia (v 3).

- The struggle is between the Seleucid line (the kings of the North, of Syria) and the Ptolemaic line (the kings of the South, of Egypt) (vv 4-20).

- The focus is on Antiochus IV, of the North, who tries to exterminate Israel (vv 21-35), as Daniel 8 reveals (see fuller details in the earlier chapters of this book).

Verse 35 switches from Antiochus IV to Antichrist with the words that the struggle will go on "until the time of the end, for it will still come at the appointed time." The Antichrist

- will exalt himself above every god and slander the God of gods (v 36) during the GT;

- will arise "at the time of the end" (v 40) when he, the Antichrist, no longer comes from either the line of the North or of the South but fights against both;

- will conquer many countries (vv 40–44);

- will establish his presence in the land of Israel (apparently to do battle) (v 45).

As in Daniel 8, Antiochus IV becomes an adumbration, a type, of the Antichrist to come (beginning with v 36). *And his reign of terror is also a type of the terror to come in the GT.*

The Tribulation Intensifies to the *Great* Tribulation Unique to World History

With this background (chs 10–11) we come to one of the pivotal verses that enlarge our concept of the suffering of the world. For the first time in all the world's consciousness there is a reckoning that all the world must pay attention to. The tribulation becomes the *Great* Tribulation.

Immediately after identifying the Antichrist as located in Israel, the next words (12:1) assert that "at that time Michael, the great prince who protects your people will arise." It is the time of the end and clearly God's powerful agent will protect Israel from extermination. We learn now that this is the *Great Tribulation*: "There will be a time of distress such as has not happened from the beginning of nations until then" (12:1).

The words demand the meaning of a *unique* time in the world's history, stretching from the world-wide flood when nations first arose after the Tower of Babel (thousands of years ago; Gen 10-11) until the time of the end (yet future to AD 2022).

- This involves at least 5000 years.

- These words must mean that there is going to be world-wide suffering—affliction not limited to Israel or the Middle East—and on a scale never seen before.

- All previous suffering from earthquakes, famines, plagues, disease, wars, genocides, and more will pale in comparison to this era, the GT.

- All these so-called "natural" disasters will join with the world-wide demonic possession tormenting all humanity and with the pouring out of the "anger of the wrath of the Lord God Almighty" (Rev 6:16; 16:1–21).

- Such suffering suggests what might come from nuclear war or other ultra-modern forms of warfare, involving lasers, satellites in the heavens, WMD's and more.

Other prophets predicted a similar time under other terminology.

- Early in Israel's history Moses warned of a future time when Israel would go into exile because of idolatry. "When you are in distress and all these things have happened to you, then in the last days you will return to the LORD your God and obey him" (Deut 4:30). The "last days" include the events of the times of the end.

- Much later than Moses, but prior to Daniel, Jeremiah writes: "How awful that day will be! None will be like it. It will be a time of trouble for Jacob, but he will be saved out of it" (Jer 30:7).

Jesus Christ reiterates Daniel's contribution to the significance of this event. For the first time in the Bible, in his final discourse (Matt 24:21), Jesus uses the terms "great tribulation" and describes it similarly to Daniel 12:1. Jesus even quotes Daniel by name a few verses earlier (Matt 24:15). Then John the Apostle in the Revelation uses the terminology, adding "the" (Rev 7:14).

The Great Tribulation is not called the "great" tribulation without reason.

The angel assures Daniel that his "people, everyone who is found written in the book (of life; 7:10; 10:21; Rev 20:12, 15), will be rescued" (v 1). Thus, in the midst of the worst suffering imaginable, God will rescue his own. The New Testament reveals that God will rescue Christians from his wrath (1 Thess 1:10; Rev 3:10; 7:3–4). This will first occur at the Rapture (i.e., Rexit)!

Isn't it time for you, the reader, living during the GT, to take notice? God will give you special protection from his wrath (Rev 7:3; 9:4).

The GT *Determines* the Destinies for All People: Heaven or Hell

Since it is a time of "great tribulation" unparalleled in history many will die (the Revelation tells us just how many: one-half of all people). Therefore, it is fitting that immediately the interpreting angel tells Daniel that there is going to be a resurrection of all to one of two destinies: heaven ("everlasting life") or hell ("everlasting shame and contempt" = judgment) (v 2). The former involves those who have insight and lead many to righteousness; they will have the glow of heaven and shine like the stars (v 3). We can infer that the rest will experience the blackness and darkness of hell.

The angel then tells Daniel to seal up the words of his prophecy until the time of "the end" when knowledge of it will increase (4).

The Text Reveals the Length and Outcome of the GT

Two questions wrap up the book of Daniel (vv 5-13). Both concern the GT. An angel asks: "How long will it be until the end of these wonders"? And Daniel asks: "What will be the outcome of these events"? In other words: How long is the GT? What will be the outcome of the GT?

The answer to the first question no doubt troubled Daniel. The end will come when the Antichrist smashes the power of God's people by the end of 3 ½ years. Clearly this verse parallels that of 7:25 where the Antichrist, called the "little horn," defeats the "saints" of the Most High and tries to change the "set times and the laws." The little horn comes out of the ten nation confederacy, the fifth kingdom that succeeds the Roman Empire. By repeating the essence of 7:25, this verse validates half the length of the GT.

Troubled, confused, and no doubt alarmed, Daniel asks for more information about what will happen to his people, the Jews (12:8). The full answer gives some solace. At first the angel tells Daniel that the answer ("the words") is closed and sealed till the time of the end (12:9). Then he adds that "the many (God's people) will be purified" and will understand. In contrast the "wicked" will continue to be wicked and not understand. No doubt these words refer to the unfolding of the meaning of prophecy that will happen in the time of fulfillment, at the end.

Months Lengthen the Last 3 ½ Years of the GT

The angel speaks about two enlargements about the GT (vv 11–12). From the time of the "abomination of desolation" to the end of the 3 ½ times there will be 1290 days (v 7)—which is 30 days longer than 3 ½ years (or 42 months or 1260 days; see Rev 12). We note that this is now the fifth (cf 7:25; 8:13, 24; 9:27) and last reference to the abominable act that Jesus also will cite (Matt 24:15). The added days may mean that the GT will require an added month to transition from the GT to the reign of Christ; or an additional month occurs in the GT pointing to a period of transition from the first half to the second half.

Then the angel pronounces a "blessing" on the one who "waits for and reaches the end of the 1335 days" (v 12). This adds seventy-five days (two and a half months) to the GT. Perhaps it simply reflects that those who persevere beyond the end of the GT will be those who are "purified and refined" (v 10); or, again, it may be a period added to the front of the GT as a transition period.

The book of Daniel concludes with the angel's wonderful promise to Daniel (v 13). He is to go his way in rest until the end. Then at the end he will experience resurrection (as one of those identified in 12:2) and receive his "allotted inheritance." Truly this is a RIP for Daniel.

Clearly the "end" refers to the last 3 ½ years of the GT and especially the resurrection of the saints from the GT (Rev 20:1–6) after the GT concludes at the Battle of Armageddon (see the last chapter). This resurrection finds its parallel with the Rapture that occurs at the beginning of the GT.

Seven Observations Summarize the GT from Daniel

Before turning to how the New Testament presents the Great Tribulation, here is a summary of what we have learned from the book of Daniel.

1) It is a period of seven years, marked by the rise of the Antichrist as the head of the greatest world empire of the ten kingdoms that flow from the Roman Empire of the past (Dan 2; 7).

2) At the beginning the Antichrist makes a seven-year covenant, an agreement, with Israel and promises to protect and prosper her (Dan 9:26).

3) In the middle of the seven years the Antichrist breaks his covenant and turns against Israel, seeking to destroy her and the God who raises up Israel as his witness among the nations (9:27).

4) The last 3 ½ years mark the worse suffering in the world's history, both for Israel in particular and for the Gentiles (12:1). Among other wicked deeds, the Antichrist will seek to change "the set times and the laws" (7:25), assume divinity, and attack God and his people.

5) A similar time in the 2ⁿᵈ century BC prefigures the GT. The evil Greek King, Antiochus IV, serves as a type of the Antichrist in his attempt to exterminate Israel (Dan 8; 11).

6) God will demonstrate special care and protection for his people by the "stone cut out of the mountains without hands" (2:44–45), and by the Son of Man (7:13–14)—both titles for Jesus Christ.

7) At the end of the GT Jesus Christ will destroy the Antichrist and set up on earth his everlasting kingdom composed of people from all nations (7:26–27).

Chapter 15

The Great Tribulation Drives the World to Its Knees

The Leader, Benjamin Christos, had taken charge of the major governments of the world. In one conflict after another the Leader had easily subdued the lesser countries of the world. His reputation as an indominable conqueror with military prowess led the formerly powerful nations, including the USA, to sue for peace. China, which now boasted the most powerful military on earth, had to bow to his brilliant strategy of destruction that he promised to pursue if China refused his authority.

The Leader especially targeted the USA. It had been the world's leader in promising freedom and prosperity. Now the Leader had to humiliate it.

Bill Archer had seen first-hand how the Leader imposed his will. All the military, from the top brass on down, had been "re-educated" to give both outward and inward compliance to his mystic persona. The number one priority was not how to defend the country but how to please the Leader, how to give political subservience to him.

On the education front the Leader had nationalized all public schools by declaring a national emergency. The earlier pandemic of 2020-21 had provided a template for how to get the teacher's unions into compliance so that their highest commitment was to the state rather than local communities and school boards. Now the Leader had free reign to impose a curricula that placed obligation to the Leader and his government supreme over all other disciplines. The "three R's" were totally immersed in the Leader's plans. History was rewritten.

The whole point of education was to raise up a generation who despised America's history, cancel it, and replace it with a new focus that would form a future vastly different than the past. As part of the "cancel culture" strategy, monuments, libraries, and institutions were all supplanted and renamed after the Leader and his underlings.

The predominance of anarchist movements of the past, such as BLM, critical race theory, black panthers, and others were all refocused to promote the Leader and his cause. "LLL" ("Long Live the Leader") became the cry.

The algorithms that the government had constructed for every person made it easy to identify who was a friend of the new state and who wasn't. Every cell phone was easily traced. The tattoo or small particle embedded under the skin could be scanned at the entrance to any public or private business. Any courageous, brave statesman who thought to resist and to spark a rebellion against the Leader was summarily terminated before the eyes of a watching world. The objective was to intimidate everyone into silence, then compliance. And it worked. The Leader had his spies throughout every layer of society.

Several evangelical churches had been at the forefront of resistance to the Leader and his pseudo-religious claims. Along with many Christian day schools and colleges they had mounted a strategic maneuver to circumvent the Leader's control. They appealed to the right of freedom of religion located in the First Amendment. But by the time the US Supreme Court finally agreed to hear the class action case the Leader had enlarged the Court from nine to seventeen justices—by votes of his lackeys in the Congress. The Court rejected the case, ruling that a state of emergency gave special powers to the Leader.

The Leader imposed his religious convictions and his "sacred" book on the conservative Christians. Overnight Evangelical churches and schools disappeared from the public consciousness. Those pastors, administrators, teachers and other leaders who refused to bow to the Leader's demands found themselves identified as enemies of the state and were summarily imprisoned and executed. Virtually every neighborhood was bathed in blood.

The Leader targeted every Christian and others who refused his "code for living." He clearly identified them by their algorithm. He voided their credit card numbers and SS accounts. Christians could not buy food or fuel or garden seeds or animal feed or parts for their vehicles or anything on credit. The Leader cut off all utilities (gas, electricity). He froze all bank accounts and other financial resources. No one could obtain cash. He stopped Social Security payments to retirees. Veterans could not obtain benefits. With the Leader's spies everywhere, even the black markets could not function. Clearly starvation was the future for all Jews and Christians, and even martyrdom. The Leader made a public spectacle of these people, branding them as vermin who needed to die to save the rest. Any who reached out to the Christians was similarly branded.

But Bill and other Christians took great courage and consolation from the promises of eternal life as found in the Book of Revelation.

The Leader eagerly embraced various scientific pursuits. He accelerated the plans of the USA and China to colonize together the moon and to reach Mars. He pushed for the development of revolutionary modes of transportation, home-building, and more. The applications of AI were almost unbelievable.

But the most far-reaching step the Leader took was to change the calendar. He boldly declared his intent to erase the memory of Jesus Christ. BC and AD were replaced with BL and AL. The Leader justified this great change by appealing to his dominance of the world and his initiation of a new era as great as the former era that came with Jesus Christ. He was, after all, Jesus Christ Returned and Replaced.

As his most despicable, arrogant act the Leader visited the newly finished temple in Jerusalem and had the hologram of himself installed there so that he might be worshipped as divine. This act resurrected what the Roman emperors had done 2000 years before.

Bill and other Christians recognized what it was--the act of desecration that both Daniel and Jesus had prophesied as the identifying act of the Antichrist. Biblical prophecy was true after all!

Now the identity of the Leader was beyond dispute. But so was his coming destruction at the hands of Almighty God at the Battle of Armageddon. Bill took up his Bible to read these texts again for the first time.

Chapter 15

The Great Tribulation Drives the World to Its Knees

As we turn to the New Testament for what it declares about the Great Tribulation (GT), much of its nature has already been revealed in the book of Daniel. The writers of various books in the NT are well acquainted with Daniel. Thus, much of our task in describing the GT is already done, thanks to the extensive disclosure of Daniel. Yet much more appears here.

The following texts unfold greater truth about the GT: the words of Jesus (Matt 24–25); and those of Paul (2 Thess 2), and John (1, 2 John; Revelation—the last book of the Bible).

Jesus Christ Directly Addresses the GT

The testimony of the New Testament about the Great Tribulation (GT) begins, as it should, with Jesus Christ. He elaborates on what Daniel had to say.

In a certain degree of irony, and in the quest for the truth, the temptation of Jesus is strategic. In his culminating temptation of Jesus, Satan offered him "all the kingdoms of the world" if Jesus would worship Satan as God (Matt 4:8–9). Just before he was crucified, in his Olivet discourse (Matt 24–25), Jesus shows that he already is the sovereign over all the kingdoms of the earth. They are in rebellion against God.

Jesus will return to conquer them at Armageddon and implant his own everlasting kingdom of peace (as Dan 2:35, 44–45; 7:13–14 assert).

Jesus Reveals the GT As Wars, Earthquakes, Famines, Deceit, and More

In his last discourse from the Mount of Olives Jesus seeks to answer two questions from his disciples (Matt 24:3).

- "When will the temple be destroyed?"

- "What will be the sign of your coming and of the end of the age?"

The disciples realize that Daniel prophesied the destruction of the temple and that this coincides with the work of the Antichrist and the return of Jesus at the end of the age—at the end of the Great Tribulation (GT). Their questions parallel the two of Daniel 12. The singular "sign" and the grammar of the verse means that Jesus's coming is the same event as the end of the age.

Jesus's answer is thorough and detailed, describing the character of the present age and the beginning of the GT without identifying it right away.

- As the end of the age approaches there will be false Christs, wars, famines, and earthquakes to bring tumult among the nations but "the end is not yet" (24:7–8).

- His followers will come under increasing danger. There will be tremendous deceit (vv 4, 5, 11, 24), so much that even the "elect" (God's people in special relationship with him) are threatened (v 24).

- They will be persecuted, killed, hated "by all the nations."

- There will be apostasy, betrayal and hatred within his people, false prophets, and deceit, and increasing wickedness.

- But Jesus encourages his followers to stand firm to the end to be saved (v 13).

- Finally, the "Gospel of the kingdom must be preached in all the world as a testimony to all nations, and then the end will come" (v 14). Jesus refers to world-wide knowledge of the Gospel.

By these words Jesus shows that the period leading up to and into the GT differs not so much from the course of history. Why worry about the events of the end from such language as this? But these are not Jesus's final words about the nature of this time. He has much more to say.

Jesus Focuses on the Midpoint of the GT: Betrayal and Deceit

Up to this point Jesus has been describing the first half of the GT. His very next words focus on the great event that unveils the Antichrist at the middle of the GT. He declares: "When you see standing in the holy place 'the abomination that causes desolation,' spoken of through the prophet Daniel—let the reader understand." Jesus is clearly quoting Daniel 9:27 where the Antichrist breaks his covenant with Israel after 3 ½ years.

In the next several verses Jesus warns of how desperate those days will be. Then he tops off the description by declaring what Daniel 12:1 also revealed. "For then there will be great tribulation unequalled from the beginning of the world until now—and never to be equalled again" (v 21). Jesus's words actually outperform the soberness of Daniel's words.

- "The beginning of the world" is a very long time.

- Historical counterparts pale in comparison: the bubonic plague; the tsunami that hit Japan; the offshore plates that will bring, according to scientists, a huge earthquake to the Northwest (and is overdue!); famines in Asia and Africa; World Wars 1 and 2 and the many wars since then; the Ukraine War; and the potential of nuclear war.

- Adding all these together will still not come close to the terror which is the GT!

It's no wonder that Jesus goes on to add to the weight of those days. "If those days had not been cut short, no one would survive, but for the sake of the elect those days will be shortened" (v 22; NIV). There is no other way to take these words than to take them literally (and frighteningly). God will mercifully shorten those days.

This then is how Jesus describes the GT. He is completely in accord with Daniel.

The Return of Jesus Christ Abruptly Ends the GT

From this point Jesus quickly moves through additional warnings about false Christs and false prophets who will do signs and miracles to deceive even the elect, if possible, during the GT. He particularly warns of false claims that Christ might be found in secret places.

In contrast Jesus declares that his coming as the Son of Man will be clear and unmistakable.

- It will shine as lightning in the sky.

- There will be the sign of the vultures eating carcasses of fallen armies (from Armageddon, Rev 19; derived from Ezek 39).

- Then "immediately after the tribulation of those days"—the GT has reached its climax—there will be signs in the heavens: the sun, moon, stars, and heavenly bodies will be shaken (v. 29).

- Then the "sign of the Son of Man will appear" (fulfilling Dan 7:13–14) and all the nations will mourn in repentance (fulfilling Zech 12:10–14).

- Jesus will come on the clouds of the sky "with power and great glory" (v 30).

- Finally, Jesus sends forth his angels "with a loud trumpet call" to gather and deliver "his elect from the four winds, from one end of the heavens to the other" (v 31).

- Elsewhere Jesus describes this event in the parable of the harvest at the end of the age (Matt 13:36–43, 49–59).

In this way Jesus declares that the GT comes to an end when he returns with unlimited power. Other texts will fill in what "power and great glory" mean, including the Battle of Armageddon (Rev 16 and 19). Contrary to what covenant theology and amillennialism assert, his is not a silent, quiet coming.

Jesus Warns about His Return

In the rest of the Olivet discourse Jesus graciously uses various illustrations to warn people about the suddenness and certainty of his return. He employs historical and cultural word pictures:

- a sprouting fig tree: his return is at hand

- standing at the door: his return is close

- the flood of Noah: final, world-wide destruction is at hand

- harvesting and mill grinding: some are suddenly taken to judgment

- the need for servants to be faithful during delay

- the parable of the virgins at a wedding waiting for the bride-groom: be prepared

- the parable of the servants: they must invest wisely what their master entrusted them during his absence.

Jesus Will Judge the Nations for Their Treatment of His People during the GT

Finally, Jesus warns that at his coming in glory he will judge the nations for *how* they have treated his people. If well, they the sheep will be rewarded with everlasting life. If evilly, they the goats will be tormented with eternal punishment (Matt 25:46).

Jesus Warns That Few Will Survive the GT

Jesus has given some of the clearest and fullest descriptions of the GT. These are unmistakable indicators for how to recognize the GT for what it is—unprecedented distress and suffering which will be not only physical but spiritual.

The most sober feature is that hardly anyone will survive these days. Yet certainly the emphasis is on believing the Gospel even if it means physical death for his sake (martyrdom). "Everlasting life" is preferable to "everlasting torment/punishment" (25:46).

Paul Warns about False Understanding of the Antichrist and the GT

We now consider the apostle Paul. He addresses the Antichrist and the GT in several of his letters, but does this most clearly in 2 Thessalonians 1 and 2. In chapter 1 Paul uses some of the strongest terms in the Bible to describe what the return of Christ will be like at the end of the GT. His words fill out what Jesus meant when he said that he will return in "power and great glory" (Matt 24:30). This text is more appropriate for the next chapter of this book where we will show how God will intervene during the Great Tribulation.

2 Thessalonians 2 presents most clearly what happens at the beginning of the GT. Paul describes the person of the Antichrist (whom we dealt with in an earlier chapter of this book) and what the GT will be like. Indeed, the occasion for Paul's writing on these topics arose from a misunderstanding of both what the GT would be like and when it would begin. And Paul's concern to correct these matters more fully informs us than what we know thus far about the GT.

Paul corrects the Thessalonian believers regarding their belief that the "day of the Lord has come" or "already arrived."

- Paul disavows such a belief: it did not come from him when he was with them and taught for a few weeks (according to Acts 17:1–9), nor from a "spirit or a message or a letter as if from us" (2 Thess 2:2).

- Paul had to correct this belief since it had shaken their "composure" and "disturbed them" (v 2).

- Moreover, the new teaching was deceitful (v 3).

The Day of the Lord by Another Name Is the GT

What is the day of the Lord that these early believers misunderstood? It is a phrase widely used in the Old Testament and carried over to the New Testament.

- It refers to the time when God will both judge the nations and come to reign over his people in blessing.

- It is a broad designation and somewhat parallel to the time of the end.

- The judgment is a time of darkness and God's wrath (Isa 13:6–11; Joel 1:15; 2:1–2 (in 2:2 it is a unique day of judgment, much like Dan 12:1 asserts); Amos 5:18–20; Zeph 1:14–18; 3:14–17; Zech 14:1–15).

- But it is also a time of deliverance and blessing for God's people (Isa 2:1–3 [the "last days"]; 11:1–9; 30:23–26; Joel 2:28–32; Zech 14:16–21; Matt 19:28; Acts 3:19–21.

- The prophets sometimes easily move from the judgment of the nations to the blessing of God's people (Joel 2:18–3:3; 3:9–16).

- Some "days of the Lord" predicted in the Old Testament have been fulfilled (Joel 2:1–11; Amos 5:18), but even they are portents, adumbrations, of what God is going to do on a greater scale at the end of time.

In his first letter to the Thessalonians (1 Thess 5:1–11), Paul warns that the Day of the Lord

- comes like a thief in the night;

- means sudden destruction when people are proclaiming "peace and safety" (v 2–3);

- is associated with sleeping during the night and with darkness, with drunkenness, and with a destination of wrath determined by God (vv 4–9).

In light of our discoveries from the book of Daniel and from Jesus Christ the day of the Lord is the time of the GT. Paul had instructed about this day but the Thessalonians had distorted the timing of the day.

New Traits of the GT: the Restrainer Removed, Lawlessness, and Satanic Deception

Paul asserts that the GT starts after (not before) two events occur.

- The "rebellion" (Gr *apostasia*) must come first, and the "man of lawlessness" must be revealed first, prior to the Day of the Lord.

- The "rebellion" may refer to the rebellion of nations (as Ps 2:13); or it may refer to the "departure" of Christians from the truth of the gospel; or it may refer to the departure of Christians at the Rapture (Rexit). We prefer the idea of the Rapture which is in the context (v 1).

Once the restrainer (probably government and law) of lawlessness has been removed (2 Thess 2:6–7), the Antichrist will appear as the "man of lawlessness" (see chapter 1 in *The Apocalypse Is Coming* for the identification of the "restrainer").

- He will lend his character to the GT, making it the time of "lawlessness" (vv 8-9; as Daniel predicted, Dan 7:25). These words suggest that much of the GT will be characterized by anarchy, rioting, protests, mob rule, vigilantism, citizen courts, rebellion, pockets of armed resistance, rogue armies, and other forms of unrest and discord—at least during the initial stages of the GT.

- The Antichrist stirs up all such discord in order to step in and by his magic formula bring order and stability.

- But it will be a totalitarian rule: his rule or no rule.

- Yet people will prefer this loss of freedom to its alternative, the chaos that rocked the world.

God Compounds the Deceit during the GT

Assisting the rise of the Antichrist to power will be deceit from Satan (v 9). Several phrases make the GT the time of unprecedented deceit.

- It will be the time when the Antichrist works his false miracles, signs, and wonders by "Satanic empowerment," with all the "deception of wickedness" for those who don't "love the truth."

- God "will send a deluding influence" so that people "believe what is false."

- The end result is that those "who did not believe the truth but took pleasure in wickedness" may be "judged."

- Note how the Apostle Paul juxtaposes truth and deceit in several ways.

The mention of "Satanic empowerment" is a reminder that again, as discussed above, there are unseen forces of darkness, i.e., demons, who are promoting evil without restraint. By various supernatural ways the world of humanity will be amazed, captivated, and mesmerized by demonic activity. They will be blind to the truth. Think of the many cults and false religions that have blinded people from the beginning until now.

We can conclude that the GT is a time chiefly characterized by great deceit because people have rejected the One who is the truth (John 14:6). They have decided for the false Christ and his wonder-maker, Satan himself. The book of Revelation will underscore these facts.

The GT in John's Epistles: The Last Hour Closes the Opportunity to Repent

The Apostle John uniquely gives to the opponent and supplanter of Jesus Christ the title of the Antichrist.

- Adumbrations and precursors of him arise repeatedly in history ("many antichrists have appeared"; 1 John 2:18), giving all such occasions the character of the "last hour." In our modern times we can think of Hitler and Stalin and Mao and other murderous dictators who have targeted the Jews and Christians for extermination.

- Everyone is an "antichrist" who gives allegiance to and worships someone else and denies that Jesus Christ is truly divine and truly human (2:22–23; 4:1–3).

- But *the* final Antichrist will take this falsehood to the point where the world will worship him, truly ushering in *the* last hour, the GT.

- *All other "last hours" gain their credibility from the final "last hour."*

- As John in his day entirely dismissed the possibility that the "many antichrists" could repent and return to the truth (2:19) so it will be in the GT.

Those who embrace the Antichrist during the GT and receive his mark become little antichrists themselves and are forever condemned and lost.

The Book of Revelation Expands on the Terror of the GT

The final revelation of what the GT is like occurs, fittingly, in the final book of the Bible. All kinds of pictures and symbols jump off the pages to complete our picture of this terrible time.

- Evil, demonic forces are in play;

- the mark that identifies the Antichrist is identified;

- one-half of humanity dies;

- the persecution of Christians and Jews;

- how the GT ends in the greatest battle of all time, the Battle of Armageddon.

Warning: Beware of Contemporary Attempts to Destroy the Witness of the Revelation

As part of the deceit of the GT, the Antichrist and his "religious" co-conspirators will do all they can to keep you from reading and studying the book of Revelation. While it has many symbols, these all mean something that is real/actual and the following interpretations reflect what Christians have in general always believed. The devil and the Antichrist do not want you reading this or any prophecies about the end lest you be convicted by the truth, repent, and be saved.

Early Warnings To Evangelical Churches about the GT

In the very first chapters we are given hints of what the GT will be like. The seven churches addressed in chapters 2–3 are faulted for their:

- having fallen "from their first love" (2:4);

- "eating things sacrificed to idols and committing sexual immorality" (2:14, 20);

- adultery (2:22) and the "deep things of Satan" (2:24);

- being "dead" (3:1);

- being "lukewarm" (3:16); and though they thought they were "wealthy" they were actually "wretched, miserable, poor, blind, and naked" (3:17). They failed to warn the world of impending judgment.

All these sins of the historical churches of John's day (about AD 90) are portents of greater evil to come in evangelical churches today.

Yet let's not forget this. At the end of every one of the messages to the seven churches there is a promise to the overcomer who strives to be faithful to the Lord Jesus. This person will "buck" the trend. Such an overcomer during the GT will have tremendous reward.

The Suffering of the GT Has Two Dimensions: Divinely Caused and Human Caused

But when we enter into the chapters (6–19) that describe the end, that is, the GT, the judgments sent by God form the emphasis of this time.

- God's judgments come in the forms of the seals, the trumps, and the vials or bowls. These are the three series wherein God's wrath is actualized on the earth on unbelieving men and women who take the mark of the Antichrist and swear allegiance to him.

- God delivers all the believers from all these divine judgments (Rev 7:3; 9:4).

Thus, there are two dimensions to the suffering of the GT in the book of Revelation.

- One dimension is what God does: he unleashes his wrath upon a mankind that has no redeeming value. They have deserted the Creator of the universe and denied the one true Savior. Their minds have become reprobate and God has abandoned them to all sorts of evil (graphically stated in Romans 1:18–32). They embrace the Antichrist as their savior and redeemer. This is the dimension of the divinely caused suffering. It is the concern of the next chapter of this book.

- The other dimension of the suffering of the GT derives from what the Antichrist, the false prophet, and Satan (the unholy trinity) bring upon the world. The preceding pages depicting the GT as taught by Daniel, the Lord Jesus, Paul, and John focus on this "man-made," the human caused suffering. In a certain sense this suffering is self-inflicted, though blindly so.

The Second Dimension of Suffering: Human Caused (by the Antichrist)

Thus, leaving the divinely-caused suffering till the next chapter, what does the Revelation tell us about the terrible suffering that the Antichrist and his programs inflict upon the world?

It is interesting that the first series of judgments (the seals, Rev 6) from God have an element in them that involves a human origin in certain respects. While they are sent/allowed by God and serve his plan (Rev 6:1–8), human beings are the agents of them to a great extent. The divine dimension contributes to the overall experience of the world in its rebellion against God.

The Four Horsemen (Rev 6) of the Seven Seals

The seal judgments are actually those that God sends. We present these in greater detail in the next chapter of this book. But it is appropriate in describing the GT to present them in summary here.

The first four seals are explained in the text. The first consists of a white horse (signifying conquest), a red horse (signifying war and killing), a black horse (signifying famine), and an ashen horse (death and Hades, signifying the *death of ¼ of mankind*).

One Fourth of the World's Population Dies

This very last feature shows how the "great tribulation" is no ordinary time of suffering from war, famine, and plagues (6:8).

The fifth seal gives no judgment on the earth but views in heaven the souls of those who have been martyred by those on earth (by the Antichrist and his followers). They cry out that their blood should be avenged (6:9–11). They are told to wait a little while until their number is complete.

The sixth seal is quite stark and overwhelming in its impact. When Jesus opens the seal, great cataclysms come that give definition to the "wrath of God" as never before (see the next chapter).

The next series of the trumpet and bowl judgments are increasingly weighty. They take place during the second half (the 3 ½ years of Daniel 7 and 12; and Matt 24:15) leading up to the very return of Jesus Christ in "power and great glory" at the Battle of Armageddon (Rev 19). See the next chapter of this book for the content of the trumpets and bowls.

What Happens to God's People During the GT?

For believers during the GT there is great encouragement. They will be supernaturally spared from God's judgments by being sealed/ protected from them (Rev 7:3; 9:4). This promise is especially comforting for the 144,000 Jews. Later a great multitude of glorified saints, Jews and Gentiles, are revealed in heaven. Though martyred by the Antichrist during "*the* great tribulation" (Rev 7:14) they worship God and the Lamb who gives them special care and deliverance in heaven (7:9–17). This section of the Revelation answers the question: What happens to God's people during the GT? God specially protects his own; and those who die are in heaven with Jesus Christ.

The Special Debut of the Two Witnesses Who Are Killed by the Antichrist

Before we get to the final series of divine judgments revealed in Revelation 16, we gain further insight about the work of the Antichrist and what happens during the second half of the GT.

Several events occur during the trumpet judgments (chs 8–9). Chapter 11 is a graphic record of God's interacting with events on earth under the control of the Antichrist. God sends two supernatural witnesses to evangelize and prophesy during the second half of the GT—during the time of the sixth trumpet (also called the "second woe"; Rev 11:14).

- They are associated with a rebuilt temple, which the Antichrist has allowed but has desecrated at the midpoint of the GT (Dan 9:26–27; Matt 24:15; 2 Thess 2:4).

- The two witnesses prophesy for 1260 days.

- They call on the world to repent while they bring worldwide plagues.

- They "torment" the earth's inhabitants (11:10).

When the two witnesses have finished their time of prophesying near the end of the GT, God permits the Antichrist to kill them. For the first time in the Revelation the Antichrist is here identified as the "beast" (see chapter 13 of this book). He arises out of the abyss and will make "war with them and overcome them and kill them" (11:7). The whole world rejoices over their death and celebrates. God permits this act for greater ends.

But after three and a half days their unburied bodies come alive.

- They are resurrected in response to God's call to "come up here"; and they go to heaven (vv 11–12).

- This event strikes great fear in the people who watch.

- Then a great earthquake destroys a tenth of the city (Jerusalem) and kills 7000 people.

- Terrified, the rest of the people give glory to God. (Interestingly, this is one of the very few places where such judgments bring repentance. Otherwise, people become more and more hardened).

Why This Episode of the Two Witnesses?

What is the intent of this episode?

- God demonstrates that even during the time of deepest darkness, deceit, and suffering, in the last half of the GT, God still has his witnesses who herald the truth and he still seeks to bring deliverance to any who repent.

- They reflect in part what the Rapture is: the immediate resurrection of believers to heaven.

- More importantly, this passage introduces the reader to the Antichrist. His origin is deeply troubling.

- The Antichrist arises from the place of demons, the abyss (see earlier chapters of this book for the implications of this origin). The text also identifies this as the same period of 3 ½ years.

Key Players in the Great Drama of the GT in Revelation 12

Several chapters fill in the total picture of what the last half of the GT will involve. Chapter 12 reveals the key players in the unfolding drama that is the second half of the GT. These are the woman, a red dragon, the male child (Jesus Christ), the beast from the sea, and the beast out of the earth.

The Woman Is Israel

The woman is a "great sign" appearing in heaven (12:1–2). "Clothed with the sun, and the moon under her feet, and on her head a crown of twelve stars," she is pregnant and about to give birth. She represents the nation of Israel with its twelve tribes.

The Red Dragon Is Satan Emboldened

Another sign appearing in heaven is a "great red dragon having seven heads and ten horns, and on his heads were seven crowns" (12:3).

- With his tail he swept away one-third of the stars of heaven and "hurled them to the earth."

- He stood before the woman and waited for the child to be born so that he might devour the child.

- Verse 9 identifies the dragon as "the devil and Satan, who deceives the whole world."

- The seven heads and ten horns and seven crowns are explained in chapter 13 where these also belong to the Antichrist.

The Man Child Is Jesus Christ

The drama continues. Jesus Christ is born to the woman; he is destined to rule the world with a "rod of iron" (as prophesied in Psalm 2). Before the dragon could devour the child, the child is snatched up to heaven. The woman escapes to the wilderness where God has a place prepared for her "for 1260 days" (12:6).

Thus, the text jumps from the time of the birth of Christ and his special deliverance to the events of the GT—from his first Advent to his second Advent. The time indicator of 1260 days is equal to the last 3 ½ years of the GT, just as we discovered in Daniel 7:25 and 12:7.

The War in Heaven

Adding to the suspense, a war surprisingly erupts in heaven during the events of the GT.

- Michael (a chief angel who was introduced in Daniel 10 and 12:1 as the "protector of Israel") and his angels wage war with the dragon (Satan) and his angels (fallen angels; demons).

- Satan and his angels lose the war and they are cast down to the earth (vv 7–9). Apparently, this means that the one-third of the angels who rebelled with Satan against God before God created the world (12:4; Gen 1:1–2) are from this point, the mid-point of the GT, denied access to heaven for ever more.

In the following verses (vv 10–12) the believers in heaven celebrate the defeat of Satan identified as the "accuser of the brothers."

- As his daily practice Satan had accused the believers.

- But they have overcome him by the "blood of the Lamb" and by their testimony even when it led to their martyrdom.

- They warn the inhabitants of earth that Satan, now defeated and full of wrath, has come to earth to vent his wrath there.

- He now knows that "he has only a short time" to exist during the last half of the GT before God fulfills his plan that will first bind him and then destroy him forever.

- This is the only place in the Bible that clearly prophesies the end of Satan before it is realized (in Rev 20).

Satan's Obsessive Anger toward Israel and Christians during the GT

During the second half of the GT Satan seeks to persecute the woman (Israel) with renewed vengeance. But God supernaturally shelters and preserves the woman in the wilderness for "time, times, and half a time" (v 14; cf Dan 7:25; 12:7). This time signals the same period appearing elsewhere as 1260 days (11:3; 12:6) and forty-two months (11:2). This demonstrates an amazing correspondence among several prophecies all pointing to the last half of the seven years of the GT (which Daniel first signals in 7:25 and 9:27).

The drama of chapter 12 closes by noting that the enraged dragon goes off to make war with the "rest of her [the woman's] children," namely Jews and Christians—they who "keep the commandments of God and hold the testimony of Jesus" (v 17).

The very next words introduce us to the work of the Antichrist during the GT (13:1–10).

The Works of the Antichrist in the GT

Chapter 13 describes the works of the satanically inspired Antichrist, here called the "beast" (13:2). We described the works of the Antichrist in an earlier chapter of this book, so it is unnecessary to go over this ground again. Here it is only necessary to comment on the conditions that will prevail during the GT.

The Antichrist brings terrifying tyranny.

- Twice the text says that he "makes war" against God's people with the entire world consenting (13:3-8).

- Universal adoration of the Antichrist and of Satan prevails. Imagine: people worship the devil! (v 4).

- The false prophet, the stooge of the Antichrist, even performs miracles, including calling down fire from heaven, to deceive the world so that all worship the blasphemous Antichrist (vv 5, 6, 13).

- Murder becomes as common as buying and selling. All who do not take the mark of the Antichrist (666) and worship him will be murdered (vv 15–18).

- All this will go on for forty-two months (v 5).

Rewards for the Martyred in Heaven and Encouragement for Believers on Earth

Chapter 14 reveals what happens to God's people who refuse to compromise. They appear in heaven in the presence of the Lamb where they enjoy the rewards of their fidelity to the Lamb.

Back on earth an angel calls on the inhabitants to "fear God and give glory to him" and "worship him." Clearly this opposes the call that the Antichrist delivers. The hour of God's judgment is at hand (v 7; this no doubt anticipates the judgments of the trumpets). Another angel announces the destruction of Babylon, which will bring great calamity to the world's people, as described in Revelation 18.

The rest of chapter 14 is one of the most graphic descriptions of judgment in the entire Bible. God will exact judgment upon the Antichrist and his followers who bear the mark of 666. No doubt the actual terms of the judgment occur in the seven bowls (ch 16). I quote the words of the judgment in the next chapter of this book. Finally, the chapter concludes with two pictures of the harvest of the wicked (vv 14–20; cf Matt 13).

The Final Seven Bowls of Judgement:

Earth As We Know It Is Obliterated

After another scene of the martyred victors in heaven and the seven angels bearing the seven bowls of judgment (ch 15), the scene shifts again to earth to the final days of calamity ending the GT (ch 16). The seven bowls are the seventh trumpet and third "woe." They are terrifying and destroy all life on earth. We relate the details in the next chapter of this book.

Yet these judgments are the response to the dimension of the humanly caused suffering due to the rebellion of earth's inhabitants. Suffice it to say that the final days of the GT reveal God's severest judgments ever given (see details about their extent in the next chapter):

- The seven bowls begin with painful sores upon all.

- Then all water becomes blood and undrinkable;

- the sun burns people, then darkness envelops them;

- then demons go out to draw all the kings of the world to Armageddon in Israel.

- Finally, the greatest earthquake since the creation of Adam and Eve shakes the earth so that all the cities of the nations are destroyed, all islands sink below the oceans, and all mountains are levelled. The capstone of this judgment is an "extremely severe" storm that rains down hailstones weighing 100 pounds each.

- The response of people is as hardened as before: they blaspheme God.

There can be little doubt that this end of the GT marks the end of earth as we know it. One event remains: the Battle of Armageddon (Rev 19).

Evil Political Power Is United with Corrupted Religious Power during the GT

Chapter 17 reveals a new detail of the GT. While the Antichrist exercises his political and military power, he does so in close alliance with all false religion. This chapter informs us that during the first half of the GT, the Antichrist will support all religions as he cements his total rise to power. He supports the woman dressed like a queen, yet she is filthy. She holds in her hand a goblet full of all the "abominations and the unclean things of her sexual immorality" (v 4). Further, she is described as "Babylon the Great, the Mother of harlots and of the abominations of the earth" (v 5). The reference is to the beginning of false worship at the Tower of Babel (Gen 11) that has continued throughout history. All the kings of the earth have committed sexual immorality with her ever since, instead of worshipping the true God as revealed in the Bible. The woman is filled with the "blood of the saints and with the blood of the witnesses of Jesus." Thus, she has martyred all the true followers of God throughout history.

The Antichrist uses the world's religions to aid his rise to world ruler. Then at the midpoint of the GT he along with the ten kings (called "horns") will turn against religion and destroy her (vv 15-16). He will then demand total worship of himself as God (as revealed in Daniel, Paul, and earlier in the Revelation), allowing no rivals. Yet this fulfills God's plan (v 17).

Chapter 18 describes in detail the destruction of the world's religions personified as a prostitute. Many enriched themselves from her. Kings (v 9), merchants (v 11), and shipmasters and sailors (v 17) lament her sudden destruction. She will never be inhabited again (vv 21–24). But the Antichrist will be eager to step into the vacuum to receive the world's adulation and worship.

Thus *the GT will be the most religious period in human memory.* This is part of the deception of the time that the Bible warns about. Probably even false specimens of Judaism and Christianity will flourish. But at the end of the first half of the GT the Antichrist with Satanic authority and power will move to deify himself.

> *Readers need to beware of being ensnared into a form of Christianity that seems all good but fails to exalt the redemption secured on the cross by Jesus Christ and his resurrection.*

The GT Comes to Its End at the Battle of Armageddon

We finally arrive, exhausted, at the conclusion of the seven years of the GT revealed in the Bible and fixed in history. The Battle of Armageddon features the armies of the world drawn to the Plain of Esdraelon in northern Israel. While the Battle is the mad design of Satan and the demons under his control (as described in Rev 16), the

Battle is God's way of bringing the world's armies under the world leader, the Antichrist, to a crushing, final defeat. None will survive.

The outcome of the greatest battle in all the world's history is not in doubt. Four "hallelujahs" proclaim the predetermined outcome (19:1–6). Jesus's return is imminent and his "wedding feast" with his saints has just been accomplished (vv 7–10).

The Forces Involved at Armageddon

The Antichrist's forces include the armies of the "kings of the entire world" (16:14) plus 200,000,000 demons (9:16). But the Warrior, Jesus Christ, comes from heaven with his armies of glorified saints (a "number which no one could count," Rev 7:9) and angels (who in Rev 5:11 number 100,000,000,000,000,000). Note also that both angels and glorified saints cannot be seen! Recall too that the creation itself is under the control of Jesus Christ (6:12–14; 16:1–21).

Other texts describe this consummate battle, with gory details, both in the OT (Zech 14) and in the NT (Matt 24; 2 Thess 1; 2 Pet 3). Revelation details the special names, clothing, and implements of Jesus Christ the Warrior from heaven (19:11–18; an earlier chapter of this book explains the details). In the concluding verses we discover how the GT ends at Armageddon (vv 19–21). (Note how the last detail below was prophesied in Ezek 39). (Note more details of the B of Armageddon in *The Apocalypse Is Coming*, ch 14).

And I saw the beast and the kings of the earth and their armies, assembled to make war against him who sat on the horse, and against his army. (20) And the beast was seized, and with him the false prophet who performed the signs in his presence, by which he deceived those who had received the mark of the beast and those who worshipped his image; these two were thrown alive into the lake of fire, which burns with brimstone. (21) And the rest were killed with the sword which came from the mouth of him who sat on the horse, and all the birds were filled with their flesh.

Thus, the story of man's greatest act of rebellion comes to an end. All opponents of Jesus Christ are killed/destroyed. The Antichrist is no more, just as Daniel prophesied (Dan 7:11, 26).

The Terrifying Concentration of Evil during the Second Half of the GT

Notice the tremendous alignment of strategic, evil events that unfold during the last half of the GT:

- Antichrist's breaking his covenant with Israel;

- his attempt to destroy Israel;

- the testimony and death of the two witnesses;

- Antichrist's power to conquer death, drawing the world's amazement;

- Antichrist's claim to world-wide worship by means of the idol made by the false prophet;

- the mark (666) of the Antichrist without which people will die;

- the trumpet and bowl judgments (catastrophic and worldwide);

- the Antichrist's destruction of "Babylon the Great Harlot" (all false religion)";

- the Antichrist's consolidation of all political, military, economic, and religious power in himself;

- the end, the destruction of the Antichrist in the everlasting lake of fire.

With all the impact that the prophecies have on our thinking about the end, let's not forget the bedrock of what the Christian faith is—the cross of Christ. I quote Oswald Chambers (*My Utmost for His Highest*, 330): "In external history the Cross is an infinitesimal thing; from the Bible point of view, it is of more importance than all the empires of the world." This book concentrates on the course of the world empires and their demise, but let's not forget the centrality of the cross. Only by the cross can anyone escape the coming judgments.

Chapter 16

God Takes Revenge on a Rebellious World

Seven Years of Carnage and Death Until the End

Bill Archer began to make his way through the rubble to his buddy's house. Bill had bowled with Tony for several years and Bill counted him among his closest friends.

Bill decided to make the mile walk to Tony's; he wanted to know if his neighborhood was in as much chaos as his own. While many of his neighbors had lost almost everything in the great earthquakes, they had become, strangely, very religious. He observed that many of his neighbors had suddenly embraced the idea that Jesus Christ had already returned to earth. His neighbor, Sam, came up to him and claimed that Jesus had visited him and even done a miracle in healing his wife's broken leg. Others swore up and down that Jesus had appeared to them as well. When Bill asked how Jesus could appear in so many places at the same time his neighbors answered with the quick retort: Don't you believe that Jesus is God, that he can do anything?

Such a question caught Bill off guard. He didn't know what to say. But he was deeply troubled. On his way Bill passed by street evangelists proclaiming that Jesus would appear in their neighborhoods, too. Someone thrust a religious pamphlet into Bill's hands. The title was almost completely smeared but it said something about how to recognize the signs of Jesus's presence. Still, Bill was deeply stirred. Having just placed his faith in Christ as his Savior Bill felt that all the frenzy about finding Jesus in one's house was going too far—or was it?

Bill recalled Jesus's words from the last discourse he gave to his disciples. He warned them that such claims that he could be found in this or that house were not to be believed. Because when he did return to earth his coming would be recognized world-wide. He would come in "power and great glory" so that instantly all the world would know. There would be signs in the heavens. This is what Jesus said, and Bill refused to be taken in by the new "prophets." But how could they be explained?

All of this new religiosity made Bill hasten his walk to Tony's. As he passed over several cross streets, Bill was shocked by what he saw. About a hundred feet down one street he observed a middle-aged man running around his house totally undressed. Farther down the street, he observed a city patrolman shooting off his service revolver into a tree. The noise was deafening, but the neighbors were cheering. Across the street a man chased a woman with a lasso.

At another corner the convenience store was being vandalized by three hooded thugs. Broken glass was all over the sidewalk. When the clerk tried to stop the rampaging one of the men dressed in black clubbed him repeatedly until he lay in a pool of blood in the street. The vandals rushed out into the street with arms full of drinks and snacks and soon disappeared.

As he rounded the corner and came to the head of Tony's street, Bill couldn't believe his eyes. There in the middle of a circle of ten or twelve people was Tony. He was practically undressed. Dancing in a frenzy he had cut himself several times and blood was flowing. The people in the circle screamed for him to cut more and more. When a husky neighbor came out of a house and lassoed Tony to restrain him, the men and women yelled obscenities at him. Tony was able to snap the rope as though it were a string. Others in the circle began taking their clothes off.

All of a sudden Tony began screaming in another, deeper voice what seemed gibberish at first. But then Bill realized that he was hearing wild cries invoking Satan. Tony was imploring Satan to take his body as a living sacrifice. The people began chanting with Tony. Soon several were passing a knife around and cutting themselves. More and more blood ran down the gutter. Some began collapsing from exhaustion and lack of blood.

Then Bill saw foam coming out of Tony's mouth. He was wild-eyed: his eyes were almost bulging out of their sockets. His hair was plastered from blood flowing from his scalp. His hands and arms were shaking uncontrollably. Others in the circle began to mimic Tony.

Neighbors began pouring into the street and began yelling at the people in the circle. Then Bill saw Tony run into his house and returned with an AR-15 rifle. Shots rang out and several neighbors were hit. Now even more blood was flowing.

Just as Bill thought, "Where are the police?" a black and white pulled up with lights flashing. Two officers jumped out. But instead of trying to stop the crimes the officers holstered their weapons and joined in the melee. It seemed that their commitment to public safety had vaporized as they committed to mass hysteria and bloodshed.

"How could this be?" Bill thought. But just then he remembered the warning that he read from the Book of Revelation. Near the end of the Great Tribulation hordes of demons would be released from the abyss and take possession of vast numbers of humanity.

This must be what demon possession and oppression look like, Bill thought: self-mutilation, murder, sexual deviancy, lawlessness, great deceit, and unnatural acts of power. Many in the circle were praising Satan for the freedom he had given them. They worshipped a head bust of the Leader who had appeared last month to take control of the world.

Bill became conscious of his own predicament and safety. Tony saw Bill and began yelling at him to join the circle. For a moment Bill entertained the thought of trying to help Tony, his friend. But he shuddered at the thought of being possessed by demons. Instantly Bill's mind was filled with the promise of the Bible that God was with him, that he had within him the Holy Spirit sent for the very reason of delivering Christians from the unseen spiritual forces of darkness.

Fearing a bloodied and shrieking Tony who was approaching with his weapon, Bill began backing up, then turned and ran for home. Shots rang out but none hit him.

"I never imagined just how deceitful and destructive demon possession could be," he reflected. "Friends become enemies. The book of Revelation is true after all."

Chapter 16

God Takes Revenge on a Rebellious World

Seven Years of Carnage and Death Until the End

We come to the final chapter in this series that deal with the three great movements that culminate history. First comes the rise of the satanic-inspired Antichrist to usurp control of the world's governments. Then unfolds the seven-year Great Tribulation which brings the worse suffering that the world has ever known (including earthquakes that level mountains and swallow islands, volcanoes, tsunamis, wars, anarchies, pandemics and pestilences, famines, and death). Third, God reveals his *divine* judgements that will wipe out one-half of all humanity, and eventually the rest of humanity at the Battle of Armageddon.

This is the most frightening chapter of this part of the book. Frightening because the end is frightening. Imagine: all history and the contemporary world of humanity cease to exist—they come to an end!!

Is this all really going to happen? We address this matter in this chapter and in the postscript.

How to Read This Chapter

As indicated in earlier chapters, you can read all the content of this chapter to get a full understanding of God's final judgments. Or you can read only the bold paragraph headings to get a quick overview of the contents of the chapter.

Part 1

Anticipation of the Great Tribulation

Before proceeding to show from the book of the Revelation just what God's vengeance at the end of the age will be, we want to lay a foundation of various truths that will help us understand that time. The next few pages present some principles to help us deal with the enormity of suffering then. They show that the judgments of the Revelation have precursors from history.

In the Great Tribulation (GT), Judgment Surmounts Grace

God is Both Loving and Holy

The matters of salvation and forgiveness give proof to the love of God "for the world." John 3:16 proclaims: "For God so loved the world that he gave his one and only Son that everyone who believes in him should not perish but should have eternal life."

This verse is probably the favorite verse of Christians. It most clearly describes how everyone can be saved based in the love of God.

But note the word "perish." God is also holy and will punish those who rebel against him, who spurn his offer of salvation and think that they can save themselves. The verses that follow (3:18b–19) assert:

> He who does not believe has already been condemned, because he has not believed in the name of the one and only Son of God. (19) And this is the judgment that the light has come into the world and men loved the darkness more than the light; for their deeds were evil.

Verse 36 strongly warns about rejecting God's offer of salvation: "The one who believes in the Son has eternal life; but the one who does not obey the Son will not see life, but the wrath of God remains on him."

Note the word "wrath." End-time wrath begins during the great tribulation and ends at the end of it—at the Battle of Armageddon. This is the only time of special, divine wrath.

In his beloved "Upper Room Discourse" given just before he died, Jesus said that he was about to send the Holy Spirit. He would convict the world of sin, righteousness, and judgment (John 16:8–11).

The Warning of 2 Peter 3:7-10: God's Patience Has a Limit

The Apostle Peter soberly warns that there will come an end to God's patience—with his toleration of evil.

> By his word the present heavens and earth are being reserved for fire, kept for the day of judgment and destruction of ungodly people. (8) But do not let this one fact escape your notice, beloved, that with the Lord one day is like a thousand years, and a thousand years like one day. (9) The Lord is not slow about his promise, as some count slowness, but is patient toward you, not willing for any to perish, but for all to come to repentance. (10) But the day of the Lord will come like a thief, in which the heavens will pass away with a roar and the elements will be destroyed with intense heat, and the earth and its works will be worthless (or, burned up).

The GT Is the Time of *God's* Wrath

The GT is God's appointed time of judgment, of displaying his attitude toward sin. God has determined the timing of this period and how it will unfold (see below the various series of judgments). The GT is part of his plan. As with the flood of Genesis, he is the cause of the GT.

First: A Great Principle Is Illustrated by the Bible and History:

God Delivers the Righteous from the Judgment Falling on the Unrighteous

A quick survey of earlier judgments in history demonstrates the principle: humanity can become so evil that God must intervene in order to save a few and to prevent the entire extermination of the human race. God will not destroy the righteous with the wicked (Gen 18:25).

The greatest illustration of this principle is the Flood at the time of Noah (Genesis chs 6–8). God destroyed all humanity (except for the family of Noah) because the hearts of people were "only evil continually" (see Gen 6:5). During the GT the culpability of humanity will be even worse, since people now have greater knowledge of God's love and the gift of his Son that people during Noah's day never knew.

God saved Lot and his family from the destruction of Sodom and Gomorrah (Gen 13:13; chs 18–19). Indeed, Peter cites three examples (2 Pet 2:4–22) of this principle: the angels; Noah; and Lot (vv 4–10). Another example is that of Ebed-Melech. During the time of Jeremiah, about 600 years BC, God delivered him from the Babylonian Captivity because he "trusted" God (Jer 39:16–18).

The Same Principle Prevails During the Time of the End

At the time of the end this same principle prevails. Jesus promised to keep his people "from the hour of trial coming on the earth dwellers"—words referring to the wicked of earth (Rev 3:15). And he has kept his promise. Not long ago, by the Rapture, God delivered the righteous, perhaps numbering in the billions. We call this "Rexit" because it is the exit of believers at the Rapture. Those unbelievers who remain behind go through the GT and suffer the evil lawlessness of the Antichrist and the wrath of God poured out in a manner never before seen on the face of the earth. But even during the GT many will be saved and protected from God's wrath. They will live on into the millennial kingdom (so Rev 20).

Jesus Christ Is the Agent of All Judgments during the GT

How could it be that the loving Lord Jesus Christ could administer this wrath?

The response is this. What else could God do when this world rejects and spurns God's offer of salvation in Christ and instead gives its adulation to the fake Christ, the Antichrist?

Jesus has addressed judgment and wrath on several occasions. In fact, Jesus speaks four times more frequently about hell and judgment than he speaks about heaven.

For example, in Luke 13:1-5 Jesus raised the question about those whom Pilate murdered or the thirteen on whom the tower of Siloam fell. He asked whether they were worse sinners because of what happened to them. His answer regarding both groups was this: "No, I tell you, but unless you repent, you will all likewise perish." The point is that all "tragedies" bringing death are portents of eternal death unless people repent beforehand.

This principle was never more important than for those living during the GT.

How Severe Is God's Judgment During the Great Tribulation?

As Great as the Flood *Was*, The GT *Is* Greater

Jesus himself compares the two events of the Flood and his return, and they occur in contexts of the time of the end (Matt 24:37–39).

- For the coming of the Son of Man will be just like the days of Noah. (38) For as in those days before the flood they were eating and drinking, marrying and giving in marriage, until the day that Noah entered the ark, (39) and they did not understand until the flood came and took them all away; so will the coming of the Son of Man be.

- Using some of the strongest language the Apostle Peter also compares the Flood with the coming of Christ and the day of judgment (2 Pet 3:3–7).

Jesus Finds Warning of the End in the Story of Jonah

It Involves Not Only the Story of a Great Fish But a Warning for the End Times

It is appropriate to mention here the example of Jonah because Jesus pointed to him on two occasions for two different reasons. Jonah's experience in the belly of the great fish for three days and nights illustrates the time for how long Jesus would be dead in the grave prior to his resurrection (Matt 12:38–40). The other reason is that Jonah is a "sign of the times" (Matt 16:4). He illustrates the reality that at the end people need to repent but refuse to do so (unlike those of Nineveh). The people of Nineveh "will stand up with this generation at the judgment, and will condemn it" (Matt 12:41), Jesus warned.

If the people of Nineveh condemn the generation of Jesus's day, they will have even greater reason to condemn the present generation existing prior to and after the Rapture. Thus, even during his time of ministry on earth Jesus gave many indications that at his second advent he will exercise the judgment of God.

God's Intervention by Judgment Was Prophesied by Daniel

Virtually all the prophets of the Old Testament, as well as passages in the Law and in the Psalms, proclaim that God intervenes in judgment by various ways. The previous chapters of this book show that Daniel strongly exposes the divine interventions of judgment (Dan 2; 7; 9; and 12).

Why Is God's Judgment So Severe During the Great Tribulation?

Answer: The Extent of Evil

The only justification for such suffering and destruction during the GT is the great evil of humanity. The restraining effect that the Spirit exercises through Christians acting across cultures was largely eliminated when the Rapture occurred. With the Spirit's influence diminished, people are left to imagine and pursue all sorts of the most loathsome and sordid sins and wicked behavior ever conceived.

The sin that was Israel's worst and that led to the demise of the nation in the 6th century BC, after about 1000 years of prosperity, was idolatry. And the idolatry of the GT—the worship of the Antichrist and his image made by the false prophet (Rev 13)—will be on a scale never seen before (as shown below).

During the GT People Refuse to Repent Even in the Face of Unprecedented Suffering

In addition, in the latter half of the GT humanity will add to their culpability by becoming so hardened in their rejection of God and his offer of salvation that they will refuse to repent. On several occasions Revelation reports such intransigence and hardness of heart when the judgments of the seals, trumpets, and bowls of wrath occur (Rev

6:15–17; 9:6, 20–21; 16:9, 11, 21). These judgments are God's *active* demonstrations of his wrath.

Just How Wrathful Is God's Wrath... and Why?

Two Words Tell Us

As a further underpinning of the depth and breadth of God's anger during the time of the GT it is helpful to reflect briefly on the meaning of "wrath" and its usage in the Bible.

Two Greek words are used to describe God's anger: *orges* and *thymas*. It is common to understand that *orges* (in Rev six times) refers to a settled attitude of anger, sometimes with the purpose of revenge. The term *thymas* (used ten times in Rev; seven times of the wrath of God) refers to an outburst, temporary attitude (see RC Trench, *Synonyms of the New Testament*, 130-31). The second word may lead to the first. Sometimes one is dependent on the other, in both ways. Either word expresses the "strongest of all passions, impulses, and desires" (Trench, 130). The word *thymas* may be more passionate but more temporary than *orges*. The latter word often points beyond the frame of mind to the outcome, the judgment (*BDAG, A Greek-English Lexicon of the New Testament and Other Early Christian Literature*, 579). Both terms occur together in Revelation 16:19 and 19:15. The terms reinforce each other and mean something stronger than a single use of the term (*BDAG*, 365).

Why is it necessary that God exercise anger? The answer goes to the nature of who God is. God cannot love good unless he hates evil. The two are inseparable (Trench, 134). There is not a more "utterly prostrate moral condition than the not being able to be angry with sin—and sinners" (Trench, 134).

Note these last statements. Unless God acts in wrath against sin he cannot be loving. These sober reflections apply especially to the judgments of the Revelation.

God Must Bring the Evil of Humanity to an End

The end times (a popular phrase but one not used in the Bible) are the *times of the end*. There cannot be ongoing cycles of blessing and cursing. God has his plan in place to terminate rebellious, (immoral, idolatrous) Gentile nations and to bring his eternal reign/kingdom in heaven to earth just as Daniel 2 and 7, and Psalm 2, prophesied.

Jesus taught us to pray this: "Our Father, who is in heaven, hallowed be your name. Your kingdom come, your will be done, on earth as it is in heaven..." (Matt 6:9–10). The "Lord's prayer" will be finally answered!

The Apostles Agree That God Will Exercise Wrath at the Time of the End

It really comes as no surprise that the Apostles reaffirm the wrath of God and that the agent of God's judgment in the GT and after it is the Lord Jesus Christ.

Paul affirms God's wrath on several occasions: Romans 1:18; 2:5, 8–9; 5:9; 9:22. In 12:9 Paul is quoting the Old Testament about God's taking vengeance (Deut 32:35). Hebrews (10:30) also cites this text. In his most severe text Paul expands on God's vengeance in 2 Thessalonians 1.

All these texts should be understood as pointing to the time of the Great Tribulation as the time when God exercises wrath.

Several texts from Revelation affirm that the GT is the time when God's judgment will be "righteous and true" (Rev 14:7; 15:3, 4; 16:7; 19:2). Thus the wrath, and the judgment that it reflects, occurs only in the GT. The verses of Romans are not pointing to the "great white throne judgment" after the Millennial Kingdom (Rev 20:11–15).

Paul even identifies government as God's servant as the restrainer of evil doing. It is "an agent of wrath to bring punishment on the wrong-doer" (Rom 13:4).

The Thessalonian Epistles Speak About God's Wrath

In the Thessalonian Epistles, Paul writes several times that Christians will be "rescued from the coming wrath" (1 Thess 1:10). Regarding the Jews who killed the Lord Jesus and who prevent Paul from preaching to the Gentiles Paul writes that the "wrath of God has come upon them fully" (2:16). He encourages his readers that they might be "blameless and holy in the presence of our God and Father when our Lord Jesus comes with all his holy ones" (3:13). He informs his readers that the Rapture, the return of Jesus Christ, gives assurance of their resurrection before judgment, whether living or "sleeping" (4:13–18). Finally, he warns his readers that after the Rapture the "day of the Lord" will come unexpectedly upon the unbelievers, not allowing any to escape (5:1–3). In contrast "God has not appointed" believers "to suffer wrath but to receive salvation through our Lord Jesus Christ" (5:9).

In every one of the chapters of 1 Thessalonians the thrust is that believers are spared from the time of God's wrath. Instead wrath is designed for unbelievers.

When we approach 2 Thessalonians the instruction regarding God's wrath is different. In chapter 1 Paul goes directly to that event at the end of the GT when Jesus Christ returns (at the Battle of Armageddon portrayed in Rev 16 and 19). These are among the starkest words about the destination of those who have embraced the Antichrist and received his mark (Rev 13–14). To the persecuted believers suffering for the kingdom of God Paul writes (2 Thess 1:6–10):

> For after all it is only right for God to repay with afflic-
> tion those who afflict you, (7) and to give relief to you
> who are afflicted, along with us, when the Lord Jesus
> will be revealed from heaven with his mighty angels
> (8) in flaming fire, dealing out retribution to those who
> do not know God, and to those who do not obey the
> gospel of our Lord Jesus. (9) These people will pay the

penalty of eternal destruction, away from the presence of the Lord and from the glory of his power, (10) when he comes to be glorified among his saints on that day, and to be marveled at among all who have believed— because our testimony to you was believed (NASB).

It is clear that Paul is pointing to the great time of wrath upon unbelievers, first to the whole course of the GT, then to its culmination at the return of Jesus Christ with "power and great glory"—words that Jesus himself used (Matt 24:30). While the word, "wrath," does not occur here, words that are equally strong do: God will "repay with affliction"; "in flaming fire dealing out retribution"; "pay the penalty of eternal destruction." Believers could never come under the scope of such terms.

When Paul wrote that believers escape the wrath to come (1 Thess 1:10) we can understand why: the GT will be extremely terrifying. The words reinforce what Paul says in Romans 12:19, that God is the "avenger" who will "repay."

Clearly Paul's words are similar to how Jesus describes his return in Matthew 24 and Luke 21. Moreover, Jesus Christ the bride groom does not "beat up" his bride (Rev 19:7, 9; 21:2, 9)!

This reality of the meaning of wrath makes it one of the strongest arguments for the pre-tribulation Rapture.

The Wrath of God Is Consummated during the GT

In light of the strong words of the other apostles given above it is not surprising that such strong words occur in the Revelation. And all these words deal with the wrath of God in the context of the Great Tribulation (which was true of the preceding texts but the GT was not mentioned).

Part 2

Seven Years of Carnage and Death

The Greatest Demonstration of the Wrath of God Occurs in the Revelation

Truly the capstone of the Bible's teaching on the intervention of God in judgment at the end of the age occurs in the final book (appropriately) of the Bible, the Revelation. The title of the book comes from its first words: "The Revelation of (or revealing by) Jesus Christ" (Rev 1:1). The contents of the book come from God the Father: he gave them to Jesus Christ who via an interpreting angel "signified" [literally "signed"] them to his servant John who wrote them for God's servants (v 1). Jesus Christ is the central focus of the entire book, indeed, of all prophecy (Rev 19:10).

Following the introduction Jesus reveals himself in a glorious way to John (reflecting his appearance to Daniel in Dan 10). He then commissions John to write to the seven churches "the things he has seen, the things which are, and the things which will take place after these things" (1:19). This verse sets forth the pattern of the book: chapter 1 reveals the things already revealed to John; chapters 2–3 reveal the present status of the seven churches; and chapters 4–22 reveal the future.

Jesus addresses each of the churches in chapters 2–3. Then John is transported in vision to heaven where he beholds God the Father on his glorious throne surrounded by a multitude of differing heavenly beings (ch 4). Then John sees the glorified Jesus Christ who is announced as a King of the tribe of Judah but appears as a Lamb. *In the entire universe* he is the only one worthy by means of his atoning death to take a seven-sealed scroll (a rolled-up book) from the hand of the Father and to open it. This seven-sealed book contains all the judgments, and the expressions of wrath, in the format of three series of judgments.

The Fact That Wrath Occurs during the GT and Not Just at the Very End Supports the Pre-Tribulation Rapture

There is a strong argument here for the pre-tribulation Rapture. For while several verses make it clear that God's wrath is poured out during the GT (Rev chs 6–19), it is never mentioned in Revelation again after this time. That is, wrath is not mentioned in 20:11–15 which describes the great white throne judgment. It is then that all humanity who have died in rebellion against God are consigned forever to the second death, the lake of fire. There is no mention of wrath then because it is a time of rendering judgment and exercising justice. Wrath has already been expressed during the GT.

The Issue of How to Interpret the Revelation

This is a powerful argument for the pre-tribulation Rapture (the Rexit!). Many who denied the pre-tribulation Rapture did so by denying that the "Great Tribulation" (terms of Jesus in Matt 24:21 and John in Rev 7:14) is a time, a period, of wrath. This post-tribulation view argues that the Rapture occurs just before the end of the GT, just prior to the bowls of wrath (Rev 16). So the promises of God to deliver his people from the "coming wrath" (1 Thess 1:10; 5:9; Rev 3:10; etc) refer to the judgment only close to the very end, perhaps a few minutes, or at the most, hours before. By this view the GT is not much wrath. Somehow the Rapture, by this view, comes a few minutes or hours prior to the Second Coming of Christ. The Rapture and the Second Coming are one, composite event.

This view also engages some special pleading about interpretation. Certainly, its defenders say, the Book of Revelation cannot be interpreted by grammatical-historical interpretation. It is in the genre of apocalypse—full of symbols and signs. It cannot be interpreted literally but figuratively. Thus the seven years of tribulation are not really seven years; the tribulation is going on now. The seals, trumpet, and bowl judgments are going on now. The Antichrist is not *the* Antichrist; the B of Armageddon is not an actual war. Israel is never going to be restored during and after the tribulation; the church has replaced Israel; and on go the assertions.

But the big question is: If we are not going to abide generally by a literal interpretation, what do the symbols mean and who decides what they mean? Where and when do the symbols stop? For example, why should the very return of Christ be real/actual? And note Jesus's words that the Great Tribulation is to be a unique period (Matt 24:21). It is certainly not unique if it is going on during the entire age from the first to the second coming of Christ.

The GT Is a Real Event

The following verses describe the GT of seven years as the time of God's wrath (about a dozen times: Rev 6:16, 17; 11:18; 14:10, 19; 15:1, 7; 16:1, 17, 19 [2x]; 19:15 [2x]). Revelation 3:10 is important here. It states that Christ will keep believers "from the hour of testing which is coming on the whole world to test the earth dwellers." The "hour" is a period of time. In addition, the text says that during the last series of judgments called the bowls (Armageddon is the 6th bowl) "the wrath of God is finished" (Rev 15:1; repeated in 16:17 about the last bowl). The occasion for wrath is over. If the bowls are going on now, by the post-trib view, then so is God's wrath. But then the warnings that GT wrath is yet coming evaporate; such wrath never comes.

Dear reader, now that the historical event of the Rapture (a real Rexit) has come and gone the argument is settled. Since it is a real

Rapture prior to the Great Tribulation (pre-trib) then the GT of seven years is actual.

Two Crucial Points: Jesus Is the Agent of All the Judgments and All the Judgments Are Actual Events

Two points are important: Jesus is the one who breaks the seals— who unfolds/reveals the judgments, thereby signifying that he is the agent of all the judgments. They come to pass by his authority and power. He approves and exercises them. Yet this authority derives from the Father on the throne (ch 4). It is from the Father's hand that Jesus takes the seven-sealed scroll.

Second, each judgment is highly symbolic but must be interpreted in light of the Revelation and earlier Scripture. By such a process all the judgments unfold as historical events.

The Seven-sealed Scroll Is the Source of All the Judgments Occurring During the GT

The introduction of this seven-sealed book is significant. It contains all the statements of judgments and the intervening discourses that take the reader from chapter 6 through chapter 19. These chapters describe those judgments that come during the Great Tribulation (GT), from the beginning of the seven-year period to the end of it. These chapters lean heavily upon the book of Daniel and other Old Testament prophets, on Jesus's words, and on Paul's and John's epistles. Chapters 20–22 are the final chapters of the Revelation and reveal what happens after the GT. Jesus will reign for a millennium (1000 years), followed by the "great white judgment throne" (ch 20). Then comes the making of a new heaven and earth—the everlasting state of believers (chs 21–22).

The seven-sealed book contains the three series of judgments: the seven seals, the seven trumpets, and the seven bowls or vials which are "poured out." The seventh seal encloses the seven trumpet judgments, and the seventh trumpet encloses the seven bowls. Thus each series contains the following, more heavy judgments. When Jesus successively breaks each seal, a new judgment is revealed and actualized.

The Seven Seal Judgments Occur First

The First Four Seals; Rev 6

The first series of judgments are the seven seals (ch 6). The picture is a rolled-up scroll which has seven seals on subsequent places in the scroll. After the first seal is broken, the judgment is revealed. Then upon further unrolling another seal stops the rolling. Thus another seal must be broken before the contents of the second judgment is revealed. And so on.

The first four seals reveal four horses and their riders. They are called forth ("come") by the four living creatures/beings who are described in Revelation 4 as surrounding the throne of God in heaven. Jesus breaks each seal and a living creature invites the horse and its rider to come.

- The first seal reveals a white horse with a rider having a bow. He receives a crown and goes forth "conquering and to conquer" (6:2). The meaning is that the judgment concerns conquest and expansion. Comparing this judgment with the next ones makes it impossible to identify this rider as Jesus Christ.

- The second seal reveals a red horse with a rider who has a large sword. He is given the power to take peace from the earth and to have people kill one another. The meaning is that war and other deaths would ensue.

- The third seal reveals a black horse whose rider holds a pair of scales. The message about the price of wheat and barley, and the protection of the oil and wine, means that famine and scarcity are going to overcome the world.

- The fourth seal reveals an ashen horse whose rider has the name of Death. His companion is Hades. They are given power over ¼ of the earth's people, to kill with the sword, famine, and plague, and by wild animals. The meaning is horrific: *¼ of earth's population will die.*

When Do the Four Seal Judgments Occur and What Do They Mean?

Do They Unfold in the First Half of the GT or Before It Even Starts?

Upon reflection, we realize that these seals correspond to the disturbances that Jesus predicted would come on the earth prior to the midpoint of the GT (Matt 24:3–14). Thus it may be that these seal judgments perhaps begin even prior to the beginning of the GT and overflow into the GT. Conquest, war, famine, plagues, and death have occurred throughout history. The fact that the fifth seal differs from the first four suggests that the time of the first four may be different than the last three.

The fifth seal has no judgment in it but reveals the saints in heaven asking how long before their martyrdom would be avenged (v 10). The answer that they should "rest a little while longer" until the number of the martyred is complete suggests that the GT is underway, and even far along.

Because there is a certain ambiguity, from this standpoint, it may not be clear when the seven years of the GT begin (apart from the Antichrist making the covenant with Israel; Dan 9). This may help explain why the Rapture is seemingly not recognized for the worldwide impact it should have. The "disappearance" of the saints is "hidden" among the other worldwide calamities and catastrophes or for other reasons.

Yet the four seals point to unprecedented intensity: note that *¼ of earth's population dies from these four judgments*. Hence they unfold most clearly and intensely during the first half of the GT.

- How terrifying it will be to live through 3 ½ years of recurring wars, famines, and plagues that take the lives of *two billion people*.

- This means that almost 100 million Americans will perish.

- We get a foretaste of the plagues by the pandemic of 2020-2022. Perhaps as many as 1,000,000 Americans alone will die, which is more than one in every 350 people!

Or think of how the numbers apply to your hometown. The picture is stark!

It's important to realize that God's people might be among these numbers, especially if these catastrophes begin prior to the start of the seven years of the GT. The promise in Revelation 7:3 and 9:4, to spare God's people from his judgments of the trumpets and bowls, may include these seal judgments (but probably not).

It is clear that the judgments representing the wrath of God begin here, but they are going to get much worse, as the next verses make clear. They are all focused on and destined for the "earth dwellers," a term reserved for the wicked who reject God (as stated in Rev 3:10; 6:10; 13:12, 14; 17:2, 8).

The Actuality of the Series of Judgments Is Supported by the Plagues of Egypt

- These judgments find their OT correspondence with the plagues on Egypt by which God brought about the Exodus of Israel.

- Many have the same content: water turning to blood; darkness; famine; disease.

- Were the plagues on Egypt real/actual? Really, it makes no sense to take them as less than real. How else did Israel escape from Egypt? All texts about the plagues assume them to be literal, i.e., historical.

- The Exodus is so embedded in Israel's history that it is the stated reason for keeping the Sabbath day, the Fourth Commandment (Deut 5:12–15). The Exodus could hardly be discounted as unreal and yet become part of the Ten Commandments.

- The Gentile nations heard about the Exodus and feared the God of Israel (Deut 4:6–8; Josh 2:10–11).

- The Exodus is frequently recounted in the OT and in the NT.

Thus, if the judgments on Egypt were real, these too in the Revelation must be. The earlier ones serve as types of these that come at the end of the age. And as types point to greater, fuller antitypes—their fulfillments—so the judgments of the Revelation are worse than the plagues that came on Egypt. Those of the Revelation affect the entire world, not just Egypt.

Leading opponents of the pre-tribulation Rapture also claim that these judgments are symbolic for another reason. They argue that a literal interpretation of these judgments would lead to the extermination of humanity!

But isn't that where all the judgments are heading?! Note that during the tribulation ½ of humanity perishes; and after Armageddon none of the wicked survive (Rev 19:21).

The Next Three Seal Judgments; Rev 6:9–20

Chapter six continues with three more seal judgments.

- The fifth seal (6:9–11) does not contain judgments inflicted on earth but moves the scene to heaven and the martyrs who have been put to death for their "testimony." They ask how much longer they must wait till their deaths are avenged on the wicked of earth. They are told to rest for a "little while longer" until the number of martyrs is complete. The answer obviously anticipates the greater judgments of the trumpets and bowls to come in the latter half of the GT.

- The sixth seal (6:12–17) brings a "great earthquake" on earth and disruption of the sun, moon, and stars in the heavens. Every strata of society, from the great to the lowly, are affected. Hiding in caves people scream out to the mountains and rocks to kill them and hide them from the presence of God in heaven and "from the *wrath* of the Lamb" (6:16). They acknowledge that no one is able to survive, to stand, now that the "great day of their *wrath* has come" (v 17).

The last words celebrate the arrival of the latter half of the GT. The word "wrath" has not been used for the six seals until here, where it occurs twice. Clearly the words anticipate the coming judgments of the trumpets (chs 8–9), bowls (designated "bowls of wrath," ch 16), and Armageddon (chs 16, 19).

- Where is the seventh seal (recall that this is a seven-sealed book of the Lamb)? It is broken in 8:1.

In the meantime, Revelation 7:3 reveals that the trumpet judgments are momentarily held back until God seals his people on their foreheads from them. The sealing represents ownership. As Israel in Goshen was spared from the Egyptian plagues (as the book of Exodus reveals), so God will preserve his people from his wrath encapsulated in the trumpet and bowl judgments (so also stated in 9:4).

A Large Number of Jews and Gentiles Are Spared from the Trumpet and Bowl Judgments

The rest of Revelation 7 identifies the 144,000 Jews who are sealed from the next series of God's judgments. Then another vision reveals the total outcome of those delivered at the end of "the great tribulation" (7:14). An innumerable number of saints from all nations are glorified around the throne of God, where the Lamb is their Shepherd. The blessings of the new heaven and earth (described in chs 21–22) are anticipated in the words of the interpreting angel. A similar scene occurs in chapters 14 and 15.

While the Rapture delivered all Christians then living from the period of the GT, many unbelievers will become Christians during the GT. Those who are not killed by the Antichrist will go on to live during the Millennial Kingdom.

With this background the interpreting angel reveals the next series of judgments.

The Seven Trumpet Judgments Are the Second Series of Judgments (Rev 8–9)

The First Four Trumpet Judgments Increase the Suffering

The next judgments involve Jesus's opening the seventh seal, which has within it the seven trumpet judgments (Rev 8 and 9). These come in answer to the prayers of the saints (8:1–5).

- The first trumpet is hail and fire with blood that consumes 1/3 of vegetation.

- The second trumpet is a burning mountain that changes 1/3 of the sea into blood and destroys 1/3 of the creatures in it and the ships on it.

- The third trumpet is a burning star falling on and poisoning 1/3 of the fresh waters, and many people die from drinking it.

- The fourth trumpet strikes the heavenly bodies (the sun, moon, and stars) so that their time of shining is reduced by a 1/3, affecting the night.

Just how these judgments occur or what the mechanisms are is not given. But this obscurity should not detract from their expressed certainty and consequences. The 1/3 fraction is carried on to the last three trumpet judgments.

The Last Three Trumpet Judgments Are Terrifying "Woes" That Emphasize Demon Possession

The next three judgments (ch 9) are more intense and terrifying than the first four (which pattern was also true of the seal judgments). The first four struck the physical world but these three strike humanity directly. These are also called "woes," signifying the more frightful nature of the judgments. Usually "woe" is an interjection signifying pain, but here the word occurs as a noun meaning "calamity." Thus "Calamity! Calamity! Calamity!"

What makes them so frightful? Two of the three are devoted to the reign of untold hordes of demons over people—to demon oppression, possession, and conquest—and there's nothing people will be able to do about it. Indeed, people welcome the possession: they worship the demons. Only those who bear the mark of God (so Rev 9:4) will escape such terror that comes on those who have the mark of the beast. These words argue strongly that those who are Christians and have the Holy Spirit cannot be possessed by fallen spirits (demons). They are protected.

The Fifth Trumpet Judgment: Demon Possession for Five Months

When Is This in the Seven Years of the GT?

We Are Probably Down to the Last Six Months

- The release of a great horde of demons (symbolized by scorpions that sting) from the abyss (the source of demons) to possess for *five months* (stated twice for emphasis) all people world-wide who rebel against God. This suggests that the abyss is emptied of its demons. The fact that they come from the abyss clinches the argument that the symbols represent actual demons. This understanding cannot be dismissed by claiming that the text is set in apocalypse literature as though it does not depict actual events.

- Even though people "long" to die to escape the torment, they will not be able to (Rev 9:4–6). This means that their wills are captured by the beings they *worship.*

- They have a king over them who directs them, an angel named Abaddon (in Hebrew; the Greek is Apollyon), meaning "destroyer." The name clearly indicates their purpose: they are forbidden to kill people but will destroy them in other ways (9:5). Having a king means that there is order, planning, deliberation, compulsion, singleness of purpose, and direction to the whole demon occupation. It also suggests that such a horde cannot be stopped.

- Thus, *they destroy human identity, intermingling human nature with demonic nature.* Human personality no longer has a mind, a heart, a will, or attitude that is human but now is "transgendered" with demons. Schizophrenia (a divided mind) occurs on a level never seen before.

- While death would be preferable, death is impossible because demons are in control. Obviously, demons won't commit suicide; and they can't die a physical death anyway.

- People are more demon-like than human-like since their fallen nature is reinforced.

- This judgment alone must involve billions and billions of demons.

- This is the first "woe."

How terribly frightening is this time. It prevails probably for the last six months of the GT. Yet it pales in comparison to the next expression of wrath.

The Sixth Trumpet Judgment: Worse Demon Possession and Suffering

But No Repentance

- the release of 200 million horsemen (probably figurative for demons again) under four angels from the River Euphrates;

- they kill 1/3 of mankind by the plagues of fire, smoke, and sulfur (9:15–19). Contrary to the fifth trumpet, multitudes now die.

- This is the second "woe."

- Among the survivors not one repents (just as in the previous judgment) (9:20–21).

- The survivors engage in all kinds of sinful activity that violates the last half of the ten commandments (see below).

We may ask: why does no one repent? The Revelation tells us that people continue to worship the demons that possess them (imagine that!—which illustrates the power of demonic possession) and idols of various materials. They continue in their murders, witchcraft, sexual immorality, and thefts (9:20–21). The "witchcraft" refers to the taking of hallucinogenic drugs—a practice within the mystery religions of the time and an interesting connection with demonic possession.

People don't repent because of an obvious reason: the demons don't let them repent. If people worship the demons that possess them they want to do the demons' bidding. Demons can never repent; it contradicts what demons do and who they are. And people are fully absorbed into demon identity.

Does 200 million challenge our credulity? It should not. The numbers recall Jesus's encounter with demons. On one occasion they possessed a man and made him "extremely violent" so that he threatened people (Matt 8:28). The demons identified their name as "Legion, for we are many." The fact that Jesus permitted them to come out and possess 2000 pigs indicates that there were, at least, that many demons (Mark 5:9, 13).

The killing of one-third of humanity means that together with the 5th seal a total of ½ of humanity has died. Over three billion of earth's population have died.

When Does the Release of This Horde of Demons Occur?

Probably in the Last Month of the GT to Allow the Armies to Gather to Armageddon.

What A Demon-Filled World Looks Like When Demons Rule

For a few moments let's imagine what it means when evil angels are freed on a scale never before experienced among humanity on earth. The text (Rev 9:20–21) says that people continue to break the second half of the ten commandments in the context where demonic possession reaches unparalleled heights. This argues that these immoral acts are instigated by the demons who possess people. That is, unprecedented demonic activity in the world's peoples means that sin and crime, lust, immorality and evil, will fill the earth. It means a world full of demon-possessed adulterers, drug addicts, homosexual predators, child molesters, gay men and women, transgenders, transvestites, queers (all the LGBTQ+ people), pederasts, bestiality addicts (all the preceding are covered by the general word "sexual immorality"), murderers, and more.

Even usually moral people, who would otherwise never engage in such immoral behavior, will be impelled by demons within to engage in the most vile of deeds—and to love doing so.

All restraint by the internal voice of a conscience has been silenced by the internal shout of demons screaming, "Do it! Do it! Do it!" Every human being is possessed not by one demon but by a legion of them. Imagine the internal (and external) chaos.

The will to do something will no longer be human generated but demonic. Love and kindness will be supplanted by hatred, rivalry, and brutality. Pride and arrogance replace humility and kindness as the new "virtues" to cultivate, expand, and reward.

Just imagine what the world will be like when every activity, every thought, every desire, every plan, every relationship, every commitment, every institution, every longing, every hope, every taste, every sight, every smell, every sense—is possessed, directed, and exploited by demons!

There is no restraint because the "restrainer" has been removed, as Paul prophesied (2 Thess 2:6-7).

The distinction between people and animals is largely erased. The distinction between human beings and demons is largely erased. There is a new, hybrid race of demons/humans like the Nephilim (Gen 6:4).

Diversity, equity, inclusion are the catchwords of the Antichrist, and he will enforce them.

This is a token of what it means to have demons taking charge of daily life. "Cancel culture" will be a reality on a scale that even its most ardent exponents never imagined.

Now you know why fallen, hardened humanity must be eliminated!

As you read these words, you can understand why we've written this book. You need to accept the gift of life in Jesus Christ before the fifth and sixth trumpet judgments arrive. After them virtually no one is able to be saved; the demons won't permit it. In the whole history of humanity on this planet there has never been a more evil, harsh environment than this time in the GT—not even before the Flood in Noah's day.

Revelation 10-15 Provides Background Information for the Last Series of Judgments

The seventh trumpet (and third woe) contains within it the seven, final bowls of wrath (described in ch 16).

Prior to the final series of judgments, several chapters intervene between the trumpet and bowl judgments. These are meant to give background to explain other details of the GT. See fuller treatment of these details in earlier chapters of this book.

- Chapter 10 declares that in the coming bowl judgments the "mystery" of God is finished. There will be no longer delay (10: 6–7). "Mystery" points back to the mystery of Daniel 2:18–19, 28 where it encompasses God's plan whereby he brings his reign in heaven to earth to end the rebellion of seven Gentile empires (see previous chapters of this book). John is commissioned to prophesy again—mainly to predict what the final bowl judgments encompass.

- Chapter 11 reveals the work of the two witnesses who serve God and cannot be destroyed for 3 ½ years. Then the Antichrist (see the earlier chapter of this book on the Antichrist) arises from the abyss and is allowed to kill the two near the end of the GT. The chapter concludes with a proleptic view (preview) of the final, bowl judgments that will end God's wrath and bring about the end of the nations of the world at Armageddon. Then Jesus Christ will begin his kingdom over the world (11:15–19).

- Chapter 12 introduces the major players of the final period of the GT. They are the nation of Israel symbolized by a pregnant woman (1–2); Satan symbolized by a red dragon who seeks to devour the newborn child (3–4); the birth of the Son (Jesus Christ) destined to rule the nations (5–6); the war in heaven between Satan and his angels and Michael and his angels, which war Michael wins (7–9); and the saints' celebration of Satan's being cast down to earth (10–12).

- Chapter 13 describes the Antichrist as the red beast with seven heads and ten horns. He receives world-wide control and worship. His companion, the false prophet, enforces the code of 666 for economic survival (as discussed in earlier chapters of this book).

- Chapter 14 records four events. There is the song of triumph by the 144,000 martyrs in heaven; the declaration from two angels inviting people to fear God and declaring that Babylon had fallen; a third angel warning of the very great wrath to come on those who take on the mark of the Antichrist; and the actions of two angels harvesting grain and harvesting grapes to symbolize the judgment that caps the GT. The wrath described in this chapter is the starkest in the entire Bible.

- Chapter 15 reveals a heavenly scene in which triumphant saints praise God as righteous and true in his ways. It also reveals the seven angels who are given the seven bowls full of the final expression of the wrath of God.

The Climatic, Catastrophic Bowl Judgments (Rev 16)

What Time Is It?

It Is Probably the Last Week or Two of the GT

When the seventh trumpet is blown, the seven bowls, the final judgments, are poured out. These are God's judgments sent to afflict the earth's inhabitants. They belong to the dimension of the divinely caused suffering.

The bowls come at the very end of the 7th year of the GT—probably in the final days of a week or two. While they are successive there is evidence that they compound the suffering by each coming quickly while the others are still existing. In other words, they add up. Judgment #1 is still afflicting people at the time of the 6th bowl (Rev 16:9–10).

The bowls are also final and complete, and catastrophic. While the previous series were partial (the fourth seal brought death to ¼ of the world; the 6th trumpet brought death to 1/3 of the world), these are complete. *By their end the ½ of mankind that have survived and who follow the Antichrist will all be dead.* But remember: there is still a large number of Christians who survive because they have the seal of God upon them to shield them from God's wrath (Rev 7:3; 9:4).

Bowl #1: harmful, painful sores/boils afflict all people who have the mark of the beast (which is everyone except those believers bearing the protective mark from God; Rev 7:3; 9:4) (v 2).

Bowl #2: all the sea water becomes blood and all life in it dies (v 3).

Bowl #3: all fresh water becomes blood. The reason is announced: people *deserve* this judgment of blood because they shed the blood of

God's people. God's judgments are "true and righteous" (vv 5–7). In this way God takes revenge.

Bowl #4: the heat of the sun intensifies so that it scorches people. The probable implication is that people burn to death. There is no place to find relief. But instead of repenting, people blaspheme God (vv 8–9). Does this mean that our atmosphere is thinned out? Or that the sun's fusion spirals out of control? Perhaps unprecedented solar flares explode.

Bowl #5: the throne of the Antichrist and his kingdom (which consumes the world) becomes darkened. People continue to blaspheme God because of the ongoing pain from the first bowl (vv 10–11). This is the opposite of bowl #4. Perhaps there is a realignment of heavenly bodies so that they block out the sun. Perhaps the tilt of the earth shifts. Perhaps the orbit of the earth changes. The orbit becomes elongated, for a while bringing earth much closer to the sun, then much farther away from it. With darkening comes cold—extreme cold. Whether fueled by fossil fuels or the "new green" sources, electric grids world-wide are overwhelmed and fail. Perhaps Bowls 4 and 5 are the consequences of a comet or huge meteor which strikes the earth. Perhaps one half of Earth's people are scorched while the other half freeze to death.

Bowl #6 adds to the terror by portending the end of history. The angel pours out his bowl on the River Euphrates. The river dries up so that three unclean spirits identified as demons go out from Satan, the Antichrist, and the false prophet. They lure the kings of the East and of the whole world to the place in northern Israel, *Armageddon* (vv 12-16). The Battle itself is described in chapter 19 (see below).

Bowl #7 is the most terrifying judgment of them all and brings all the judgments to climax (vv 17-21). "It is done" a voice cries out from the throne. Indeed, God's venting of his wrath is at an end. The bowl is composed of a complex of terrors:

- lightning and thunder;

- the greatest earthquake since the creation of man. No doubt this accounts for many of the following features;

- the collapse of all the cities of the nations including the "great city"; all is rubble;

- the fall of Babylon (probably symbolic of the destruction of all the Gentile empires, including the Antichrist and his kingdom);

- all islands disappear and all mountains are levelled; and an "extremely severe" plague of hailstones each weighing about 100 pounds strike people. People blaspheme.

Clearly this bowl is the accompaniment to and aftermath of the Battle of Armageddon (see below). The finality of these bowls is beyond question. The earth as we know it is destroyed (2 Pet 3).

God's Final Act of Wrath Is the Death of All Humanity Arrayed against Jesus Christ at Armageddon

In concert with the pouring out of the seven bowls of God's wrath just described (16:1–21), and to conclude them, arrives the greatest battle of all time, Armageddon. It is unique in

- its scope (all nations are represented);

- the supernatural elements involved (note the bowls above);

- the physical appearance of Jesus Christ descending from heaven as Warrior;

- its geographical location—Israel, at Jerusalem and Megiddo (which has been a strategic fighting place throughout history beginning with Thutmose IV of Egypt);

- its conclusion: all human combatants arrayed against Jesus Christ are conquered and destroyed (later to be resurrected, judged, and then consigned to the lake of fire, the second death; Rev 20).

The glorious Lord Jesus Christ is triumphant. As the Warrior from heaven he enters into combat. There is no question about the outcome. See earlier chapters.

As the consequence of the Battle and the 7ᵗʰ bowl of wrath every single, surviving person in allegiance to the Antichrist dies (Rev 19:21).

No Follower of the Antichrist Will Be Alive after Armageddon

After Armageddon the only survivors in the world are the millions who are allied with Jesus Christ and who are under the protecting seal of God (Rev 7:3; 9:4; 14:1). They continue on to reign with Christ in the new, millennial kingdom (Rev 20:1–6). Even greater numbers will go on into the new heavens and earth (Rev 21–22).

One book, the earth's history, is closed. Another book unfolds without an end, like a never-ending scroll (an analogy used by C.S. Lewis in "The Last Battle," of the *Chronicles of Narnia*).

We hope that you, dear reader, have trusted in Jesus Christ as your Savior. The preceding chapters show how terrible the suffering from God's wrath will be for those who side with the Antichrist and refuse to believe the Gospel of Jesus Christ. But the ultimate suffering to come to unbelievers is everlasting in the lake of fire (Rev 20:21). The prospect of temporal suffering as a Christian during the GT should never serve to keep you from repenting and embracing eternal life found in Jesus Christ.

***All non-Christians should be frightened into belief. Recall John 3:16** (above).*

Conclusion

As we've indicated previously, Jesus was pro-active in preparing his disciples for the trials that they would endure following his death and resurrection. The prime example is found in what he told them at the Last Supper, just hours before he was betrayed by Judas. His teaching on that occasion is found in the fourteenth through seventeenth chapters of John's gospel. Once again, we encourage you to spend some time there.

Jesus fully understood not only what was to befall him during the coming hours, but also what was to come upon his followers. When we think of what is lined up for believers during the Tribulation, the parallels between you and the disciples in the Upper Room are many. As you read through those chapters in John, remember that what the Lord Jesus taught them applies also to you (John 17:20). But of all the incredible resources and encouragements he shared, there's a particular one that we're obliged to offer at the close of this book.

Our Lord was aware of every circumstance that lay ahead. He also knew all the strengths and weaknesses of those who loved him. Including Simon (Peter), of course. Here's a portion of a short conversation that occurred between the two during the Last Supper:

> Simon, Simon, Satan has asked to sift all of you as wheat. But I have prayed for you, Simon, that your faith may not fail. And when you have turned back, strengthen your brothers (Luke 22:31-32).

You know what it's like when someone addresses you by name—twice. It's an attention-getter. But it's what Jesus said next that might have stood up the hair on the back of Peter's neck. Satan had asked permission to put Peter and the rest of the disciples (the "you" is plural) through the ringer. Well, through the sifter. Think either of some screening device or of Satan's own fingers. The latter may give it a bit more impact. Now it's metaphorical, of course. Even so, how would you feel, knowing that you were about to be placed in the evil one's hands?

But wait, see what the Savior says about all this. First, "Satan has *asked*...". We noted above that the devil's access to Peter (and the rest) for this testing could only come by the Lord's own divine allowance. And that allowance could only come with presumed restrictions (see Job 1:12 and 2:6 for a similar request). This fits together with what John said about Christ's protection of all the saints (1 John 5:18). There's a real difference between getting a workout from Satan and his bringing you to utter destruction. Latch on to that perspective.

But this is only the half of Jesus' promise. For next, he tells Peter, "I have prayed for you." Now, just chew on this for a few moments. We are generally grateful when someone says they're praying for us. But how about if it's the One by whom all things came into existence (John 1:3), by whom all things *continue* in existence (Col 1:17), who is the inheritor of all things (Heb 1:2), who is always heard by the Father (John 11:42), and who lives continually to appeal to God on our behalf (Heb 7:25)? This is the One who will be praying for you—and out of whose *own* hands you cannot be taken (John 10:28; see also Rom 8:31-39!!).

Jesus prayed for Peter that his faith would not fail. He was thinking of Peter's being left standing in victory at the end of the game. Yes, Peter fumbled badly when he denied being a disciple after Jesus had been arrested (Luke 22:54-61). But that was what Peter "turned back" from, to a life (and death) of responsible discipleship.

You, my friend, will indeed make it to the end of what God intends for you in the days ahead. May you have the same confidence in it that Paul had:

I have fought the good fight, I have finished the race, I have kept the faith. Now there is in store for me the crown of righteousness, which the Lord, the righteous Judge, will award to me on that day—and not only to me, but also to all who have longed for his appearing (2 Tim 4:7-8).

May you look forward to hearing—addressed to you personally—the words of the Lord of Glory:

Well done, good and faithful servant. You have been faithful over a little; I will set you over much. Enter into the joy of your master (Matt 25:21).

About The Authors

John F. Balch, MDiv, is retired from over 30 years of service with the National Cemetery Administration, primarily as a Budget Analyst. Prior to his employment with the federal government, he served as a pastor for eight years in Grants Pass, Oregon. His theological and pastoral training was taken at Western Seminary, Portland, Oregon, from which he graduated in 1978. His undergraduate degree is from Michigan State University (BS, Fisheries and Wildlife). He is a veteran of the US Navy.

Since concluding his pastoral ministry, John has steadily maintained a teaching ministry in Portland area local churches that has focused on the exposition of both the Old and New Testament. He currently partners with his co-author in James' podcast *Apocalypse Is Coming*.

John has written a series of short but unpublished commentaries on the biblical texts of a number of major choral works including Bach's *St. John Passion*, Beethoven's *Christ on the Mount of Olives*, Handel's *Messiah*, Mendelssohn's oratorios *Elijah* and *Paul*, and Mozart's *Vespers* and *Requiem*. These were produced while he was a member of the Vancouver (WA) *Bravo!* Chorale and were designed to provide both performers and concert-goers with an understanding of the biblical background and message of these masterpieces.

John's interests include classical music, birdwatching, model railroading, and rugby. He met his wife Hedda while attending seminary. She was born in the Netherlands and immigrated with her family to Oregon when she was six. They have a son and grandson who live in

Arkansas. They enjoy friends, neighbors, gardening, and trips to the Oregon Coast.

James B. De Young, ThD, is Senior Professor of New Testament Language and Literature at Western Seminary, Portland, Oregon, where he has taught New Testament Greek and related courses since 1975. His training includes Moody Bible Institute (diploma), East Texas Baptist University (BA), Talbot Theological Seminary (BD, ThM), and Dallas Theological Seminary (ThD). He has been a regular contributor to the Evangelical Theological Society and initiated the section on hermeneutics. He has ministered abroad in Mexico, Europe, and Afghanistan. He has served in Damascus Community Church since 1971. For over a dozen years he has led an annual fall retreat on critical issues facing Christians today.

James and his wife Patricia have lived in semi-rural Damascus, Oregon, since 1971. During this time he has served Damascus Community Church in various ways. He has also served on the city council of Damascus (2013-16) and as the appointed mayor (2019-2020). They have reared four children and now have twelve grandchildren, all living in the area. Their family gatherings for camping and the celebrations of Christmas and birthdays are delightful occasions.

De Young has spent his life in teaching the Bible and the biblical languages. He is dedicated to empowering Christians to discern and apply biblical truth in an increasingly pluralistic, hostile culture. This has been the focus in all of his articles and various books: on biblical interpretation, Greek syntax, homosexuality, Islam, women in ministry, submission to the state, and in his several books on universalism (2017; 2018; including *Burning Down the Shack* (2010)). His most recent book is a comprehensive study of the Antichrist: *The Apocalypse Is Coming: The Rise of the Antichrist; the Restrainer Removed; and Jesus Christ Victorious at Armageddon* (2020). See his web site: jamesbdeyoung.com.

The present book grew out of the conviction that the Christian church has largely neglected the teaching of the Bible about end time events (eschatology). When the pre-trib Rapture occurs there will be a great need for explaining what has happened to those "left behind" and who believe the Gospel. This book will disciple them with the biblical truth about the Antichrist, the Great Tribulation, and the wrath of God poured out during this time. Our goal is to equip these new believers to persevere until this time of tribulation is completed at the Battle of Armageddon. Until the Rapture this book will similarly equip Christians through the present time of suffering and persecution.

This same concern for renewal and revival led De Young to start a podcast with John Balch called "Apocalypse Is Coming." Hear it at www.anchor.fm/james-de-young where many of the topics found in this book are discussed.

At the time of this writing De Young was completing another book presenting the pre-trib rapture as the key to all eschatology and exposing the shortcomings of Reformed eschatology.

9 781662 851773